Rosalyn Yalow
NOBEL LAUREATE

Her Life and Work in Medicine

Rosalyn Yalow
NOBEL LAUREATE
Her Life and Work in Medicine

A Biographical Memoir by
EUGENE STRAUS, M.D.

PLENUM TRADE • NEW YORK AND LONDON

Library of Congress Cataloging-in-Publication Data

On file

ISBN 0-306-45796-2

© 1998 Eugene Straus
Plenum Press is a Division of Plenum Publishing Corporation
233 Spring Street, New York, N.Y. 10013-1578

http://www.plenum.com

In memory of Bernard Straus

Contents

Preface

Through the years my mother has told me
that it was fortunate that I chose to do
acceptable things, for if I had chosen
otherwise no one could have deflected me
from my path.

ROSALYN SUSSMAN YALOW, PH.D. 1996

$\mathcal{T}$he goose was cooked. Wild rice, plum pudding, candied yams, heaped and steamed upon their platters. Giant peasant breads and bat-long baguettes waited to be torn asunder, sitting next to gallons of sparkling cider and wine, ready to flow in rivers of excess. Never mind the hearty array of cheeses, fruits, tarts, cakes, cookies, and nuts, all set about and raided by a band of small children who with their flushed faces squealed cheers of delight. "I have a dress like that. It's pretty," said a 10-year-old to her friend. "But my mom said I didn't have to wear it." "You're soooo lucky!"

Now the grownups grew silent, shushed the little ones, and raised their flutes to toast this New Year's Day of 1995. It was 2 P.M. and as the host, I was ready. Looking at the assembled dear friends, family, and colleagues, I raised my glass to propose a toast to the fullness of their coming days. There were children home from college, friends with new babies, young associates off to new jobs, and lots of good stuff on the plates. As I held my glass aloft the phone rang. I waited for my wife to answer and her eyes said, "You better take this one right now."

I don't know if anyone made a toast that day, but by nightfall I was thinking of the little girls and their hard way to go.

This is a story of triumph and tragedy, joy and despair. It is about the strength and weakness of remarkable individuals who have made an imprint upon society. And it is a tale of a society that both promotes and blocks the path of struggling but brilliant individuals. The characters include some of the most creative and productive scientists of our time. Still, it is not a sentimental remembrance. It is an unfinished story and a cautionary tale.

The book is in the form of a biographical memoir. I took on the challenge of writing it after the shock of New Year's Day, 1995, because I think that children and adults should know about Dr. Rosalyn Yalow. The facts and flavor of her career illuminate the circumstances that surround women in science and medicine. Women, and other disadvantaged groups, have a particularly difficult path in these areas. But the problems that Rosalyn Yalow was up against in the sciences also inform the challenges that women contend with in such diverse areas as politics, business, law, education, and other fields.

The 1937 biography of Marie Curie,[1] the discoverer of radium, by her daughter, Eve Curie, has inspired young women for nearly three generations and focused attention on the fact that women are not only capable of doing science but also can achieve distinction. More than half a century later, at the turning of the millennium, we must realize our daughters are still at a disadvantage. Adults and children together should consider whether girls who aspire to science and medicine are given a fair chance in the nation's laboratories, clinics, hospitals, and graduate schools, and whether they hit a glass ceiling.

There are individuals who can enlighten and inspire others with their brilliant minds, achievements, unyielding dedication, and their position of simply being out in front of prevailing convention. Rosalyn Sussman Yalow is a figure of mythic proportions, and all the more so because she has feet of flesh. From a poor and uneducated family, she fought her way to the greatest heights a scientific career can attain, winning every prize imaginable and more than fifty honorary degrees. She became only the second woman to win a Nobel Prize in medicine. The first, Gerty Cori, was the daughter of a wealthy industrial chemist and shared the prize with her husband and scientific partner. Why is it that nearly one hundred years after Marie Curie shared her first Nobel Prize with Henri Becquerel and Pierre Curie there are still so few prominent women in science and medicine? What did Rosalyn Yalow have to face to realize her goals?

There can be no doubt that women have been kept out of serious science and barred from leadership positions in medi-

Figure 1. Rosalyn Yalow receiving the Nobel Prize in medicine or physiology from King Carl Gustaf XVI of Sweden.

cine. While a relative few have been able to succeed, they have done this against great odds. Still, like no one before or since, Rosalyn Yalow was not to be denied. This book, unlike Ruth Lewin Sime's wonderful biography of Lise Meitner[2] or the essential writings about Rosalind Franklin,[3] Frieda Robscheit-Robbins, and other women scientists,[4] does not have to "set the record straight" for someone who was denied her just recognition. Yalow is not the woman denied, overlooked, or exploited. No, try as they might, no one was going to thwart Yalow, or keep her from the credit she deserved. Yet, in struggling over and around obstacles and getting to the top, she reveals how far we have come, though not far enough, and in studying her life and career you may discover what changes in society should lie ahead.

Here is the other side of the coin, rarely seen, where the woman's face appears in bold relief and she is not held up for her goods. Where she forces herself to the very top of the man's world. It had not been done before, not in the world of medicine. From her story we can learn about our American values, about our scientific establishment, and about our own ambitious impulses. If we fail to use the lessons of trailblazers like Yalow then we all have a harder way to go.

Acknowledgments

I thank Rosalyn Sussman Yalow, who, while foregoing all rights to editorial or stylistic control, gave her complete cooperation to this work. I am indebted to her daughter, Elanna, and her son, Benjamin, for both their help and friendship. This book could not have been written without the cooperation of the many Yalow and Berson family members, friends, and colleagues who gave generously of their recollections, thoughts, and opinions. I am especially grateful to Mildred S. Dresselhaus, Johanna Pallotta, Maurice Goldhaber, Rolf Luft, Sherman S. Lawrence, Estelle Sussman, Ruth Wollman, Seymour Glick, Jesse Roth, Jeffery Kelman, Radha Korman, Edmund T. Lonergan, and Stephan Kass. I thank my mother, Pearl Straus, and my children, Alex, Allegra, and Sylvie Straus, for their encouragement.

I thank my wife, Bette Korman, for her encouragement, criticism, and the warmth of her creative flame.

I thank my editor, Linda Greenspan Regan, for her firm and gentle guidance and for her magnificent blue pencil.

1

The Witness

Ros Yalow and Sol Berson were the
Toscaninis of the field . . . Most others
were, if not organ-grinders, followers.[1]
ROLF LUFT, M.D.
Professor Emeritus of Endocrinology
Karolinska Institute, Stockholm

It is an undeniable fact there is no way for
a smart woman to be public without being
seen as a treacherous Lady Macbeth figure
or bitch goddess.[2]
ERICA JONG

$\mathcal{R}$osalyn Yalow's neighbor, George Rifkin, is in his 80s and nearly blind. He knew something was wrong because he had called and no one answered. He hadn't waited long at the door, letting himself in with the key he had hoped he would never need. The front door opened into the living room where Yalow always slept on a cot. The curtains, as usual, were drawn. Outside it was a bright and beautiful day; inside it was dark and quiet. George called out, "Ros?" No answer. He groped forward toward a shape on the floor. "Ros?" The shape thrashed wildly, then lay still. He didn't touch her, stumbling to the kitchen for the phone and the list of numbers that he knew would be on the refrigerator door. He called the ambulance, then called Yalow's son.

On New Year's Day, 1995, her son, Benjamin Yalow, was in Oregon visiting a friend. At 2:00 P.M. in New York, I set aside my champagne and good cheer to receive Benjamin's anguished phone call. "George Rifkin just phoned," he said, his voice working for control. "He went to my mother's house to wish her a happy new year and found her on the floor, covered with blood. She's in a coma. George has called an ambulance. They should be there by now, I'll be on the first plane back."

Rosalyn Yalow lives in a modest one-family house on Tibbett Avenue in the Bronx. It is a quiet street at the foot of the great hill that separates upscale Riverdale with its mansions, manors, and luxury spa-infested apartment buildings from the real Bronx. She chose her home as she did her husband, and her scientific partner, with care and calculation, and she has attributed much of her success to these choices.

Tibbett Avenue is a transition, a border zone between the modest and the great. It is tree-lined, faux-Tudor, and clean. Beneath the street, deep under the houses, Tibbett's Brook runs down from Yonkers to its subterranean opening into the Harlem River. Few who live there know of the flow under foot or that they sleep above a hidden stream. Around the turn of the century the Harlem River was a shallows spreading five blocks north of its current location. To allow commercial traffic from the Hudson to Long Island, the Harlem River was moved south and deepened, and Tibbett's Brook, then navigable, was driven under.

The Yalows have the biggest yard on the block with lovely rose bushes and a small pear tree. A large and fruitful cherry tree has always defined the property and shaded not only the house but also the garden where peas and tomatoes were grown in summer (Fig. 2). In former years Rosalyn would put the cherries up in Ball jars and give them to the favored few. This year the tree was taken down. It had grown old, the center eaten by carpenter ants, and Yalow's son, Benjamin, who lives in the basement apartment, feared that it would fall and damage the house. Without its crowning glory, the house looks like the others on the block, waiting for something to happen, for a reawakening.

When I reached George Rifkin on the phone he told me that the ambulance had come and taken Rosalyn to the nearest medical center. He didn't know what had happened to her. She looked very bad, he said. I quickly told our New Year's Day guests that there was a medical emergency, excused myself, and rushed to the hospital.

I had worked with Yalow for over fifteen years. I had been her mother's physician, her son's physician, and our families had ties of friendship and professional associations going back to the time of my childhood. In 1950, in the most crucial moment of her career, she had gone to my father seeking a partner for her research. As a nuclear physicist, she had not taken a single course in biology, but she knew just what she wanted to do, and she knew what she needed. She wanted to apply the newly available radioisotopes (unstable radioactive elements that are byproducts created by nuclear reactors) to crucial aspects of biomedical science. It was the dawn of nuclear medicine and Yalow saw her future there, using radioactive isotopes to measure body spaces, like the volume of blood that circulates in the vessels, and to study the body's metabolism of hormones by incorporating ra-

Figure 2. Rosalyn Yalow in front of her house on Tibbett Avenue in the Bronx.

dioactive iodine into their structure and then tracking them like following a bear with a radio transmitter around its neck.

In 1947 she had taken a job as a consultant to the Radio-isotope Unit at the Bronx Veterans Administration Hospital. By 1949 she had set up her laboratory and begun publishing studies using radioactive phosphorus and sodium, and then, with the flush of her first success, she felt there was something missing. Yalow wanted a vision to complement her own, a more medical approach. She needed a partner, and she wanted someone special. It would have to be a physician with unusual insight and energy. She had already worked with a number of bright physicians but they didn't have the spark, the imagination that could augment her own so that together they might become more than the sum of their parts. So she went to Dr. Bernard Straus, Chief of Medicine at the Bronx Veteran's Adminstration, to discuss her idea for a partner and to get advice. Straus had noticed the young physicist who, in her thirst for ideas and approaches, would attend clinical conferences and pick up concepts and information with uncommon speed and assurance. He knew she was going places, and he was delighted to help.

"There is a young physician who has just taken a clinical job. He has no training or background in research, but he is the brightest physician I have ever trained," Straus said. "He can be difficult. He's very quick and impatient. But he's wonderful, and I think you two will get along. I'll arrange a meeting—just the two of you—and if it goes well, we will convince him to give up his new job. His name is Solomon Berson."

They met and hit it off famously. "After half an hour I knew he was the smartest person I had ever met," she remembers, and she treasures that first memory of meeting him. Those who knew Yalow and Berson in the early days have their own renditions of that first meeting. The two scientists played math games for hours. They began discussing insulin because Yalow's husband was a diabetic. . . . According to Yalow, none of the stories are true, but it was the beginning of what is generally considered to be among the most dynamic, productive, and interesting partnerships in the history of science. That meeting was the birthplace of a partnership that would, for the first time, bring an American woman to the highest level of scientific accomplishment, and, like her radioactive tracers, her career can guide us to understanding more profoundly the plight of women in science and society.

In 1950 Yalow brought Berson into research, but soon he would be saying, "Stick with me and your name will be up in lights." Less than twenty years later, Berson and Yalow, like a single name known to everyone in the world of biomedical science, were certain to be awarded the Nobel Prize. Their development of radioimmunoassay (RIA), a method of measuring infinitesimally amounts of virtually any substance, revolutionized biomedical research and clinical medicine.

RIA, like a fine molecular microscope, could find and measure substances that previously had only been estimated using cumbersome and inaccurate biological assays. This method came to Berson and Yalow when they were studying the metabolism of insulin. They had been tracing the fate of insulin by attaching radioactive iodine to molecules of beef insulin and injecting tiny amounts of the radioactive insulin into normal subjects and diabetics. They were searching for an answer to one of the most important and perplexing problems in medical science: Why do most diabetics have high blood sugar if their insulin-producing cells are normal?

There are diabetics who are frequently lean and who develop the disease in childhood; they rapidly lose the insulin-producing beta cells in the pancreas and thus lose the ability to keep their blood sugar within the normal range. Yet, there is another type of diabetes, one that was harder to crack. It was well known that the majority of Type II diabetics (the ones who are generally overweight and develop the disease as adults), have pancreata containing plenty of beta cells with lots of insulin. It was known that in Type II diabetics the insulin is normal in its ability to lower blood sugar and after a meal it is released into the bloodstream as in normal people, as the blood sugar rises. Berson and Yalow wanted to see what happened to insulin once it entered the bloodstream in Type II diabetics as compared to normal subjects. So they labeled trace amounts of insulin with radioactivity, injected it into human volunteers (those with and without diabetes), and took blood samples every few minutes for several hours to determine how fast the insulin was metabolized and disappeared from the bloodstream.

They found something completely unexpected, something that they hadn't even considered. In diabetics who had never been treated with insulin, the radioactive insulin circulated in the blood and was metabolized just like in normal people. But in people who had previously been treated with beef or pork insulin injections the radioactive insulin became attached to a large protein in the blood plasma. It was as if, in the treated subjects, the small active insulin molecule, like a little child, was taken into the arms of a sheltering adult and ushered through the bloodstream so that it might be kept in circulation.

This unexpected finding had implications that went beyond the question of insulin metabolism. The young investigators quickly characterized the large plasma protein that was binding radioactive insulin in the blood of insulin-treated subjects. It was a globulin, a large protein like an antibody molecule, and it clearly appeared in response to injections of insulin. Yalow and Berson concluded that treatment with insulin injections immunized patients so that they developed insulin-binding antibodies. In other words, the injection of beef or pork insulin called forth the large sheltering molecules that took the little insulin molecules into their midst and kept them in the bloodstream. It is this property of taking up insulin that makes the globulin (that has appeared in response to injections of insulin) an "insulin-binding antibody."

Berson and Yalow prepared their data for publication in the meticulous style that was already their hallmark, but the most prestigious scientific journals rejected their work, first *Science* and then the *Journal of Clinical Investigation*. Berson and Yalow were incensed because they were unable to convince the peer reviewers and editors with the logic of their position and because the editors, in rejecting their insistence that the globulin was an antibody, accused them of "dogmatism" and characterized their writing as "incoherent." The scientific world was not ready to accept the fact that a molecule as small as insulin could stimulate the human body to produce antibodies. Letters flew back and forth, passion flared, and then, in the midst of the battle, they accepted a compromise to drop the term antibody in the title of the paper and call the protein an insulin-binding globulin. Still, they would not forget. It was more than a semantic argument, there were important scientific issues at stake. The dispute would affect their attitudes about peer reviewers and editors and form their style of dealing with adversity. Yalow would finally settle the score some twenty-two years later. Nonetheless, at that moment they moved past the argument because they were on to something even more exciting.

Yalow and Berson had observed that radioactive insulin could be displaced from the sites on the antibody molecule that bind the radioactive insulin by the native insulin in the patient's blood samples. In other words, the radioactive insulin simply competed with the native insulin for a special place on the big antibody molecule like kids trying to sit on the same chair. When they determined the precise amount of radioactive insulin pushed off the antibody molecules by a known volume of a patient's blood and compared that with the displacement produced by known concentrations in standard insulin preparations used for treating diabetics, they were measuring insulin concentrations in human blood.

They called the method radioimmunoassay: *radio* because the antigen (substance foreign to the body that initiates an immune response, e.g., antibody production), in this case insulin, was labeled with a radioactive isotope of iodine (^{131}I); *immuno* because the antigen (insulin) was binding to an antibody and so at the heart of the method was an immunologic reaction between an antigen and its antibody; and *assay* because they were measuring something. Because almost any molecule can be an antigen, meaning that when injected into an animal in the proper circumstances almost any substance can be antigenic and stimulate the production of antibody molecules that are finely tuned, absolutely specific in recognizing only that stimulating antigen, Yalow and Berson understood that their method would have many applications.

RIA, as it soon became known, can be likened to the children's game of musical chairs, if we may extend this metaphor. In an RIA, radiolabeled antigen competes for antibody binding with the native antigen in a patient's blood sample. The antibody molecules, with their special ability to fit and bind specific antigen molecules, are the chairs. The antigen molecules are the kids. We can see only the kids playing the game if they are wearing party hats. The radioactively labeled antigen (for example, insulin-[131]I: insulin molecules that have been labeled with ^{131}I, a radioactive isotope of iodine) are kids wearing party hats. The molecules of a patient's own insulin in a small volume of blood plasma are kids without hats.

In playing the RIA game, we can use as many chairs as we like because we can adjust the antibody concentration in the assay. We can have as many kids with hats as we want because we can add as much labeled insulin as we like. What we want to find out is how many kids without hats are in a small volume of the patient's blood plasma. We start the game by putting three ingredients into a test tube with a buffer solution (a room with music): antibody molecules (chairs), labeled insulin (kids with hats), and the small volume of patient's plasma (containing an unknown number of kids without hats).

When we stop the music, the number of kids with hats that are left standing (the number of insulin-^{131}I molecules *unbound* to antibody molecules) is determined by the number of kids without hats (the number of unlabeled insulin molecules in the patient's blood plasma). So we determine the amount of insulin in someone's blood, say yours, by observing how a small volume of your blood affects the binding of radioactive insulin to insulin-binding antibody in a test tube.

If you have a high blood insulin concentration (lots of hatless kids in the game), then at the end of the assay many radiolabeled insulin molecules will fail to bind to the antibody (lots of kids with hats left standing). The higher your blood insulin concentration, the fewer radiolabeled insulin molecules will be able to bind to the limited number of antibody molecules because the places are simply taken by the greater number of your own insulin molecules from your blood sample.

By 1955 Yalow and Berson were already well known and respected for their quantitative work in the areas of iodine and albumin (albumin is a major protein constituent of blood plasma) metabolism. But the ability to measure peptide hormones was quite a trick. These are the vital little proteins that act as chemical messengers and regulate body functions, like insulin. Some of these circulate in the blood in concentrations as low as 10^{-12} moles per liter, which is about the concentration of one teaspoon of sugar mixed in a lake measuring sixty-two miles long, sixty-two miles wide, and thirty feet deep. Yalow and Berson quickly realized they could apply the method to a vast array of endogenous (produced by the body) and exogenous (introduced from outside the body) substances, because antigenicity, the ability to elicit an antibody response, as they had shown for insulin, was a far more general characteristic of molecules than had previously been thought. The commercial possibilities for RIA were enormous, and indeed RIAs have made fortunes for commercial laboratories and producers of assay kits.

"We never thought of patenting RIA," Yalow says, looking down her nose as though a dead fish had been placed before her. "Of course, others suggested this to us, but patents are about keeping things away from people for the purpose of making money. We wanted others to be able to use RIA. Now some people assume that I'm sorry, but I'm not. Anyway, we had no time for such nonsense."

The antibody is the heart of any immunoassay because, like a deft and educated hand, it must grasp only one specific molecule, its antigen, the very molecule that called it forth from the lymphocytes of the immune system. In the assay, that same antigen must be picked out by the antibody from whatever number of other, even similar, molecules it encounters. In other words, almost any chemical can stimulate antibody production. Because of this, they created a tool that could be adapted for work on almost any biological problem, be it a question relating to insulin metabolism in diabetics or to determine why some people get hepatitis after a blood transfusion or whether a patient has too much or too little of a specific medication in their blood. The flow of vital scientific data began to pour from their unlikely little laboratory on Kingsbridge Road in the Bronx.

Yalow and Berson never had a large or well-equipped laboratory, but their rapid application of RIA to a variety of scientific issues captured the imagination of the scientific community. Along with the brilliant young physician-scientists who flocked to their mom and pop shop from the early 1950s through the late 1960s, they first transformed the science and practice of endocrinology (the study of hormone action) by developing assays and studying insulin, growth hormone, adrenocorticotrophic hormone (ACTH), parathyroid hormone (PTH), among others, and then showed the way to new vistas in hematology, gastroenterology, virology, and pharmacology, while teaching the rest of the scientific world their methods. The result was exponential progress in virtually every aspect of medicine and biological science. Every clinical, research, and commercial medical laboratory in the world was using their method. Every pint of blood was checked for contamination with it, and chances are good your blood has been analyzed by RIA.

Berson and Yalow, Yalow and Berson, magic team, man and woman, physicist and physician, were fast, sharp, yet vastly different in temperament and training. They inspired awe, and the scientific medical community was at their feet. Their methods and scientific paradigms were being used to determine the presence of all kinds of substances in every tissue and body fluid, to characterize the molecular form of the materials, and, most important, to precisely measure their concentrations. Suddenly, physicians and researchers wanted to go to the Bronx V.A. Hospital to meet and learn from the masters. And they came from everywhere: Guillemin, Rosselin, and Assan from Paris, Isidori and Negri from Rome, Samols and Hartog from London, Thomopoulou from Athens, Devlin from Dublin, Gomez-Mont from Mexico, Scott from Auckland, McGarry, McKenzie, Colle, and Schucher from Montreal, Beraud from Lausanne, Brauman from Brussels, Pimstone from Capetown, Jadresec from Santiago de Chile, to mention just a few.[3]

The guests would stay for a few days, a week, a month, and leave the Bronx with the secrets of RIA. They left with handson experience using the new method that was changing the world, and with the blessings of the masters. Many also took with them some of Berson and Yalow's precious antisera, the small volumes of guinea pig plasma containing specific antibody molecules, to enable them to begin to work quickly when they got home. For many, it was a gift of a new direction in their work.

All returned with stories of what it was like to be around Berson and Yalow as concepts and approaches to problems flew between them and around the lab like tennis balls. "It was like bouncing ideas around," say many of the people who worked in the lab. It was the free exchange of ideas and the opportunity to participate that excited the visitors and the fellows alike. Berson and Yalow were overpowering in the defense of their data when controversy arose, but they didn't try to stifle the competition. They didn't try to sell their antisera, and the suggestion that they patent their methods, as Yalow indicates, was met with frank derision. It can truly be said that they gave of their knowledge and materials and bade the scientific community to go forth and multiply. It is also true that they were intensely competitive, disinclined to collaborate with others, and frequently harsh and unforgiving in their criticism.[4]

The work in their laboratory was very intense because they drove themselves hard. Yalow, who worked longer hours in the lab, also wanted to fulfill her role as wife and mother. But there were some precious quiet moments in the lab. Yalow had found the guinea pig to be the best species to produce antisera. In the little room that housed them, she opened herself to feelings of tenderness for the animals. Very early in the morning, she would come with lettuce from home to supplement the guinea pig's diet. Before anyone else had arrived, she would take each guinea pig from its cage, cradle it in the crook of her left arm, and feed it with her right hand. All the while she would talk to it, calling it by its name (they were named according to their distinguishing colors), "black right ear, white left ear, brown back," or "black head, white body," cooing, soothing, entreating the animal to be happy, and cajoling it to produce the most wonderful antiserum. "Yes, my little black head, white body, yes, isn't this lettuce sweet? Are you drinking enough water? Why isn't your bottle empty? I'll give you fresh water anyway. You're such a cute one, so handsome, and your gastrin antisera is the best in the world." When the animals were injected with antigen, or bled for their antibody containing plasma, she would hold them, nuzzle them, kiss the tops of their heads, whisper to them.

An observer, never having seen Yalow in such a tender moment, would be visably astounded. She would say that it was this that brought the good antibody, this soft sweetness, more than the right combination of antigen injected according to the precise schedule that he had read in the little green antibody notebook for each animal. No, she would say, anyone can make the antigen preparation and inject it and then take blood from the animals on schedule, but you must talk to the guinea pigs. You have to love them if they are to give you the special antiserum that you need. She believed that she had the touch, and treasured her relationship with each animal (Fig. 3). So here was the formidable Dr. Yalow in the earliest morning or latest night, communing with her guinea pigs. The few who observed this were shocked and amused by the depth of her belief in this unscientific notion, but soon the moment would pass, the lab would be bustling again, struggling with ideas, techniques, and the grind of hard work, and the whispering, romancing maiden was nowhere to be found.

The Radioisotope Unit of the Bronx V.A. Hospital generated the special air of excitement and discovery that fills only a few places from time to time. It was an air rich in the noble elements of intellectual curiosity, honesty, hard work, and enormous expectations. And it was free of the fumes of commercial exploitation, something that would be hard to imagine in today's competitive medical marketplace where, as reported in the the *New York Times*, tests for the chromosomal defect causing Down's syndrome in the fetuses of pregnant women are held up because the holder of a patent demands a $9 royalty for the performance of each test.[5] Many people still recall how their first breath in that atmosphere was intoxicating, even addicting. And, like a team playing behind a pitcher throwing a no-hitter, even if no one mentioned it, everyone felt that The Prize, the one they called "The Big One," was on its way.

Sitting in their cramped office, their identical desks facing each other and pushed together to provide a large work surface, Berson would put his feet up after a long day, smile, shake his

Figure 3. Rosalyn Yalow with one of her precious guinea pigs.

head, and exclaim, "They pay us to do this!" His satisfaction seemed complete; he would express his exuberance like a musician playing a cadenza: a song to the development of a scientific concept, or a rif about Etruscan art, or Middle Eastern history. He would liken scientific discovery to artistic creativity. As he once said in an interview, it was "the thrill of perceiving a little corner of the universe into which no one has previously been privileged to glimpse. But unlike the truly virtuous, the immodest researcher hardly hesitates to publish the fruits of his labors and loses no opportunity to talk about them even if strained to visit the far corners of the globe for this purpose. Small wonder then that he at least secretly enjoys, if he does not overtly relish, any external approbation of his efforts." Soon Yalow would get up and make tea, thinking of the next experiment. But there was trouble in paradise.

In 1968 Sol Berson left the V.A. to become chairman of the Department of Medicine at the Mount Sinai School of Medicine. There had been other opportunities to leave the V.A. for a larger stage—he had been offered chairs of medicine before—but this time something in him told him to make the move. Mount Sinai, after all, was a new school of medicine. It had a bright future, and perhaps he thought that the great team's accomplishments in research were more than assured, and mostly behind them.

Yalow was against the move and refused to relocate their laboratory to the medical school. She could have gone to beautiful new digs, a larger laboratory, an exalted position at the medical school; all these were in the package that was offered to Berson. Nevertheless, Yalow liked the old place, it felt like home, producing gold from that unlikely mine with simple tools that she fashioned with her own hands. She felt that Mount Sinai would have distractions, internecine politics. She feared that she would be marginalized, that Berson would be drawn away from her and the scientific work by the pressures of a complex medical center, that she would be pressured to collaborate with other scientists while Berson was off administering his department.

Berson's predecessor in the chair of medicine at Mount Sinai had been Dr. Alexander B. Gutman, discoverer of the enzyme alkaline phosphatase, and the world's authority in the area of gout. Yalow knew that Gutman had a female research partner, T'sai Fan Yu, M.D. Her picture adorned the walls of the Capital Medical Center in Beijing, China, where she had been trained in medicine. A brilliant, accomplished scientist, she was hardly known at Mount Sinai, and that was hardly the fault of Gutman. It was simply that she was a woman, and women do not hold important positions in medical schools. Yalow had no intention of becoming a Yu, running a lab across the hall from the chairman's office, removed from the center, a satellite, a Ph.D. in the belly of the M.D.'s world, though it would hardly be the fault of Berson.

Yalow tried to persuade Berson to stay, but the lure of building a great department in a great medical school was too great.

After a brief struggle Berson left for Manhattan, and Yalow stood her ground in the Bronx. For some time Berson tried commuting to the Bronx to work at night, going over data, discussing future projects, but it became too taxing, and his hands were full at Mount Sinai, full of the extraneous things Yalow had predicted, and empty of science. It wasn't right for him, she would say. Berson was a scientist, not an administrator, not a politician, and Mount Sinai would kill him, she would say.

Hadn't Berson gone off to India for a month and returned to find that rival department chairs and the dean had snatched beds from his medical service, reducing its size and therefore its importance? Yes. Hadn't he become enraged, stormed out of meetings, threatened to quit? Yes.

Didn't Berson rub hard against the old guard at Mount Sinai? Yes, indeed. Yet he believed he would lead them to places they had never dreamed of through the power of his ideas and with his glorious vision of a medical center driven by a powerful research engine. But they would not follow. The dean and president (one man with two jobs) had a different vision, a more practical view, one based on the rewards of clinical practice, and a view that was certainly more in line with what was to come. The Golden Age of American medicine, begun with the end of World War II, with the triumph of idealism over racism and fascism, with enthusiasm for the boundless power of science and technology, had brought respect and power to creative and talented researchers like Berson. During that brief Golden Age, ideas, discoveries that solved problems and opened new ideas, held the higest value. Scientific imagination and the ability to make things work in the laboratory were prized above the commercial exploitation of medical technology.

But the Golden Age was fading, and a new age was already dawning—the age in which medicine would increasingly be seen as a cash cow, an industry like any other, to be run by managers, business people with, or without, M.D.s. Solomon Berson, removed from the clinical world, was a complete stranger to the concept of medical economics. He was a man for whom the idea of manipulating medicine for corporate profit was unthinkable, disgusting; he was lost in this world, and was thus achieving nothing. Yalow made it clear that Berson had made a mistake, a big mistake by leaving her and their mom and pop shop at the V.A. in the Bronx, and so she became a symbol of hostility to the men at the medical school.

Only an irretrievable outsider could have felt the way she did. As a woman, a Ph.D., she had no hope of cracking into the board rooms of power medicine. Her hostility to the great medical center came primarily from her perceived exclusion, and that was not specific to Mount Sinai. Women, Ph.D.s in physics, simply were, and still are, marginalized in all medical centers. As a more astute judge of people and institutions than Berson, Yalow also felt that medical centers were not places where science came first. She was nothing but a woman scientist. Berson had the gender and the medical degree at least to masquerade as one of "them."

By 1972, I was a young physician training in Berson's department at Mount Sinai. My primary interest was in research and I had some grant money and space in the laboratories of Dr. Kurt Hirshorn. Hirshorn, who would go on to become chairman of the Department of Pediatrics, characterized the best of the Golden Era: a brilliant, humane, good humored physician-scientist, who was at home in the laboratory and at the bedside. One day Berson called me to his office. He had been out for several weeks and explained that he had suffered a small stroke.

"I'm all better now," Berson insisted. "But I don't want anyone to know about this, not even Ros," he said, flashing a mischievous smile and taking a lung-filling drag on his inextinguishable cigarette. In retrospect, the stroke was probably caused by a silent, painless heart attack. "And I want you to do something for me which will be good for you as well. I want you to go up to the Bronx V.A. and work in the lab with Ros. You'll have to talk with her. She will have to agree. She's the boss up there. I can only get to the lab once in a while now."

When Yalow said she would have me, I was off to the Bronx V.A. Heading there I had ambivalent feelings, since I would be working in the very building where administrators had fired my father in 1954 after he had built the Department of Medicine to the point where it was the pride of the system. Under pressure from "Tail Gunner Joe" McCarthy's demands that government agencies be cleansed of the subversive elements that the senator saw everywhere, my unfortunate father was visited by the FBI and encouraged to finger fellow workers. Instead, he kept the FBI at bay until their targets were out of the government's employ, and still refused to cooperate. Many years would go by before he would get a regular job. He made a living by writing articles for popular medical publications and by establishing a small private practice. However, upon reflection, I realized that nearly two decades had gone by, and it was hard to resist the charisma of Sol Berson.

With the possible exception of his leaving for Mount Sinai, Berson manipulations were always in the best interests of all concerned. Perhaps, if he had taken a chair of medicine after winning the Nobel Prize, things might have been different. The Nobel Prize confers a certain aura of special insight and authority that while it may be destructive to the creative process by elevating the recipient out of the essential give and take of scientific discourse, definitely smooths the way for the laureate.

One month after I started working at the V.A., Berson was found dead in a hotel room in Atlantic City. Just a few days before his fifty-fourth birthday, he had been attending a scientific meeting and had suffered a massive heart attack. The relationship with Berson was the center of Yalow's life. His death was her low point, both professionally and personally, and the pit from which she later rose to her greatest glory. I was there for that struggle. I am the witness.

2

Dumped

I have respect for people only because of
the qualities they have, not because of
their position.
ROSALYN SUSSMAN YALOW, PH.D., 1996

$\mathscr{W}$hen I arrived at the hospital, Rosalyn was gone. The house officer in the emergency room didn't remember her name, but he remembered a rather dirty old lady who had suffered a stroke. They had refused to admit her, or in technical lingo, she had been "dumped." Lots of old people stricken by strokes are dumped, since they may not be insured and thus would run up hospital costs to maintain them as they lie in a coma, waiting to expire. So they are transported instead to the municipal hospital, the place of last resort.

The tragedy is not that a great icon of medicine had been dumped. It may be ironic that Yalow had often been invited to that hospital's parent university to lecture, to receive an honorary degree, and that the presidents and deans had lined up just to touch her hand, to be remembered, and the professors had hung on her every word. The tragedy is that a desperately ill human being had been turned away as have so many others like her.

I had to find her. I would have gone to the nearest municipal hospital, but the house officer had remembered that when she left his emergency room the ambulance driver said they would take her to Montefiore Hospital, a private institution near her home. When I arrived, her cardiologist, Ira Rubin, was at her bedside. "She's comatose, and bleeding from the stomach," he told me. "They dumped her! Gene! Can you believe it!"

"Sure," I said. "She's not wearing that Nobel medallion around her neck. They saw a stroked-out senior citizen, no I.D., kind of ragged. . . . A GOMER (Get Out of My Emergency Room)."

"But she's got a serious G.I. bleed going. She could have bled out in the ambulance."

"I guess they lucked out."

Rosalyn had the physical signs of a basilar artery throm-

23

bosis. The CAT scan confirmed a big clot in the basilar artery at the base of her brain. A mean looking area of inflammation in her stomach wouldn't stop bleeding, and she couldn't receive anti-coagulants to prevent extension of the clot because of her bleeding stomach. Her chances of regaining consciousness seemed slim at best.

When her son Benjamin arrived, I said there was a small chance that the clot might dissolve spontaneously. Though this seemed unlikely, I had known of a few such rare recoveries. If this happened, she would wake up, and might be in the same shape she was in prior to this event.

Two years earlier Rosalyn suffered an unusual stroke that left her right side without proprioception—the ability to recognize the position of body parts. "My right arm doesn't talk to the rest of me," she would say. Stoic, intrepid, she responded as she had to other of life's disappointments: never complaining, making the best of what she had. She tried writing left-handed. She walked with difficulty and rarely again climbed the stairs to her bedroom. She lived downstairs, using only the half-bath near the kitchen and sleeping in the dining room. Benjamin did the shopping, got her clothes from upstairs, did the washing, and took care of everything.

But still, Yalow persevered, going to her office at the V.A. every day. She was picked up by a car service, returned home by Dr. Herbert Rose, assistant chief of staff for research. Moreover, she persisted in the fights that had concerned her for many years: the public's fear of nuclear power, what she regards as myths about the dangers of radioactive materials, microwave towers, irradiated food, and basement radon. Like Marie Curie, she had made her mark with radioisotopes and she feared that irrational and phobic attitudes might limit their use. And, like Curie, who died of the effects of radiation on her bone marrow, Yalow is less fearful of radioactivity than are most lay people, or other scientists, frequently defending nuclear weapons testing and supporting the safety of nuclear power. She figured that she was on the right track when she was alone in debates at the National Academy of Sciences, or when she was booed at the Bronx High School of Science for advocating nuclear power. Even hobbled, she likes a good fight.

She had based her calculations concerning radiation damage from atomic bomb testing and other radiation associated risks on published government data.[1] Whether she was influenced by political concerns or was simply, and uncharacteristically, completely trusting and uncritical, Yalow never considered that the government's data might be false. Only very recently, it has become apparent that the government has obfuscated the truth in these matters. For example, in August 1997 the National Cancer Institute revealed that fallout from atomic bomb testing in Nevada from 1951–1962 contained greater amounts of thyroid cancer-causing iodine than was previously revealed to the public. It is now clear that the increase in thyroid cancers (10,000–75,000 more cases), found mostly in children and young Utah females, was due to atomic bomb test fallout. Similarly, documents[2] made public by former Department of Energy secretary Hazel R. O'Leary showed that throughout the 1950s, when the government was maintaining there were no health hazards from nuclear tests, the Atomic Energy Commission regularly warned the Eastman Kodak Company and other film manufacturers that radioactive fallout could damage their products.[3]

Only a few weeks before Yalow went into a coma, she had expressed her sorrow at the current state of research in the areas of medical science with which she is familiar:

> It's a different life in science now. The current attitude is to keep things you discover secret, to keep others from learning so that you can exploit what you are doing to the maximum. We tried to train people in the use of radioisotopes in medicine. We tried to open the field of nuclear medicine. We weren't helping the competition; we were creating the competition. And it's a shame, but today there's no future in anything with the word "nuclear" attached. People don't trust anything that has to do with the word nuclear or radioactivity. This is having a bad effect on nuclear medicine. Now the smartest people aren't going into nuclear medicine, and there are few people being trained in the field. But the distrust goes beyond radioactivity, the whole approach to research in science is being cut back. In to-

day's funding situation a young person can't feel safe about sustaining a career in scientific research, so if someone wants to get married and raise a family it's a very risky proposition. We're simply not getting the best and the brightest going into research the way we did in my day. It isn't just medical research, it's all research. You just can't tell students that there's a great future in research, and so we're not getting the brightest students. I'm glad I'm old.

On the evening of January 1, 1995, Benjamin Yalow signed DNR (Do Not Resuscitate) orders for his mother. This meant that if she had a complication, like a cardiac or respiratory arrest, there would be no attempt to save her. He was well aware of her wishes and of her attitudes concerning terminal illness and death. "I see no reason to exist in an unsatisfactory fashion," she would say. Like Curie, she spoke of her own death in calm, practical terms, absolutely without emotion. Rosalyn, who had had a long history of cardiac arrhythmias, lay there, comatose, bleeding, her heart beating irregularly. It looked like the end. Many doctors came to the bedside. They were curious, supportive, helpful, anxious to share anecdotes about the great woman, about her late husband, both of whom they had known and cared for, medically and personally, over many years. No one thought she would live.

After having borne a long flight across the country and many hours at his mother's side, Benjamin Yalow went home alone, exhausted, expecting that his mother would be gone by morning. In his early forties, never having left his mother's home, he was always the good son. Having already lost his beloved father, he was visibly shaken and could be expected to break. He had been misjudged before. But, as with the poor old woman on the litter who was turned away from the hospital emergency room, things are not always what they seem.

3

Woman in the Dunes

Anyone planning to argue with Rosalyn
Yalow would be well advised to be
properly prepared.[1]
J. EDWARD RALL, M.D., PH.D.
Senior Scientist
National Institutes of Health

If I were writing my story, it would be one
page long.
ROSALYN SUSSMAN YALOW, PH.D., 1996

$\mathcal{D}$ays passed with little to be done for Rosalyn, other than old-fashioned watching and waiting. She began to look more frail, smaller, and older than her seventy-three years.

Montefiore felt like home. Yalow and I had cochaired the Department of Clinical Sciences at Montefiore until 1984, and her husband, Aaron, had worked as a radiation physicist at Montefiore back in the 1950s. We knew many people there. Everyone was concerned and anxious about her condition, and even after the parade of physicians and hospital dignitaries trickled down, a strong current of genuine feeling and the desire to be helpful remained. Each day Benjamin and I went to the hospital to visit Yalow in the intensive care unit. It was hard to hang around there doing nothing while the staff was busy dealing with intravenous lines, monitor alarms, bladder catheters, bed changes, and the myriad essential functions they performed so well for someone who increasingly had little chance of surviving.

Benjamin stayed strong under extraordinary pressure. Having always lived at home, he felt the place dominated by the presence and the will of his mother. Her litter of medals, prizes, plaques, and testimonials—just the ones for which there was no room at the office—lay in piles on bookshelves and chairs, gathering dust, yet somehow creating an effect of sublime decadence, a clutter of stardust. Aaron, his father, with whom he had been close, was now more than two years dead. Aaron had a brilliant mind and had been a physicist like Rosalyn, but he worshiped his wife and allowed her to rule.

Benjamin's piles also lay around. Envelopes on the living room chairs and sofas, letters from lawyers, banks, insurance companies, and doctors, were all neatly arranged by Benjamin. These were documents of his father's estate, ever-so-slowly nearing completion, like a semi-permanent remembrance, as though Aaron would be there as long as the papers remained. There were also thousands of science fiction books—Benjamin's passion—piled on the floor, waiting to be read, again. And the house seemed to be collecting the remnants of an epic struggle between a begrudging world and a lone woman. There it sat: darkened by drawn curtains, in need of repair, distorted by the rearrangement of living space, perched over a buried river. Of the whole family, only Elanna, the Yalows' daughter, had fought her way out.

To add to the difficulties, Benjamin, still grappling with his father's death, and now with his mother dying, had recently quit his job. After more than twenty years at the City University of New York's Computer Center, a shake-up of the department had created instability and uncertainty regarding operations and directions. Stress in the workplace had thrown Benjamin's irritable bowel syndrome into high gear. He had decided to quit and do his computer work as an independent contractor. As difficult as this change was, it did provide Benjamin some relief, and he could become more deeply involved in the world of organized science fiction fandom, a place where he is well known and respected and feels at home. And science fiction has been a better home than most. After half a life of being considered "weird," first for prodigious precociousness, later for his astounding range and depth of interest and knowledge (including mathematics, all manner of science, the complete compendium of matters military, especially the technology of weapons, and sports of all kinds), he at last found the kind of respect and love he deserved in "the community." The science fiction community loves Benjamin for all the things that confuse what they call "normal" people, and they showered him daily with hundreds of e-mail messages of support and concern, as they had when his father was dying.

After several days the DNR orders expired, but Rosalyn was no better, so they were renewed. Benjamin was in close touch with Elanna, who lives in California, giving her the daily bulletin. There was no use in her coming, but she would have been there if she had been needed—if there had been something for her to do. Through the battles of a lifetime, battles familiar to most families, Elanna maintains her love and respect for her mother. But she has a husband and two young sons, and she is the president of a national firm that employs more than five thousand people. She has a doctorate in educational psychology from Stanford, and her company sets up and manages daycare centers. Elanna travels a great deal, while her husband, who edits computer books, works at home. She doesn't come to New York to hang around. "The apple doesn't fall far from the tree," said one family member in describing Elanna.

I went back to the first emergency room where Rosalyn had been taken by Hatzollah, the Jewish ambulance service, and dumped by the hospital. I wanted to read the record of the evaluation made there, and I wanted to find someone to explain the hospital's declining to admit a patient in her condition. I was directed to a clerk who told me that they kept no records at the hospital pavilion, that all the records were stored at the parent institution, and that I should call and then make a formal request in writing. When I called I was told that there was no record of anyone named Yalow, not on January 1, 1995, not ever. There were no responses to written requests.

"My first impression of Rosalyn Yalow,"[2] says Maurice Goldhaber, professor of Physics at Brookhaven National Laboratory, "[is] when she came to the University of Illinois in '41 or '42, the only girl to get a Ph.D. among the many hundreds of students . . . There were other women students but they all married and dropped out. There was one quite bright one who married one of the male students who got a physics Ph.D. She dropped out and became, I think, a teacher, and had seven children. She came from a Catholic family with twelve children, and she told me that her parents told her that they would never tell a child that it's a last child because there could always be another one. Anyhow, on this principle she had seven. Well, Rosalyn got married there too, but she went a different way. She and Aaron met there. They were both my students. So I first knew her as Rosalyn Sussman. And then they got married, and Aaron, in spite of his diabetes did reasonably well. He was certainly the weaker member of the family, but he did well. Maybe she took good care of him. Anyway, my first impression was that she was very aggressive. I said that to some of my American colleagues, I was not so long here from Europe," Goldhaber laughs, leaning back into his chair in a cluttered office at Brookhaven, where for many years he served as director. He is a warm person, sharp, quick, witty, and without pretension. "Perhaps you shouldn't tell her this, but, of course, the other professors, being American, they took this 'aggressiveness' as a compliment. But for me, it wasn't entirely a compliment."

Goldhaber, Yalow's thesis advisor in the Department of Physics at the University of Illinois, was born in 1911 and points out that this was the year that Ernest Rutherford discovered the nucleus of the atom. "I came of age at a time when nuclear physics also could be said to have come of age with the discovery of the neutron by James Chadwick in 1932," he wrote in his article "Reminiscences from the Cavendish Laboratory."[3]

Yalow's mentors at Hunter College (Herbert Otis, Duane Roller, and Jerrold Zacharias), having recognized her talent, gave her the vision to go into a wider world so that she could meet and study with big leaguers like Goldhaber. Goldhaber, an Austrian Jew, had begun his studies in nuclear physics in 1930 at the University of Berlin. There, along with Leo Szilard, Valentine Bargmann, Max Delbruck, and Hartmut Kallmann, he attended the physics colloquium where the front row was usually occupied by Max Planck, Albert Einstein, Max von Laue, Walter Nernst, Erwin Schroedinger, Otto Hahn, and Lise Meitner. By 1942, Goldhaber had already emerged as a major figure. His 1934 paper with Chadwick[4] defined the mass of the neutron and was influential in its acceptance as an elementary particle. Most important, Goldhaber, unlike some others, was willing to take on a female student.

He had met and later married Gertrude (Trude) Scharff, when she was a fellow physics student in Berlin. Trude got her Ph.D. there, before Goldhaber who left for Cambridge in 1933 because of the growing anti-Semitism. At Cambridge he worked under Rutherford, who was the Cavendish Professor. Goldhaber continued his friendship and collaborated with Leo Szilard, the theoretical physicist, who, upon learning of the discovery of nuclear fission in January 1939, immediately sounded a warning: Neutrons would be emitted in the fission of uranium, and this might lead to a chain reaction and the construction of bombs.

In 1938 Goldhaber took an assistant professorship at the University of Illinois. Trude soon joined him, and they were married. She could not get a job at the university because of a nepotism rule. This was an important reason for their eventual move to Brookhaven, where they could both work. Illinois, realizing what they had lost, repealed their nepotism rule shortly after the Goldhabers departed. So Goldhaber was keenly aware of the rarity of female physics students, especially in the United States, and he knew that Yalow would have difficulty getting a job.

Yalow also anticipated problems ahead. Before she was admitted to Illinois with a teaching assistantship, she had obtained a part-time job as a secretary to Dr. Rudolf Schoenheimer, a leading biochemist at Columbia University's College of Physicians and Surgeons. Yalow was a first-rate chemist, Jerrold Zacharias had assured Schoenheimer. Still, Yalow was told that she would have to start as a secretary and work her way into the lab. The secretarial job was supposed to provide an entry into graduate courses, via the back door, a common opening for women in science. She had to agree to take stenography courses. Yalow was willing to do that, willing to do almost anything for a career in science, now that her professors were behind her, and having been inspired by Eve Curie's biography of her mother, Marie Curie, which had just been published.

As a junior at Hunter College, she remembers "hanging from the rafters in Room 301 of Pupin Laboratories at Columbia when Enrico Fermi gave a colloquium in January 1939 on the newly discovered nuclear fission." One would expect that Fermi mentioned the essential role of Lise Meitner's physics in the realization of nuclear fission. Yalow does not remember. In 1939, only months after the discovery of fission and Meitner's flight from Germany, this woman of Jewish origin was well known in

America. Meitner could have become an inspiration to many women. She should have shared the Nobel Prize with her long-time collaborator and friend, Otto Hahn. But in the heat of the Nazi period, Hahn took the award and the credit, and in a short time Meitner was all but forgotten. Maybe that was the lesson Yalow learned: A woman could be involved in a decades-long partnership, play a major role in a momentous discovery, and then be shoved aside. She would learn stenography, too, if she had to, so she enrolled in a business course. But she quit it the minute she heard she was accepted at the University of Illinois. Tearing up the steno books, she exulted in what she felt was, for a woman, "an achievement beyond belief." She was to start as a graduate student, a candidate for a Ph.D. in physics, and she had been offered a teaching assistantship in the Physics Department. The teaching assistantship paid $70 a month plus free tuition. "I was the first woman to have a graduate assistantship in physics there since 1917," she remembers. "And I remember when I first got there I was given a list of housing on campus that wouldn't take Jews."

At the first meeting of the Faculty of the College of Engineering she discovered that she was the only woman among its four hundred members. Nonetheless, she insists that, "It is evident that the draft of young men into the armed forces, even prior to American entry into the World War, had made possible my entrance into graduate school."

At Illinois the administration was not sure whether they had ever awarded a Ph.D. in physics to a woman. Perhaps before World War I they might have, they told her, but certainly not since. This did not worry Yalow, even though her undergraduate coursework in physics had been minimal for a major, since Hunter College had only begun to offer a physics major during the second semester of her senior year. She therefore began her studies at the University of Illinois by sitting in on two undergraduate courses, taking three graduate courses, and working as a half-time assistant teaching the freshman course in physics.

In the end, she finished in three and a half years—at least one full semester before anyone else. She had done twenty-two courses and her thesis. She earned twenty-one As in her courses and one A− in the electrodynamics laboratory course (Fig. 4).

UNIVERSITY OF ILLINOIS—THE REGISTRAR'S OFFICE

Name Yalow, Rosalyn Sussman			Vault No. 146863

Entered	Matriculated	Matr. Number	Place and date of birth
Sept.20,1941	Sept.20,1941	133706	New York, N.Y., July 19, 1921

College	+Curriculum Major	Name of parent or guardian
Graduate	Physics	Simon Sussman

Degree Ph.D. (Physics)	Date Feb. 4, 1945	Address of parent or guardian
M.S. (Physics)	August 29, 1942	1881 Morris Ave., The Bronx, 53, New York

School last attended	Residence classification of student
Hunter College, B.A., Feb., 1941	Resident 6/8/42

ACCEPTED FROM

ADMISSION UNITS

English	Latin	History	Physics	Bookkeeping	
	German	Civics	Chemistry	Draw. & Man. Train.	
Algebra	French	Economics	Zoology	Music	
Plane Geometry	Spanish	Com. Geography	Botany	Agr. or Home Econ.	
Solid Geometry		Sociology	Biology	Sten. & Type.	
			Other Sciences	Misc. Subjects	

Descriptive Title of Course	Course Number	Sem.Hr.	Grade	Descriptive Title of Course	Course Number	Sem.Hr.	Grade
First Semester 1941-42		units					
Modern Lab. Practice	Phys. 191a	1	A				
Light	Phys. 71a	⅔	A				
Light Laboratory	Phys. 72a	⅔	A				
Intro. to Higher Analysis	Math. 71a	1	A				
Second Semester 1941-42		3					
Light	Phys. 71b	⅔	A				
Light Laboratory	Phys. 72b	⅔	A				
Vacuum Tubes	Phys. 46	1	A				
Intro. to Higher Analysis	Math. 71b	1	A				
Summer Session 1942		4					
6/8/42 - 8/29/42							
Nuclear Physics	Phys.S183a	1	A				
Dynamics	Phys.S122a	1	A				
First Semester 1942-43		8					
Dynamics	Phys.122b	1	A				
Nuclear Physics	Phys.183b	1	A				
Modern Laboratory Practice	Phys.191b	1	A				
Second Semester 1942-43		11					
Electrodynamics	Phys. 146a	1	A				
Quantum Mechanics	Phys.181a	1	A				
Research	Phys.190	1	A				
Summer Semester 1943(16 weeks)		14					
Electrodynamics	Phys. 146b	1	A				
Research	Phys. 190	1	A				
First Semester 1943-44		16					
Research	Phys. 190	3	A				
Statistical Mechanics	Phys. 163	1	A				
Second Semester 1943-44		20					
Research	Phys. 190	4	A				
Summer Semester 1944 (16 weeks)		24					
Research	Phys.190	4	A				
		28					

A CERTIFIED TRANSCRIPT WILL HAVE THE UNIVERSITY SEAL
EMBOSSED AND THE REGISTRAR'S SIGNATURE IN BLUE BELOW.
JUN 11 1896

ISSUED TO STUDENT

A transcript is a confidential document and
should not be released without the student's
written consent.

Figure 4. Rosalyn Yalow's transcript from the University of Illinois.

The chairman of the Physics Department called her to his office. He had something to say now that this woman was getting her degree. He told her that she was a good student, but "that A— confirms that women do not do well at laboratory work."

"I can't remember who that was," Goldhaber laughs. Yalow remembers. He was the acting chairman of the department, and she didn't argue or protest. A graduate student doesn't argue with the chairman. Not then, she explains. Anyway, she thought she had done well enough. Aaron and many of the others had begun graduate school with better backgrounds. Aaron had a masters degree in physics when he started. Yet she had finished first—half a year in front of the pack—and with a nearly perfect record. "Who else would sleep in the bathroom?" She laughs, remembering the nights she had stayed in the lab to work, actually sleeping on the floor in the bathroom. "I worked harder."

After receiving her doctorate in physics, Rosalyn left her new husband to take a job in New York with IT&T. Though his wife had surpassed him as a student and had already landed a job, Aaron was delighted. He had no problem with their six-month separation. Aaron has been often described as weak because of his great deference toward his wife, his scholarly demeanor, and his high-pitched voice. Still, he had the uncommon strength to guide and support an ambitious woman and to maintain his own intellect in the face of an overwhelming partner. He never boasted and barely ever spoke of his own career as a professor of physics at Cooper Union, and a very popular one at that. Nor was it known among many who dominated their own wives, among men who expected the kind of consideration that Aaron gave to Rosalyn, nor among women who deferred to men and saw his respect as strange, that she frequently turned to him for advice and help that he had given her direction, had read and critiqued every paper and every speech she wrote. Aaron felt secure enough in himself and his capabilities that he had no need to flaunt this. And, as a young man, he had displayed an adventurous spirit in the cause of politics. In 1940 Aaron Yalow decided that he would attend the Democratic National Convention in Chicago. As an insulin-dependent diabetic, it took great physical courage for him to hitchhike there from his home in Syracuse.

Despite the summer heat, he went on the road with excitement, optimism, and a come-what-may attitude. Aaron wanted to participate in the political process; he wasn't satisfied with observing and criticizing. He had the dedication of an activist and the ideals of a liberal. The trip would have been an adventure for any young man, but for a diabetic in the era before disposable syringes and needles who would have to boil his injection apparatus at least twice daily and who would be without materials to keep his insulin cool, it took determination and courage. But Aaron had none of the bluster and egotism that is often expected of men.

As Rosalyn Yalow left Illinois for IT&T, World War II raged on. Many American scientists devoted themselves to the Manhattan Project, the U.S. government project (1942–1945) that led to the production of the first atomic bombs. IT&T was a European firm and all of her coworkers were Jewish men, mostly from France, who had escaped from Europe just in time. Although she was the only female scientist working there, they treated her well, and she felt no pressure or discrimination. Still, she says, "They had to have a war so that I could get a Ph.D. and a job in physics." The refrain, along with the coy smile, confronts and evades her struggle.

"She was very clever," Goldhaber says of Yalow, remembering her early days as his student, trying to find a key to her later success.

> She did her work well. As I say, the work which we published turned out to be wrong, but that is partly my fault, and partly the speed, and we were a bit isolated during the war; you couldn't get criticism. She was aggressive, always in a hurry. Aaron was not aggressive. He was a bit, well, weak, you might say. But, strictly by chance, I gave him a more interesting problem. We didn't publish it properly. We published only an abstract. We should have made a big fuss about it. It turned out to be very important. At that time it was believed that neutron resonances mainly disappear by gamma emission, and Aaron found one which disap-

peared by re-emitting the neutron. That was a big surprise at the time. Now, of course, it's part of the folk-
lore. But I wasn't a pusher, and Aaron didn't push
himself. I suppose in their family Rosalyn was in
charge; I don't know. For research you need a little
aggressiveness. These days you need to elbow a little.
She would come to me to discuss her progress and
that's when she usually was a little impatient. If I was
busy or something, she'd want my attention. Well, in
retrospect, since she was so successful, one can say her
aggressiveness was built on something, it wasn't just
for the sake of aggressiveness. It was because she was
going somewhere. Going somewhere in a hurry. She
keeps saying that I didn't appreciate her. I don't know
why she says that.

There are elements of a woman's life that seem invisible to
men and, in the face of the constant forces that make for muddle-
ment, may be only barely perceived by women themselves. Rosalyn doesn't understand why some men didn't immediately per-
ceive her worth. She tells her story without listening to the
words. Then she tells her story, listens, and decides that it is true,
receiving validation from her effect on a male audience. She feels
that all women scientists should marry, rear children, cook, and
clean in order to achieve fulfillment, to be a complete woman.
Her yearning for autonomy, which women and men share, is a
source of ambivalence as she yearns for protection in a male-
dominated environment. She seems unaware of this dichotomy.
Where were the women who were in a position to help her? She
remembers receiving help and support only from men. Yet she
was required to give men help and support, and she asserted her
will among men, while simultaneously subjugating herself. She
insisted upon her competence, her recognition, her place. Still,
she thinks her story would be no longer than a page.

"It was a big surprise to me that a male physician would
treat me as an equal," she says. "If Sol had not been that way,
there would have been nothing I could have done about it."

4

Paper, Twine, and Collars

My hero.
Aaron Yalow

On the morning of the fifth day of her coma Rosalyn Yalow suddenly woke up and said, "Get me out of here." The clot had dissolved. She immediately began to try to take control of her situation. Her physicians at Montefiore Hospital called me to complain that she was giving them orders. Benjamin and I breathed a sigh of relief. We knew that this was a good sign, and so Elanna came to visit.

Meanwhile, the chairman of the Department of Medicine at the university whose hospital had originally dumped Rosalyn sent word through an intermediary that his facility had done the best thing for her. They had felt she needed neurosurgery and there was none there. So they let her go. The intermediary and I had a good laugh. There had been no surgery at Montefiore, no thought of it. Also, it's odd that the record would be expunged when you've done the best thing. Now that Rosalyn was alive and aware, she was once again the Nobel laureate and the member of the National Academy of Sciences. She could again have influence on institutions, funding agencies, and opinion makers. If there was any concern that she might be vindictive or sue there need not have been, because she is the last person to consider redress in the courts; she simply laughed off the incident.

"Ros' mother was the dynamo," says Sherman Lawrence, Rosalyn's first boyfriend.[1] Rosalyn met Sherman when she was thirteen. He was her beau until she went off to Illinois at the age of twenty. Now he's her lawyer, and they are still close friends. Sherman enjoys a long and successful marriage and strong family ties. He shares a plush midtown office space with his son, also a thriving lawyer.

Sherman has a relaxed confidence about him, and a voice that takes you in like a natural storyteller. "The mother was the dynamo, oh yeah! The father was a nice recessive man. And when he died I handled the estate. And that Rosalyn, boy, she took over. You know, it was just like she was in science. She was that way with everything, she made all the decisions. She was meticulous. She was determined. Nothing would stand in her way. She used to scare me."

Clara Sussman, Rosalyn's mother, was born in Berlin before the turn of the century. At that time, Jews could do well, and her family was educated and wealthy. Her maternal grandfather owned a lucrative weaving business, and his wife was a society matron from a leading family, a large and powerful woman. Clara's mother, Bertha, left Germany in the 1890s and the misfortune that drove her from home was the salvation of her family. Bertha's brothers were physicians, and quite successful. They practiced in Berlin when German medicine was the fountainhead of Western medical tradition, and they were important members of society, with all of the trappings of place and position. They had retired by the time they were killed during the Nazi era.[2]

Bertha, like her mother, was tall, intelligent, and well educated. She might have taken her place as a ranking member of Berlin's Jewish society by marrying a doctor, lawyer, banker, or even a professor. But she had married down to a handsome tailor, a "lady's man" who made uniforms for high-ranking army officers. Despite his charm and good looks, he was just a tradesman, and that brought disfavor and eventually disinheritance.

Hard times forced the couple to emigrate. In search of work the young family, Herman and Bertha Zipper along with their five children, moved to Russia. They settled in Rega where they lived for two years and had a sixth child, but when Rega failed to provide a better life they came to America. They lived in Philadelphia for a short while before relocating to the tiny village of Wellsville, Ohio. There, Herman Zipper opened a tailor shop, and Clara and her three sisters and two brothers went to school. After six long years in Wellsville, the family moved to New York City in 1895, to the German section of Yorkville on the Upper East Side. Herman opened a custom tailor shop specializing in fine clothes for the physically handicapped. He was a wonderful tailor, very careful, making patterns to fit even the most deformed individuals. He taught tailoring to his daughters, but Clara had what he called a "hot needle," meaning the clothes she made would fall apart. Clara was full of life, and not afraid of her father, who might yell and intimidate others. "Kill me, I dare you," she would say, standing before him with her arms folded across her chest. The Zippers spoke German at home, never Yiddish, and even though Herman understood English, he spoke only German.

With all of the picking up and moving on, searching for a place where a decent living could be made, Clara Zipper acquired only a sixth grade education. And while that might seem odd, coming from such successful stock, the reversal of fortune for Bertha and her family was, of course, far less catastrophic than for the family they had left in Germany. In America, Clara grew solidly into that matriarchal line, tall, strong, intelligent, and, as Sherman points out, a dynamo, with energy to spare. She met and married her husband, Simon Sussman, in New York.

Simon's family had emigrated from Russia, but he was born in New York. Raised on the Lower East Side among poor Jewish immigrants, he had only an eighth grade education. That didn't keep him from educating himself and developing a successful business selling paper and twine, and if his wife was the family's prime mover, Simon was no pushover. He was a strong man, both physically and in asserting himself as head of the household. But Clara knew how to handle her husband. Their son, Alexander, known to the family as Allie and to others as Alex, was born in 1915. Their second child, Rosalyn, was born on July 19, 1921 (Fig. 5).

Clara read all the books that Rosalyn and Allie brought home from school, and she picked up the language of what she read, even technical language from the college texts. She appeared educated, and her husband read the *New York Times* every day. "Not the *Daily News*," Rosalyn remembers. Simon, however, never read the books. "He was a reader, but mostly the newspaper, and very good with figures. My father ran the cemetery committee of his lodge. It took a lot of time, and he did it with care," Rosalyn recalls.

Figure 5. Simon and Clara Sussman with their children Alexander and Rosalyn.

Still, the family was distinctly working class and a secular Jewish family with no religious interest. Rosalyn is proud that she came from uneducated parents, thrived in the New York City public school system, and graduated from Hunter College, a public college in the city university system. It is the pride of a self-made New York woman who came up through the city's institutions, when they were strong and free and offered the promise of equal opportunity—a pride that goes to the heart of the democratic ideal. It's an attitude that says give me half a chance and I can do it, and that's all most people ever want.

Simon Sussman's first job was as a motorman on the 3rd Avenue El, the now defunct elevated line on New York's municipal railway system. From this he put enough money together to open the paper and twine business on the Lower East Side. His brother did the same, though with separate businesses, since they didn't always get along. They both did well wholesaling rolls of brown paper and the rough twine used for wrapping packages. Simon worked in a small office with a telephone, making deals, buying and selling, delivering his goods. He was a reliable, honest man. Building his business from nothing, he finessed it into something resembling prosperity.

The Sussmans moved uptown, out of the Lower East Side ghetto to the Bronx, where you went in those days if you were making it. Not making it big, but moving up to Walton Avenue, they were delighted to move to a good Jewish neighborhood. The year was 1929, Rosalyn was about eight, Allie was fourteen. Suddenly things got harder. The stock market crashed, and the Great Depression took hold. Though they never went hungry, money became tight. Clara took in homework from the neckwear trade, sewing collars, and Rosalyn worked with her mother, turning the collars as her mother sewed. The father struggled on with paper and twine, making it work as best he could, but now, for the first time, he wasn't able to overcome difficulty through sheer hard work. Businesses were folding, Simon's customer base was shrinking. He became worried, frustrated, and although he was a kind man, he could bluster.

There was power in the X chromosome; control and stability resided in the dominant matriarchal line. Clara did more collars, stitched the family seams, kept it going, maybe the "hot needle" cooled with her daughter by her side turning collars and learning to bear down, to push out trouble, and to focus on the work. Downtown the stocks were dropping, businesses flopping, businessmen jumping from the 21st floor. Up on Walton Avenue, the Sussman females, like those in many other families, worked together and hung strong.

Clara was one of those imposing, stately women, who by all accounts was in charge of her home even though her husband appeared commanding. Simon demanded absolute cleanliness, even giving the white glove treatment to the wheels of Allie's baby carriage. Clara simply did the cleaning at 4:00 P.M., just before he would get home.

At age ninety-eight she had a powerful presence and a strong constitution when I admitted her to Montefiore Hospital to evaluate her severe left flank pain. The abdominal x-ray showed a stone in her left ureter, the passage from the kidney to the bladder, and there were some red blood cells in her urine. But the ureter wasn't obstructed and I was unsure of the pain's cause. She endured that pain with good spirit, never asked for more medication, and inquired how things were going for me.

One night she had a reverie, a waking dream in which her family was gathered at an outdoor party. Everyone was there, sisters, nieces, cousins, enjoying the day in the open air. There were trees and grass, and she enjoyed the experience until she realized that she could not make it go away. When she reported this to the house staff on their morning rounds they became concerned and ascribed it to cimetidine, a medication they thought she had been taking. Clara reassured the young physicians. She had not taken the prescribed cimetidine, and, she explained, old people get a bit disoriented when they sleep away from home. Indeed, that afternoon she called me to her bedside with the solution to the mystery of her aching flank. She had developed the typical rash of herpes zoster, shingles, over her left flank and abdomen, and she went home the next morning. In a few weeks it was all gone.

Clara had had several abortions before Allie was born. She had been either unsure about wanting children or felt the timing was wrong, but that had been her decision. When her children were born she devoted herself to mothering. Simon spent his free time working for the Knights of Pythias lodge. It was a secret society like the Masons, full of ritual signs, symbols, and expressions. Simon was an enthusiastic member and eventually brought his wife, his sister-in-law, and his niece into the lodge.

An orderly man, Simon was organized and meticulous. He adored yet feared his daughter—at least Allie thought so. Rosalyn's older cousin, Ruth Wollman, who is ninety, remembers why. Rosalyn was outspoken, supremely confident, and fearless. Once, when Rosalyn was eleven and Ruth was twenty-four, the youngster embarrassed her in front of the family. "Cousin Ruthie, do you have your doctorate degree?" Rosalyn asked. "No, Ros, not yet," Ruth responded. "I'm only twenty-four, and I just have my masters." "Well," said Rosalyn, "when I'm your age I'll have *my* doctorate." Ruthie loves Rosalyn for that, for her spunk, for her willingness to speak out. She feels that Rosalyn, who for years followed her around, takes after her, although surpassing her, in that brash way of saying whatever is on her mind. Perhaps not everyone enjoyed Rosalyn's all-engines-full-ahead approach. Another time, again with the family gathered, Allie was asked to recite a poem he had learned in school. Allie was a bit shy and he declined. But Rosalyn jumped right up and recited the poem, stealing all of the thunder.

Rosalyn remembers that women and men had different interests then and that her parents didn't spend much time together. Her father was away working or at the lodge, running the cemetery committee. He was proud of the orderliness of his cemetery operation, and of how he helped the families of the lodge members in their times of sorrow and need. For her mother, there wasn't much emotional contact with Simon, and Rosalyn's memories of him are scant and distant.

Rosalyn's most active memories are of learning to read very early and of going to the library. In those days you got a library card by going to the library and reading to the librarian. When she got her first card, the librarian was amazed that a five-year-old could read so well. Allie had taught her to read. He would take her to the library each week and both kids would read voraciously. Rosalyn remembers little about the goings-on in the home except that males and females lived quite separate lives. She liked the closeness of helping her mother by turning the collars. Soon Rosalyn was taking over the rule of the roost. Even at the tender age of seven or eight, Allie referred to her as "The Queen Bee."

Allie began feeling deprived. During the tough years, when he was a teenager, he worked to contribute to the family's maintenance, yet he felt certain voids in his life. He felt the lack of material things, but even more important, he suffered through the tensions and frustrations of struggling through hard times without feeling the kind of human contact he craved. Less verbally demanding, less driven than his little sister, though he was older, he felt at sea. Already a teenager, Allie seemed to miss out on the stability of a tight working relationship with his mother. Family frustrations could be vented on Allie. He could be yelled at. He could be slapped. But he knew, and Rosalyn knew, that no one would dare slap her. Maybe she wouldn't come home late or step out of line, but in any case, they wouldn't dare. From as far back as anyone in the family can remember, Rosalyn had a no-nonsense attitude and a commanding presence.

Allie wanted to get out of the house early, before he was of college age. He wasn't happy at home, but he had to wait. Finances were difficult and he had to help. Perhaps the home wasn't the happiest home. Maybe he was the only one who knew it. They had struggled through the Great Depression. He had done what he could by pitching in, working while doing brilliantly at City College. And now it was over. After graduating he took a routine job in the post office and married young; maybe it was his escape route, and that might explain why the marriage ended quickly. Soon enough he was married again and this time to a girl of German origin, not a Jewish girl. In those days even secular Jews didn't marry German girls. It meant trouble. And that marriage soon ended.

His third wife was everything anyone could ask for, a woman Rosalyn had introduced him to. But there was trouble once again because his new wife, Estelle, wasn't an observant Jew. Even though the Sussmans had never been religious, and

Allie wasn't religious, hadn't even become a bar mitzvah—a common rite of passage even for secular Jewish boys at that time—there were troubled vibrations coming from the Yalows. By that time Rosalyn was married to Aaron Yalow and fulfilling the role of wife in a deeply religious tradition. Now that Rosalyn went along with her husband's religious practice, somehow they expected the same of Allie. The Yalows wanted this marriage to change Allie. They wanted him to be a family man, keep kosher, have children, be ambitious in the traditional sense, and go on to something beyond his post office job. Although there was no reason to believe that this would happen, Aaron and Rosalyn were clearly disappointed. This created a distance that could not be bridged between the Yalows and Allie and his third wife.

Aaron Yalow's religion was deeper than culture. It was in the marrow. In all matters related to religion he had his way. And Rosalyn had her way in all the things of the world. This was their understanding. When he spoke of religious matters or of the history of the Jews, which for him were the same, and when he debated finer points of interpretation of religious text, which were as grains of rice to a meal, he came alive. There was a glow, and he was a man distinct from the one who wandered in the empty secular world, where he knew everything about physics, but didn't live it, never quite fulfilled his potential. For Aaron, family meant children, a Jewish home, a religious life.

Aaron Yalow's parents were both from very orthodox families. His father, Samuel, was the chief rabbi of Syracuse, New York, and the upstate region surrounding the city. Though not Black Hat (not wearing the traditional black garb of the Hasid in even its least exotic form) he was in the Chabad Lubavitch movement until the end of his life (Fig. 6). The Chabad Lubavitch movement is the most active group in Jewish orthodoxy which works to bring Jews into orthodox Jewish life. As a major Lubavitch rabbi in the upstate region, Rabbi Yalow had contact with the Lubavitch Rebbe, at least yearly getting a visit during which contributions from the community would be transferred. The Rebbe is the head of the movement, revered to the point of worship, and he was considered by many within the movement to be the messiah.

Figure 6. Aaron Yalow and his father studying the Talmud in the backyard of the Yalow home in Syracuse, New York.

At the very end, after Rabbi Yalow became ill and moved to Brooklyn for his last months, there was a disappointment. The Rebbe failed to acknowledge him in his suffering. There was no prayer, no blessing for Rabbi Yalow, no message. It is hard to understand the depth of the pain and the disillusionment this caused. Rabbi Yalow was a good man; many considered him a saintly man. The family tradition had been Lubovitch for generations.

When Rabbi Yalow died, the family decided to split from the Lubovitch movement. More than a decade later, when Rosalyn Yalow became a Nobel laureate, a Lubovitch representative contacted the family with invitations to return to the fold. Aaron responded through intermediaries, indicating that there would be no return without an apology from the Rebbe. It never happened.

Although Aaron had not become a rabbi, his life centered around the synagogue, and religion was his passion (Fig. 7). An active Zionist, he worked for the United Jewish Appeal, acted as the link between his synagogue and the Riverdale community, and organized lectures for the synagogue on public affairs and other issues. Finally, he became the nexus between his wife and the world of Jewish tradition and religion.

Allie and Estelle were not religious. They were liberal in their beliefs and had no children. This distanced them from the Yalows. By the 1960s Aaron and Rosalyn, who in 1944 had both worked for the election of the left-leaning Democrat Henry Wallace, had become politically conservative in response to Zionist concerns. Interestingly, in the early 1940s they felt that Roosevelt *wasn't liberal enough.* They felt that the Left was sympathetic to the plight of European Jews, while the Right had done business with Hitler. Nonetheless, in the late 1940s through the 1950s, with the deepening of the Cold War and their concern for the well-being of Israel, the Yalows moved further and further to the right. Allie and Estelle didn't socialize much with the Yalows. No one cared to get into arguments or listen to offensive points of view, so the two couples remained cordial, but at a distance. In 1979 Allie retired, and he and Estelle decided to move to Florida (Fig. 8).

Figure 7. Aaron Yalow at the Wailing Wall in Jerusalem, Israel.

In a typical family, Jewish or otherwise, the first-born son is frequently the one who is pushed and therefore surpasses his younger siblings in achievement even if they are endowed with greater gifts. It is striking that Rosalyn had so much more drive and ambition than her older brother. Everything points to the fact

Figure 8. Rosalyn, Aaron, and Benjamin Yalow, with Aaron's sister and brother-in-law, Israel and Chaniett Lerner, and Estelle and Allie Sussman.

that Allie, like his sister, had more than sufficient intellect; he had a brilliant mind, possibly her equal, but their priorities and interests were different. He continued in a low-level post office job, never aspiring or attempting to raise himself in the known and accepted hierarchy of what others perceived as the "professional life." Allie never had a professional life. He made a living.

One analysis might demand that Rosalyn was more "masculine" than Allie. On the other hand, aggressiveness and drive, characteristics that surely are considered masculine, right down to the testosterone levels circulating in the blood, may simply be poorly defined in our popular imagination, and they are socialized out of many young women. Rosalyn Yalow's life, and her interaction with those around her, continuously challenge conventional notions of what is masculine and feminine. Where one stands between the desire for autonomy and control, and the seemingly opposed need for protection, support, and approval, may vary considerably during the course of a lifetime. It can vary during the course of a day, and ultimately, one's general position in that dichotomy may be more a consequence of socialization than of gender. Rosalyn's feeling that Goldhaber, her former professor, did not sufficiently appreciate her talents suggests a need for approval that was already under tight wraps and was subsequently suppressed to the point of apparent extinction.

If, in fact, Alex Sussman felt needy and unloved, if he craved the approval of his family, and if Rosalyn's attitudes and responses are more representative of that family, then he would have received little recognition or satisfaction for those needs. Somehow, Rosalyn and her brother had very different emotional cores. There is a stoicism that overflows its banks onto a plain where feeling is difficult, and certainly, the expression of feeling, if not extinct, is greatly diminished. Rosalyn Yalow is in that tradition. She picks up an invisible shield and marches on. She is going for something, and her eyes are on it, shedding no tears. This served her well in professional life. She put everything into her science, and she was ready to drop a cherished theory and start again if the data went in a different direction. In her personal life, she simply created her reality, made it work for her, regarded its perceived functionality as validation, and might convince some others that her creation was the truth.

According to Sherman Lawrence, Rosalyn's former boyfriend, who was hanging around the house when Allie was eighteen:

> Allie messed his own life up. He entered the post office because he married when he was young. The woman he married, the first one, was the worst thing for him. He was the victim of his own foolish decisions. Allie could have been a scientist just like Rosalyn was, if he didn't get involved in all these personal things, and he ended up a real playboy. Women kind of destroyed his life in a way, in that he didn't have an opportunity to use his intelligence.
>
> Ros and Allie just didn't get along. She didn't invite him to the Nobel Prizes, whether it was the wife he had married. . . . They got along up until his first marriage. That's what created the distance with the family: they felt that he never should have gotten married—he was young. That handicap is what stayed with him his whole life. Rosalyn felt that he should have done better.
>
> She's very unemotional when it comes to things like that. She was never anybody to show emotion. She was cold blooded as they make it. I've never seen . . . She built a shield around herself. You know what I mean? And no one can tackle that shield. . . . Even when her father died, and her mother died, she took it all in stride. Aaron too. I mean she's that way. She was a scientist all her life, never showed emotion, not openly. But a great woman! Great as they come. She would go down to Congress, oh boy! And [she was] a wife! And a mother!

If she felt her brother was frittering away his life, Rosalyn had long ago resolved that she would fight to get ahead. Rosalyn points out that Allie never even moved up in the post office. Her cousin Ruthie's husband was also at the post office, but he rose in the ranks, and he had only a high school education. No, Allie was soft, and if, as Estelle says, "he warmed people," if Benjamin and Elanna Yalow liked him, and if he was active in helping disadvantaged youth, that was OK.

But there is still a more serious purpose to life, at least according to Yalow. She never drifted, she planned, made up her mind and went for it. She believes "Allie wasn't intellectually aggressive. Whereas I, as a small child, made up my mind that people and institutions were going to need me, and I was going to let them know that they would need me." Yalow felt that a man needed to be that way more than a woman.

Sherman Lawrence recalls: "She knew what she wanted. She used to scare me. I mean, 1, 2, 3. And she was that way when she was young." Yalow met Sherman Lawrence when he was the leader (he says "The Rabbi") of the youth congregation of the Jewish Center of Highbridge, where he ran services on Friday night and Saturday. Highbridge is in the Bronx, near Walton Avenue. The local girls used to come into the Jewish Center to meet boys. One day an attractive girl walked in. She was tall for her age. Sherman, who was a freshman at New York University at the Heights, the Bronx campus, needed a date for Class Night back at DeWitt Clinton High School, where he had recently graduated and still maintained ties with friends, teachers, and organizations. She became his Class Night date in June 1935.

From then on they became "real buddies." He remembers her acting very grown up. He has a picture taken at Rockaway beach. Mature, shapely, Rosalyn was as interesting a person as he had ever met. She would go to the campus at the Heights to see Sherman, a dashing figure, the editor of the campus newspaper, and a leader of student groups. They continued to remain friends during the year Sherman dropped out of private college at New York University to ease the financial burden on his mother, and during his three subsequent years at the public City College of New York. Rosalyn understood the necessary advantages of public education, and during this period she entered Hunter College, another city school.

They saw each other all the time. Though they had no money, they knew how to have a good time for free. They would hike through the Palisades, or attend night court with a hot dog and an orangeade. Rosalyn, he recalls, was a lot of fun. She was not strictly business; she knew how to have a good time. She got along well with his mother and befriended his young sister.

Sherman got to know her romantic, adventurous side. His mother would have been happy if they had married, and he in turn got to know her family. They were a definite item. He says:

> All those years we had lots of fun together. She was a beautiful little girl. She was a beautiful soul to be with. And she was very stable, very well organized. Not like me. I was a little erratic then. But she was really stable all through college. She used to pull these surprises all the time. At Camp Swego, I was the dramatics counselor. One day I'm up in camp working, and the girls start arriving when, lo and behold, I see Rosalyn Sussman walking off the bus. I couldn't believe it! I said, "What are you doing here?" She said, "I'm not going to let you spend another summer away from me!" She had applied for a job in the girl's camp, and, of course, she got it.

That was the summer of 1939 when Rosalyn was eighteen. In the fall Sherman went off to Harvard Law School (Fig. 9). Rosalyn went up to Boston on weekends (Fig. 10). They stayed together through his first year at Harvard. They strolled the campus and surrounding neighborhoods, and they frequented cafés. But they are people who respect privacy and do not discuss issues that they consider private. It is not clear whether they had a sexual relationship, but it is understood that, as Sherman says, "we did what young people did in those days." He adds:

> When I was in law school I was in no mood to get steadier, to commit myself to anybody, and boy but she was persistent . . . I'm telling you! But she went out to Illinois and that solved the problem in that out of mind, out of . . . I mean, I couldn't make promises or anything. She met Aaron then. She married Aaron in 1942.
>
> I didn't get married until 1947. Rosalyn may not want to hear this, but the girl I went with was Rosalyn's best friend. From 1942 until I got married I used to go out with Elenore, who was her best friend [and] lived on Walton Avenue too. I went to the war, of course, and

Figure 9. Sherman Lawrence as a law student on the Harvard campus, 1939.

Figure 10. Rosalyn Sussman on the Harvard Law School campus, 1939.

when I came back Elenore used to come to the Veterans
Hospital—I was wounded overseas—every Saturday.
[Another woman], the woman who would become my
wife would come every Sunday. I was on crutches then.
I came back with my leg in a cast, and one day Elenore
couldn't come on a Saturday and sent me a telegram
she's coming on Sunday. So both of them, my wife, I
mean the woman who would become my wife, and
Elenore, came on the same day. I was in a ward with
thirty-five men and all of them screamed, "Holy Gosh!
Here comes the other one." They both came together
and they walked out together. They became friends,
and Elenore subsequently married a dentist, and that's
how I got my wife. Those two were the only girls I
knew then. It could have been Rosalyn's best friend I
married. It's one of those funny stories. And we all
keep in touch.

If the young Rosalyn Sussman was hurt or disappointed by
how her first romantic relationship turned out, she never spoke
of it, never mentioned anything to friends or family, and now will
only say that she was lucky it ended. Still, one cannot help but
consider that she wanted more from Sherman and was deeply
affected by the ending of their romance. Nonetheless, as Sherman
himself points out, she could not be expected to wallow in self-
pity or obsess on what might have been. It is likely she recognized that they were, quite literally, going in different directions
and rapidly reorganized both her schedule and even her heart. In
any case, it is a testament to the durability of her relationships,
and an example of her flexibility and control, that she continues
to this day to maintain a warm personal relationship with Sherman (Fig. 11).

Regardless of how Rosalyn felt about the resolution of her
romantic relationship with Sherman, her characteristic of immediately turning from even the greatest losses and looking only at
the way ahead is stunning, though it may seem cold. Someone
near to Rosalyn, and who loves her deeply, looked curiously at
me when I asked about Rosalyn's feelings, her heart, her soul.
"Soul?" the person asked, a mischievous smile emerging. "Since

Figure 11. Rosalyn Yalow and Sherman Lawrence, 1977.

when does she have one of those?" Sherman would argue with that. He had held a strong but tender young women to his heart. He understood her complexity, and he was acquainted with her soul. Rosalyn would disparage any discussion on the topic and suggest that it is behavior that counts.

Loyalty is certainly one of Rosalyn's strongest characteristics. She remained close to her mother and was a dutiful daughter, still grateful for the many years during which her mother bussed across the Bronx, from her home to Rosalyn's, every afternoon to help care for Benjamin and Elanna. Rosalyn Yalow never felt too smart or too grand for her family or for her small circle of friends who go back forty or fifty years. If her relationships seem to lack depth or intimacy, they are nonetheless honest, without guile, pettiness, or pretention, and they endure. She just never had the time or the inclination to develop the social arts, not after she went off to Illinois to go after her Ph.D. Once she was on her way, she had few, if any, interests beyond her science. It appears that she has paid dearly for this. Friends, family, scientific colleagues all think so, and they wonder whether her single-mindedness and intense focus on work, which limited her from developing more in other areas of her life, was really necessary. Since there were no role models for her, no variety of established ways to achieve her goal, and as she crossed hostile and uncharted ground, the question is moot. In the end, those who know her accept her as she is, although they may wish to have known her better, or that she could have been more sustained by her relationships. They lament her apparent lack of deep human contact for what they feel is a loss to her, a void in her life. They wish they could have been allowed to give her more. "I did what I did," she says.

5

Making a Way and a Place

I'm a fighter, but you have to plan and you
have to adjust. If I were young and
starting out now, I'd go into a different
field. I could never get a research grant.
ROSALYN SUSSMAN YALOW, PH.D.
1996

*O*ne week after she had arrived at Montefiore Hospital in a coma, Rosalyn Yalow was alert and wanted out of the hospital, but she wasn't the same. She would repeat herself. She wouldn't do it in front of strangers, wouldn't show that she didn't remember names that she should have known. The remarkable thing was how well she compensated for intellectual impediments by thinking her way around them.

"Are you functioning as my cardiologist?"

"Yes, I'm Dr. Rubin, of course."

"I know who you are, and you're still my cardiologist. Now, let's get me out of here. OK?"

It was 1946. The war had ended, and men were back looking for jobs. There was little future for a woman in nuclear physics. That was a fact of life, although it was an exciting time for nuclear physics, a time when, as Yalow now puts it, "it seemed as if every major experiment brought a Nobel Prize." The High Flux Isotope Reactor at Oak Ridge Tennessee was firing neutrons into the nuclei of atoms, and it is often said that a physicist looking into the "swimming pool" reactor could see the blue glow of the neutrons streaming out and believe that the intellectual creations of Albert Einstein, Hans Bethe, and Enrico Fermi were the greatest works of art of the century. Nuclear physics had been Yalow's first love. Fermi was an inspiration, but she wasn't working in nuclear physics when she graduated from Illinois and joined IT&T, and, when the boys came back, they put a man in her place. They didn't even have to fire her. It just became clear that there was no way up for her in the organization.

Yalow spent no time mourning a lost career or feeling that she was a victim. She simply decided she didn't want a career in industry anyway, so she got a job as a temporary assistant professor of physics back at her alma mater, Hunter College. It was not where she wanted to be. At that time Hunter College was a women's school, although there were a few men studying there under the veteran's G.I. bill of rights. "Girls' schools" had no cachet then, but if she was only biding her time, looking for an opening, waiting for something to happen, she nonetheless applied herself and became a remarkable teacher. She inspired many students in the few years in which she taught physics, but one went on to greatness.

"My background was very much like Ros'. I was born in Brooklyn but I grew up in the Bronx, and I met Ros when I was 17, a junior at Hunter College," says Mildred Dresselhaus, Ph.D.[1] Dresselhaus is Institute Professor of Electrical Engineering and Physics at MIT, past president of the American Physical Society, and current president of the American Association for the Advancement of Science.

> I had a rather good science background because I went to Hunter High School, and they did a fine job at teaching science—almost as good as the Bronx High School of Science. It was the best available to young girls at that time. I was the top student in math and all the physical sciences. But, just like Ros, I was told there was no career in this. I was encouraged to go into school teaching, that's what the guidance counselor told me. And because I came from a poor family, I made my expenses by tutoring, both in high school and in college, so I already had some experience in teaching. I had gone to Hunter College to become a school teacher. I didn't know anything about careers in science. Rosalyn was the first person who suggested that to me. I took the Modern Physics course that she fashioned at Hunter College, and it was a very exciting course, it totally knocked me over. And Ros told me to attend the physics colloquium at Columbia University. She was a very engaging teacher, and she invited me to her house. That was amazing, no other teacher ever did

that. Then she encouraged me to go to graduate school and seek a substantive career, and it seemed like such a long way, but she acted as if I should just go for it.

It was a time of expectations. It was a time for change and growth, for great projects, new fields, the making of vast enterprises from the smallest starting materials. An idea would grow into a new industry. There was limitless power in a speck of matter. $E=mc^2$ was not just a theory. The energy you could get from something could be multiplied by an unimaginably large number. For such incomprehensible advances there were pitfalls; there were prices for everything.

Fermi had wanted to prove that the stars build atoms into more complex elements and that matter, like biological systems, evolves. In 1941 Glenn Seaborg created a new element and named it plutonium, for Pluto, the god of the underworld. And the world of physics began to fear some dark consequence from the underworld. In a few short years, thousands of people were horribly destroyed by the products of these wondrous discoveries when we dropped a uranium bomb on Hiroshima and a plutonium bomb on Nagasaki. The devastation unleashed by these bombs tainted the beauty of nuclear physics. "I have become death, the destroyer of worlds," quoted Robert Oppenheimer, the leader of the bomb project. Leo Szilard, whose letter to President Roosevelt, signed by Einstein, had initiated the quest for the bomb, quit physics for biology after the bomb was dropped, hoping to serve humanity better. Many of those who participated in making the bomb were profoundly shocked by its actual power and by its use. Even the effervescent Richard Feynman was unable to work for some time after the bombs were dropped. He suffered from dark forebodings of nuclear doom, feeling certain that science had inextricably brought on what would eventually turn into the end of the world.

Although the Yalows never doubted the wisdom of the nuclear attacks, nor the policy of developing a massive nuclear arsenal, they could not escape the general climate of fear surrounding mid-twentieth-century nuclear physics. The coming together of nuclear physics and medicine through the use of radioisotopes—that was new and unspoiled terra incognita leading to a bright horizon. Here was nuclear physics put to a peaceful purpose, radioactivity in the service of human health.

The production of radioisotopes for use in biomedical science was an outgrowth of fundamental research into the artificial alteration of elements at the Oak Ridge nuclear reactor. People with knowledge of radioisotopes were now needed in biomedical research. The biomedical researchers did not understand and could not safely handle radioactive isotopes. The physicists generally knew little or no biology or human physiology.

By 1946 Aaron Yalow had gotten a job at Montefiore Hospital as a radiation physicist. It was Aaron who suggested that there was opportunity for his wife in the application of radioisotopes to biomedical research, and Aaron who suggested that she meet Dr. Edith Quimby. So, following her husband's advice, Yalow went up to Columbia's College of Physicians and Surgeons to see Quimby, who, quite naturally, worked under the direction of a man. Yalow went to see what they were doing, to learn the fundamentals. Estelle Sobel, who would later marry Allie, was then working there.

In 1947, not long after Yalow began an unofficial apprenticeship at Columbia, Bernard Roswit, chief of radiation therapy at the Bronx Veterans Administration Hospital, called Quimby for advice about starting a clinical radioisotope service. The V.A. was on a course of rapid development, radioisotopes from Oak Ridge were new and exciting, and an epiphany was in the making. Quimby gave the phone to "The Chief," Dr. G. Failla, who, having heard about Yalow from Quimby, told Roswit that if he wanted a radioisotope service he couldn't do better than to hire a brilliant young nuclear physicist named Rosalyn Yalow. Even if it was the old boys' network at work, it was a lucky break all around.

Americans felt that nothing was too good for our returning veterans in the aftermath of their bravery and suffering in World War II. They had saved us from the horrors of the Axis powers. Some had lost parts of their bodies and others, their minds, in the struggle. V.A. hospitals were being transformed from Old Soldiers and Sailors homes to modern hospitals with advanced research and training capability. The V.A. was in the process of becoming a great hospital system and a major player in the emerging Golden Age of medical research and training. Young physicians, back from the war, where many of them had gained outstanding experience, were offered excellent pay and superb opportunities in the V.A.

During this period of rapid change, the chief of medicine at the Bronx V.A. Hospital made arrangements for a researcher named Ludwik Gross to move his mice from the trunk of his car—his makeshift animal quarters—to a real laboratory in the hospital where he would do fundamental research. Before that, basic research was rarely carried out in a V.A. hospital. Gross would discover what would become known as the Gross Leukemia Virus. He was the first to link a virus to a malignant disease in mammals. This breakthrough would win him great acclaim.

It was at the beginning of this Golden Age that Yalow was about to meet Berson. Solomon Berson was one of many bright young men who chose the V.A. for the completion of their training. The Bronx V.A. was already becoming a fine hospital, the national flagship for the emerging V.A. system, and it would become a mecca for state-of-the-art medical research.

The Bronx V.A. fostered an atmosphere in which independent thinking was prized, even encouraging a strong exchange between the clinical and research services. It was a revolutionary new spirit—optimistic, less concerned with hierarchy, position, and protocol, and more interested in fresh ideas and an ethic to roll up your sleeves and get to work. It was the end of the war, the dawning of the victory of light over darkness. Here was a hospital for the Golden Age, a place where outstanding clinical medicine was practiced in conjunction with cutting-edge research. Within a short time Berson and Yalow would become recipients of the first Middleton Award for excellence in V.A. research, the V.A.'s highest research award, and in the years to come there would be seven other Middleton winners from the Bronx V.A. No other V.A. has had more than two.

A pioneer, George Hevesy, had used radioisotopes to measure blood volume in 1940, and by the early 1950s most hospitals were scrambling to set up radioisotope services. Edith Quimby, through Failla, her boss, sent Estelle Sobel to Lenox Hill Hospital in Manhattan in 1952 and suggested that they hire Rosalyn Yalow, who was already making a name for herself at the V.A., to consult on and supervise their radiation physics. At Lenox Hill Yalow and Estelle worked well together, co-authoring a scientific paper and becoming friends.

As their friendship developed, Estelle visited the Yalows at their home on Tibbett Avenue, and after a time Yalow introduced Estelle to her brother. She invited them to meet at the house. Estelle remembers more about what happened after they left, when Allie took her home, and they stopped in a place for something to drink. She ordered a cocktail and Allie was shocked.[2] A friend of his sister's? Alcohol! This could be more interesting than he had imagined. Indeed it was.

Soon they fell in love, and they stayed together despite opposition from the families on both sides. From hers, because Allie had been married twice before. From his, because Estelle was not as malleable as they thought she would be. The Yalows had hoped that Estelle would bring Allie into the fold, give him some conventional ambition, establish a family, a Jewish home, and that didn't happen. Allie remained his old self: kind, gentle, intelligent, unpretentious, easygoing. So the kibitzers—the contending families with their behind-the-scenes opinions, although well-meaning—were wrong. The marriage was a good, stable one, and it remained so.

Estelle is strong and independent. She has a scientific background, a master's degree in physiology from the University of Iowa, and like many others, was in awe of Yalow when she met her at Columbia. Yalow had simply come to observe in the lab of Dr. Edith Quimby, a pioneer in the applications of radioisotopes in medicine and an advocate for women in science. Estelle, who had trained with Quimby in radiation biology, was impressed with how quickly Yalow learned, how analytical and unpretentious she was. Even then, Estelle says, Yalow could talk to anyone, and no matter what their background, she could explain the most complicated concept in simple terms so they would understand. Estelle was thrilled when she got the opportunity to know Yalow better. She enjoyed visiting her house, and she was happy to meet her brother, but her relationship with Yalow did not develop further once she and Allie became involved.

Allie admired his sister. He took pride in her accomplishments, but there were problems between them. He continued to call her The Queen Bee because of the way she always seemed to command center stage. Everything and everyone formed around her, having to respond to her every need and demand, discussing her numerous accomplishments. By the time Allie and Estelle married, Yalow was well on her way to the top of her profession; after all, she had been The Queen Bee and on her way since childhood. Allie stayed in his position at the post office, and though everyone thought the job was beneath him, he didn't seem to think that way. Estelle didn't care where he worked. She loved him and felt comfortable with him. He was a warm human being with an easy manner and a sense of humor. She respected him for his qualities, not for his position.

I met Allie in 1976 at the ceremony for his sister's Albert Lasker Basic Medical Research Award, a very prestigious award in its own right, but generally considered to be a prelude to the Nobel. He seemed to enjoy his part as the proud and happy brother, but that impression might have come more from gracious good manners toward a stranger. By that time he had retired from and was working in a federally funded Joint High Schools Program whose goal was to get jobs for disadvantaged high school students. His job was to find employment for students at Seward Park High School on New York's Lower East Side. He was modest and pleasant in describing the work. Later, I read a story about him in the *New York Daily News*[3] that described him as an energetic go-getter who was driven to help the kids he worked with. They were "[his] kids," as he described them. Of fifty high schools in the program, Allie's work at Seward Park had placed the most kids in jobs, 487 in one year, more than one hundred more than the second-place school. Working tirelessly on the telephone and using persuasive methods of his own design, he was passionate about helping these kids get a break.

The very next year he didn't attend the Nobel Prize ceremony in Stockholm. Rosalyn had invited Allie, but not Estelle. Allie wouldn't go without Estelle, and he felt that he had been invited only to take charge of Clara, their aged mother. In actuality, when Allie declined to go to Stockholm, Clara was left at home. The official story was that she was too tired after having traveled to California only a short time earlier for the wedding of Rosalyn's daughter Elanna. Allie and Estelle had by then retired and moved to Florida. And then, after a few years in Florida, Allie was gone.

One day Estelle came home and Allie was dead. She had had no inkling of a problem. There was no note, and no one knew why. "After all," says Rosalyn, "Estelle was a perfectly good wife. They had a good life. They had both worked, so they had enough money. I mean, no one could understand why he committed suicide." Later she would say that someone as smart as Allie, who had an education and a sister who was a Nobel laureate, must have been dissatisfied with his own accomplishments. When Rosalyn found out, she didn't show much emotion or feeling. It never was her way, yet I am sure that she wept deep inside, in the buried place, where even she rarely visits. And now, if one asks if she was sad when her brother died, she can say yes, and I can see the hurt through the fleeting glimpse in her eye, to her guarded and protected soul.

Estelle moved back to New York. There had never been any disrespect or open hostility between Estelle and Rosalyn, not even in the period before Estelle married Allie, when she declined the Yalows' invitation to live with them so that she could learn to keep a kosher home. The difficulty between them had been played out in the subliminal language of gestures, lack of gestures, subtle expressions of the face, or invitation list—the language that family members feel in their bones, though there had never been an open break. Estelle and Rosalyn to this day are friendly. There is respect and concern. Estelle visits Rosalyn from time to time, but there is no exchange of feelings.

6

The Shield around the Maiden

[Yalow] has shown a way of being a great
scientific-medical worker and, among other
things, a very good mother and family
woman.
JOHANNA PALLOTTA, M.D.
Beth Israel Hospital, Boston
1996

Men, as well as women, must urge the
shattering of barriers to gender balance as
our issue—our joint social obligation—if
we are to achieve success.[1]
JORDAN J. COHEN, M.D.
President
Association of American Medical Colleges
1996

$\mathcal{A}$s always, Benjamin was on top of everything. He knew every lab test, what was scheduled, and what his mother was eating. When Elanna arrived at Montefiore she asked Yalow, "How are you?" "Alive," her mother answered, giving her noncomplaining, deadpan answer that in turn asks the questions: Why do you ask? and Why am I alive? It was a good visit, about an hour, and they were all glad to see each other. Before we left Yalow looked up at her daughter repeated, "Well, my right hand still doesn't talk to the rest of me." Elanna looked back, then smiled. "It's sad," was all she said.

"When I was an undergraduate, the women physics teachers at Hunter College didn't like me. I was too aggressive," Yalow smiles. The smile is proud. She knows things we don't. She was the first physics major they had ever had, and she was the darling of Professors Herbert N. Otis, Duane Roller, and Jerrold Zacharias, men who "took [me] over," nurtured her ambition, and got her a teaching assistantship at the University of Illinois.

Roller and Zacharias were well known. Roller had edited a popular physics text with Albert A. Michelson, whose passion for the accurate measurement of the speed of light led to concepts resulting in Einstein's formulation of the theory of relativity, and, in 1907, to the first Nobel Prize in science for an American. Zacharias had gotten his Ph.D. in physics at Columbia in 1932 and then tried to get a job there. "I couldn't get one because I was Jewish," he later said. Isidor Isaac Rabi was the only Jew in Columbia's physics department and Zacharias recalled that Werner Heisenberg had buffaloed the dean at Columbia to hire him. Columbia would have Jews as graduate students but, as in most of the other universities, they would not have them as

faculty. So Zacharias got a job at Hunter College, where he recalled they needed what he called an "exhibit Jew."[2] While teaching at Hunter, Zacharias worked thirty to forty hours a week for
seven years as an unpaid associate in Rabi's lab studying atomic
hydrogen. He volunteered to do this work because it was his
passion and the Hunter job was strictly teaching; there was no
opportunity for research at Hunter. Shortly after Yalow graduated, Zacharias left Hunter for Massachusetts Institute of Technology where he became a prominent professor and participated
in the Manhattan Project.

Many years later Zacharias remembered an incident in his
advanced optics course at Hunter. "The course came right after
lunch, and the girls were often logy, so I decided one day to say I
was going to make two mistakes. Rosalyn picked up three. And
she was right." She graduated from Hunter magna cum laude
and a Phi Beta Kappa.

These gifted men made Yalow aware of a wider world. They
recognized her talent. They encouraged and supported her, and
they were in a position to help. She feels that the women didn't
like her because she wanted to do extra experiments, and because
they saw her leaving behind the acceptable notion of becoming a
high school science teacher. Yalow wanted to be a physicist. She
wanted to do original experimental research. In other words, she
wanted to play in the big yard with the big boys.

It would not come easy. There would be years of struggle,
and she would not quit or turn her back on other young women
who had the potential to become real scientists. After the IT&T
experience, when Yalow came back to Hunter to teach, brushing
aside her failure to get a university or industry job in experimental physics, she somehow trusted that she would find a way into
science. She encouraged Mildred Dresselhaus, her finest student
who would go on to an illustrious career, and other young
women with talent to do the same. Still, Yalow never became an
advocate for women's organizations. Young girls would write to
her after she won the Nobel Prize, but she never responded by
organizing or joining an effort to dislodge the barriers to their
progress. Yalow would only serve as an example, responding
exclusively to individuals.

Dresselhaus, speaking of her early career, says

Ros was always there in the background. She was a very supportive individual. She was dynamic and forceful, and she pushed me into the wider world. She didn't tell me what kind of science to do—she was very flexible in that way—but she wanted me to develop myself, and she was very anxious for me to go to a top university and see where I land. She never told me about problems for women in science. She had faced that part, but she never told me about it. She felt that if you really wanted to go in a direction then nothing would stop you. She had her family, she was a strong believer in that. She always said it could be done, and that you shouldn't give anything up. She juggled a good deal to make that happen, and I did too. But for everyone who came behind her she helped them to see a clearer signal ahead.

Of course there are obstacles, even if she denies them. Of course the obstacles are there: I encountered my share and she encountered many more because she came along ten years earlier. So it was much harder when she went through. But she had the right approach. I have to support her. I support her in a lot of things. Sometimes others are critical of her. In her position today on nuclear energy, whatever, there are issues that come up, and she has a position that is unyielding. She's right and everyone else is wrong, and she lets you know it. She's confrontational. She runs her life that way. She functions that way. She has to be that way. If she weren't that way she wouldn't be what she is today. That very strong focus. The world is grey, but she is able to make black and white out of it, and that's always helped her.

When I was a student at the University of Chicago, my own advisor was very unhappy every time I won a fellowship. Every time I applied I would win. He was very angry about that because he felt that it was taking resources away from people who would use it, and he could not envisage that I would have a meaningful career.

Listen, Ros made it easier for me to become a physics student. She showed that it could be done. Now that advisor in Chicago has gone from someone who was very negative about women students to someone who is very positive about them because he sees that it can be done. So people can be educated. Ros was one of those visionaries who went around saying that for women to be in physics they had to be smarter than men. That shows she recognized barriers.

Look, there are still barriers. In the profession now there are only six percent women working in physics, and twelve percent getting out with Ph.D.s, and fifteen percent at the undergraduate level. We still hear quite a bit about the male brain being wired better for hard sciences, but however you look at it there's a distribution, and there are plenty of women who can do it. Actually, the employment situation today is so poor in physics that it will drive the men out more than the women, and with the prestige being less, there will be relatively more women for the wrong reasons. Just as in medicine, as the working conditions and the salary fall, more women come in.

We're ahead here at MIT, there are more role models. We have about ten percent women faculty, and most of them are in science and engineering. In those fields more than half have tenure. However, maybe half of them have chosen not to get married and have families, they just do their science. Ros would say they're sacrificing too much, that it's not an acceptable situation. So a role model like Ros is a great inspiration. But women still have to perform in a very stellar fashion to get attention in science.

I think that Ros overlooked a lot, otherwise life would have been too hard. Maybe she's not a feminist, but she supports women in science. She wants to see more women go into science, and she would like to see women be more successful in science. At the same time, she is against any kind of a program that would give them any advantages. She would feel that they have to get there because they're good. I've done things on behalf of women because I'm at a university where there is much work to be done on behalf of women. In her situation the sociology of science is not important, but here we have many young students that enter at day one, and they come in with equal abilities. At least in the early days the women had very low aspirations, they dropped out more frequently, their attainments were less. Why was this? I put in effort to try to understand and do something about this. She supported all of it. What she didn't support was giving women certain advantages. But she understood why in my job I had to do this and she supported what I was doing. And I don't believe she thinks I'm a feminist either.

I was anxious to see a critical mass of women students here because I believed that their performance would be better, they would be able to benefit more from the resources here, which turned out to be correct. There were four percent women students when I came here. It's an order of magnitude higher now. I think it's better for both men and women. It's improved the atmosphere. But these are the things you have to do when you're a professor in a teaching environment, which is not what her job was. I thought it was important and she didn't reprimand me for that work.

Despite Yalow's relationship with Dresselhaus, her isolation from women has been nearly complete, and she feels that they don't like her. There are few women in science, and virtually none on her level, so she works with men and considers herself their equal, at the very least. She feels that their wives generally don't like her, since she has little to say to them. If they haven't "discovered anything," haven't made important contributions to some important field, she fails to recognize anything of real interest in their experience or their conversation. As the wife of one of her former fellows puts it, "She made me feel that my husband would be loyal to her before me. And I'll bet Mrs. Berson felt the same way." At best they feel she ignores them, they feel her disinterest. There have been notable exceptions, like Dr. I. Arthur Mirsky's wife, Elenore.

I. Arthur Mirsky was part of the legend of Berson and Yalow, as many great innovators have a legend, a well-told tale of the events leading to their success. It was Mirsky's hypothesis about the nature of diabetes that Berson and Yalow were testing when they invented RIA and measured the insulin circulating in blood. Mirsky was a theoretician, a psychiatrist by training, but a fountain of ideas. He was a man who had followed his mind into the laboratory and had become the chairman of the Department of Clinical Sciences at the University of Pittsburgh School of Medicine.

The "Mirsky Hypothesis" held that the diabetes that generally occurs in adulthood, referred to as Type II diabetes, is caused by excessively rapid metabolism of insulin. According to this theory, insulin would be expected to disappear from the blood stream of Type II diabetics more quickly than in normal subjects. It turned out Mirsky's theory was wrong, but it had inspired Berson and Yalow to work on insulin. They stayed close with Mirsky, even after he retired and moved out to Malibu.

Yalow would visit Elenore in Malibu whenever she was in California, even after Arthur died. Elenore became a friend, but she was not a confidant. Yalow liked Elenore, but she did not seem to know how to get close; she could not share intimacies. Yalow has had no real female confidant, no girlfriend, no one who has gotten behind her official story. The official story is that everything has been for the best. It does not include failures, mistakes, regrets, disappointments, or tragic circumstances. Other tragedies not dealt with include not having women friends to commune with or not even being able to feel the voids in the area of friends, in the area of her understanding her children's feelings, in completely dealing with her brother's death, in the area of her expressing herself through activities now that the science is gone, and especially in her detachment from her own feelings.

Most of her social contacts and events have been professionally centered meetings, conferences, or when visiting scientists came through town.

In the 1950s and 60s Berson would tell her to sit with the ladies. She would do it, but it rankled, and she didn't always do it very well. Perhaps her annoyance was deflected onto the women. More recently, her own brand of advocacy for women has irritated more traditional feminists. She doesn't subscribe to many of the central principles of feminism and reacts to them with impatience when they displease her. Her views come so directly from a unique experience that they may appear to be elitist. As Yalow puts it:

> It bothers me that there are now organizations for women in science, which means they think they have to be treated differently from the men. I don't approve. I'd be rather hostile if men felt that they had to have professional men's organizations. I believe that if you're a woman scientist you should be in the same place as the man scientist. Science is not sexual and we should work collaboratively and cooperatively in science. I'm not sure that boys and girls have the same aptitude for science, but the ones who go into science should have the same capability and opportunity. If there isn't equal opportunity, then the laws should fight for equal opportunity. Now the big problem is that we don't have the mothers or the maids that I had.

"I think that Ros would change her mind about women's organizations," says Dresselhaus,

> If she looked at the data regarding, for example, the women's committee within the American Physical Society. I wasn't a big advocate of it when it was formed, but after twenty years the number of women going into physics after the women's committee was formed in 1971 has increased, and the slope with relation to men has gone up by a factor of seven. Of course, it didn't only have to do with this committee, but it had some

effect. So I was proven wrong, and I supported them, and I became chairman of that committee twenty years after it got started. We need these committees because men may pay some lip service but they're not willing to put in the work to improve things for women in science.

I agree with Rosalyn that there is only one science. There are some advocates out there who think that when women do science the science changes. I can't see that. I think that the facts are the facts and whoever discovers the facts, they will discover the same facts. So, I agree with Ros on many issues, but some of the interventions have to be pioneered by women, because men will not put in the time and effort. They will not put their necks out on the line. I think that when I talk to Ros about that, more and more, she comes to my way of thinking about it. I think she's a persuadable person. She has very strong beliefs, but she looks at data, and she will change if she's made a mistake. Like everyone, that's easier for her when it's about science.

Men do not generally recognize that the worlds of big science and medicine, both the academic and clinical spheres, are hostile to women. Men are so familiar with the institutions that we are not conscious of the fact that they are designed as hierarchies with powerful male figures controlling opportunities for training, practice, recognition, promotion, and all aspects of development. The structure is responsive to the pattern of a male life, to a linear career progression with no concern for childbearing or nurturing, where male standards of behavior predominate. The atmosphere, particularly in the early and most impressionable phases of careers, is rather like an old-fashioned ball team or combat unit with small groups working long hours under stressful conditions. Dominance, ambition, and competitiveness are prized. Sensitivity, responsiveness, deference, accommodation are considered more the qualities of a social worker.

Yalow was a lone woman in that world, yet she thrived. Nonetheless, she was rooted in her womanhood, which, despite the stereotypes we are indoctrinated in, includes an aggressive nature, one that could not be eradicated by the forces of a sexist culture. So she never really fit in. She was always an outsider. If anything, she got tougher:

> When it came time for me to have children I was too important to be fired. The rule at the V.A. was that you had to resign in the fifth month of pregnancy. Resign, not get leave, and so in those days I always teased around saying that I was the only person to have an 8 lb. 2 oz. five month baby. They absolutely could have made me resign. They got rid of other women. The woman who worked with the animals, our veterinarian, was forced to resign. They could get another one of her. But I wasn't concerned because they needed me. Everybody knew they needed me. And I was working with Sol. So I wasn't forced to quit. By that time my relationship with Sol was such that I figured that I wouldn't have any trouble, so I worked until the day before I delivered. The V.A. was a male organization— even the technicians were all male—and it's very likely that without Sol I would always have been a second class citizen, because I was a nonphysician and a nonmale. The V.A. was a male organization and hospitals are physician organizations. I was most fortunate that Sol Berson didn't treat me like a second class citizen.

Still, Berson wanted her to sit with the ladies because he felt that, as a woman, it was her place. As advanced as he was, including appointing women to important positions in his department at Mount Sinai, some of his attitudes and expressions were formed by sexist tradition. Things have changed since the 1950s. Medicine and science have been opening to accept more women. Before 1970 women were fewer than ten percent of medical school applicants. Now they represent about forty-two percent. And they get accepted at a rate of about forty-seven percent, virtually the same chance as men.[3] In 1970 women made up about eight percent of all U.S. physicians. By 1990 it was seventeen percent, and it will be thirty percent by 2010. No wonder there is so much being written about the feminization of medicine. Are we now to expect that more talented women, like Rosalyn Yalow, are going to enter the profession and make the kinds of careers for which they are qualified?

Women physicians earn about forty percent less than their male counterparts. They seek, or are tracked into, lower paying positions. They work fewer hours per year and tend to spend more time with each patient. What sort of medical careers will most of the entering women have?

Clearly, giant corporations have taken over medicine. The insurance companies and health maintenance organizations (HMOs) want most services to be rendered to their customers·by minimally trained primary care providers who see thirty to forty patients per day. It is simply not possible for highly trained physicians to see a patient every fifteen minutes as scheduled by HMOs. There are too many details to be clarified, too many questions and answers to be explored, too many possibilities that should not be ignored.

When a patient comes to see a physician there is usually a problem, and a physician is trained to delve deeper than the quick conclusion, to explore beyond the superficial analysis, to know and weigh the possibilities. But, when a customer goes to see a provider, and when the provider lacks the depth of training and experience required to understand the possibilities, and when that provider is under extreme pressure to close the encounter within the allowed fifteen minutes, one can see that a superficial analysis of the problem could occur. A highly trained person generally does not want to care for "customers." That is why there has been a severe cutback in the training of specialists and subspecialists and an expansion in the training of primary care providers.

The development of HMOs has resulted in many customers getting their care from physician's assistants and nurse practitioners. While this system is highly efficient in terms of making money for the corporation, even the primary care physician will know little after a few years of seeing customers every fifteen minutes. The relationship between the healer and the patient—the center of all true healing—cannot be made into a unit of production for corporations without losing most of its essence. It is within this context, as Dresselhaus points out, that women are finally getting their share. And affirmative action, which might help women move up from the ranks of primary providers, is getting the boot.

There are 125 medical schools in the United States today. How many females chair Departments of Medicine? Many would be surprised to learn that there is not one. As for Departments of Surgery? One. Departments of Psychiatry? Two. How about Pediatrics? Pediatrics has been known as a woman's field: ten. Less than ten percent of all women on medical school faculties are full professors, while thirty-two percent of male faculty are full professors. Ninety-three percent of all tenured full professors in clinical departments of American medical schools are men. And despite years of efforts to bolster the presence of women in medical education, male medical school professors today outnumber women professors by 10:1.

Have we really come that far from the time of the Civil War when James Barry, M.D., a woman who became Inspector General of Hospitals, had to pretend to be a man?

Any senior physician in the academic sphere who has not seen countless acts of gender bias and sexual harassment ignored simply has lying eyes. In 1992 the Association of American Medical Colleges asked graduates if they had been subjected to sexual harassment or gender discrimination during medical school. Sixty percent of women said yes. A study of five successive classes at a midwestern medical school revealed that thirty-four percent of the women had personally experienced gender discrimination and sixty-two percent had observed discrimination against classmates. If a woman has a problem, she's going to have to take it to a man. That's American medicine today: Everything is changing, but white men still rule.

The situation is no different in university science departments. Although currently, we read optimistic hypotheses about the improving status of women in science in books like Yentsch and Sindermann's *The Woman Scientist* and inspiring biographical features of woman scientists like the *New York Times'* June 11, 1996, piece on Dr. Shirley M. Tilghman. I believe Nancy Hopkins' letter to the editor of the *New York Times* was more to the point and indicates that the issues Yalow faced still define the problem of a woman's career in science:

> To the Editor:
>
> The molecular biologist and geneticist Shirley M. Tilghman (*Science Times*, June 11) is what heroines are made of. But young women who don't grow up to be a Dr. Tilghman should not be too hard on themselves.
>
> I'm a tenured professor of biology at Massachusetts Institute of Technology and have just participated in a review of equity issues and numbers of women in the M.I.T. science departments.
>
> As of 1994, there were 252 men and twenty-two women in the six departments of science combined. In biology, the percent of faculty members who are women is the same as when I arrived twenty-three years ago.
>
> We talked with almost all the women faculty members in science. Younger women who are doing it all— jobs and family—told us that the numbers of women on the faculty will remain small because the pool of women who would choose such a life style will never be large.
>
> As for the tenured women, the prejudice that most encounter is such that one wonders why many of them stay on at all. You have to ask what affirmative action means. It does not seem to mean "women are welcome here." This is true even though we have a dean who is committed to change and who is supportive of women faculty members.
>
> As for having children as well as this job, for women of Dr. Tilghman's generation it was much harder than it is today. Of seventeen tenured women faculty members in the six departments of science, only seven have children.
>
> There won't be many women scientists at the top until prejudice against them abates and until it becomes fashionable to admit that children take more of a woman's time than a man's. The system needs to

change to make the playing field equal. We owe it to young women to make the institutional changes needed so that more can have it all—or even have it at all.

Nancy Hopkins[4]
Cambridge, Mass., June 12, 1996

Rosalyn Yalow was in water so treacherous that she was unwilling or unable to recognize the danger, but it is a fact that most female talent still gets forced under, like Tibbett's Brook, the river running under the Yalow home, and no one even knows it's there. Of note, recent studies show that young women entering science with female mentors drop out at a higher rate than those with male mentors. One woman quoted in Project Access, a Harvard study of the attitudes of more than 800 scientists who began their careers with prestigious postdoctoral fellowships between 1952 and 1987, said that, "The more you got to know (the mentor), the more you realized she'd given up all personal life to be a scientist."[5]

Yalow insisted on having it all: career, family, home. She had the determination of a pioneer, the will to make difficult situations work for her, the ability to focus so hard that everything but what she wanted dropped away. In the process she created reality in the image of her needs. She forced herself to the surface, but, rather than denouncing the obstacles, she is still more apt to deny the effort to push her down.

So I didn't pay any price for working so hard, and I never felt any gender bias. My husband was a physicist who actually introduced me to medical physics, so he was happy to live with my success in the field. And we lived a mile away, and we had a good maid, so it never seemed that I was away from the managing of the house. If they needed me, I was there. If they didn't need me, I was in the lab. There was never the feeling that my children were being neglected, so my children didn't pay a price.

Everyone who knows Rosalyn Yalow marvels at her insistence upon seeing things as she would have them. Her determination is also remarkable, and these characteristics of percep-

Figure 12. Rosalyn Yalow, 1941.

tion and determination are linked. How did she come by these
traits? Yalow points to a story her mother told me to emphasize
that fundamental aspects of her character came very early, perhaps at birth.

It is an important issue, the question of the wellspring, as it
reflects on traditional assumptions of male and female aptitude
and behavior. Yalow was an exceptionally bright girl in high
school. She had an unusual interest in math, because her math
teacher, Mr. Lippy—she still remembers his name—took special
interest in her gifts, as did Mr. Munsack, her chemistry teacher.

Figure 13. Rosalyn Yalow posing for the camera, summer 1940.

English teachers? "Who can remember?" Certainly her interest and ability in math and science were unusual, but it would be unusual in a young boy as well. If Allie had had Yalow's interests and determination, that too would have been rare. It is certainly a minority of young girls and boys who have special talents and are devoted to math and science. But Yalow was not unique; other girls have such ability, but it is usually socialized out or directed into high school teaching.

"Math and science came very easily to me," says Mildred Dresselhaus. "I did a lot of work on my own. In the New York City school system you got your textbooks in the first week of school and I would read the textbooks as soon as I got them. The

Figure 14. Aaron Yalow and Rosalyn Sussman at the Field Museum, Chicago, 1941.

first one I would read was the math book, the science book was next, then the history and the geography books. I had a certain order, my brother did the same thing. It was our system. I had a natural interest." Dresselhaus' brother also became a distinguished scientist.

Young Rosalyn Yalow was focused. She was a disciplined girl who did her homework and tried to excel (Fig. 12). But Yalow

Figure 15. Young Rosalyn with her brother Allie.

was going to do what good girls do: get married and become a teacher. She was a handsome girl, with black hair and a good figure. She could smile, she could cajole, and she could flirt. She liked to pose for the camera like a beauty queen (Fig. 13). And having a close relationship with her boyfriend, Sherman, she had the romantic notions of any young person.

I asked Sherman if she expressed her feelings, back when she was a teenager. Did she say how she felt about him?

"Oh sure! We could talk about everything. We were real buddies!"

But then, as she left the Bronx for her graduate studies, something changed and she roared into Illinois on a different

Figure 16. Rosalyn and Allie Sussman, 1942.

course. Life was closing in, choices were being made, and one road stretched out straight ahead. From that time forward she drove with a certain determined relentlessness, in the same way she drove a car: just sat down and went for as many miles as the road held, stopping only for fuel. How could the trip have been different?

Clara Sussman was ninety-nine and still sharp when she told me the story, one last time, about when she realized that her daughter had some extra determination. It was when Rosalyn was three, just after Clara had taken her to a children's show. They had stopped in a store for some groceries, but then, back on the street, her daughter insisted on walking home a new way. Clara said no. Rosalyn insisted. Absolutely not, Clara demanded. Discipline and good behavior were valued in the Sussman family. At this point in the story Clara would shake her head with a kind of wonder at something beyond understanding. "She just sat down on the sidewalk and would not move."

Her daughter got her way, and seventy years later she still savors the victory. "I just sat down," she smiles, "and there was nothing my mother could do. A crowd gathered. We were going my way, or we weren't going to go at all." But her smile, nearly complete, leaves a speck of room for something unsaid. Was there something Clara might have done? Were there other elements in the power struggle?

"Was Allie there?"

"I don't know, I don't remember," Rosalyn says. Neither did Clara. The little girl always focused more of her mother's attention. She was already The Queen Bee. So there she stands, in an old photograph, triumphant at age four or five, her boxing gloves held high in the pose of victory, and her right foot holding her brother to the ground (Fig. 15).

"Allie was just as smart as I was," Rosalyn insists, "but I was more aggressive."

7

A Good Deal and True

She used to say to me, "Boy, it's good I didn't marry you, because I never would have gotten the Nobel Prize. You never would have tolerated what Aaron tolerated, seeing me running back to the lab. . . . Good I never married you, that's the best thing that ever happened to me." I said, "You're right, one hundred percent."
SHERMAN LAWRENCE

When my daughter Jackie was born some years after my time at the Bronx, Dr. Yalow flew to Boston and insisted I get live-in help, which she helped me to do, so that I could go on with my career.[1]
JOHANNA PALLOTTA, M.D.
Beth Israel Hospital, Boston

$\mathcal{S}$he had been through hell: a night of thrashing on the floor, five days in a coma, and two weeks recuperating in the hospital. However, she is from a line of long-lived women. Clara died two weeks short of her hundredth year. Clara's sister Rose lived to one hundred and two, sister Sue to ninety-seven, and cousin Ruthie is in her nineties and living alone. Yalow, at seventy-five, didn't see the need for it all. She may be "as cold-blooded as they make them," as Sherman grudgingly says with clear, if peculiar, admiration. She may be unemotional, scientific, detached, but her hard-nosed critical analysis is applied to herself with the most icy objectivity. "I've lived a long life. I've done what I wanted. I've been successful. It's enough," she told me, within hours of regaining consciousness.

We discussed alternatives but there was no choice. Yalow accepted her debility and prepared to fight on. When she returned home the wounds on her legs from banging against the bed were still encrusted, and the carpet around her bed was dark with dried blood. She picked up her routines: teetering down the steps to a waiting cab each morning; the long slow walk to her office in the research building at the Bronx V.A. Hospital; reading, dictating editorial comments, speeches, some physical therapy, perhaps a meeting; then the hard walk with the four-pronged aluminum cane—struggling from her office back to the hospital lobby; the drive home with Arline or Herb; back up the six steps to the front door; reading at the kitchen table while she ate dinner from the microwave; and into bed by 8:30 P.M. You needn't have seen her in the salad days to understand her ability to turn her heart off like a faucet was serving her well. The shield that covered her emotions gave her the fearsome control of her feelings. She would need these skills more than ever, and she would have to strengthen them, because now she would need protection at her core, at the place that no one sees and a place even she seems unaware of. She would need protection from her own emotions. For one of the first times she was in a fight she didn't relish.

Rosalyn Sussman met Aaron Yalow September 20, 1941, the very first day they arrived at the University of Illinois (Fig. 17). They married in June 1943 (Fig. 18). For Aaron it was love at first sight, and he would stay in love with his "Rosie" (pronounced Rahzee) for more than fifty years. Until his dying day, he helped her in every way possible, delighting in her brilliance and her accomplishments, never demanding, and always being supportive. It took Rosalyn a bit longer to engage.

What was it that attracted her to Aaron?

He was the only Jewish physics major around. No, there was one other, but he was a head shorter than I was, so he was out. In those days Jews socialized with Jews, and Jews married Jews. And Abe Sacher took us under his wing. Sacher had started Hillel, the Jewish student organization, there at the University of Illinois. We were clearly the most famous students in Hillel because we were physics graduate students. We were the first Jewish graduate students in physics since 1933. It wasn't that Illinois was anti-Semitic—we had three senior faculty who were Jewish—it was that they couldn't get Jews jobs after they graduated. So it wasn't anti-Semitism that kept them from taking Jewish students; it was just practical. Before the war effort physics was difficult for Jews in the States. You had Rabi and a few others, but it was hard. Zacharias' experience was not unique, and it was well known. The physics community was very small. It still is. Europe was much better.

In the beginning, Rosalyn had difficulty accepting the degree of Aaron's religious dedication. She had learned the fundamentals of Judaism and the kosher laws from Sherman, but Aaron

Figure 17. Rosalyn Sussman and Aaron Yalow in 1942.

Figure 18. Rosalyn and Aaron Yalow on their wedding day.

took religion to a different level. They couldn't go out to eat because there were no sufficiently kosher restaurants, and Aaron dedicated Friday night and Saturday to strict observance of the Sabbath. But because he was the only eligible Jew in the department, they got together. Mostly they studied together. In fact, Rosalyn remembers little about the Illinois years except how hard she worked.

Aaron's twice weekly letters home to 714 Irving Avenue in Syracuse, almost all beginning "Dear Family," document his deep involvement with his family. They speak of his concern for

Jewish culture and religion just before a full realization of the holocaust took hold in the world's consciousness, and they show his pride and joy in the woman who would become his wife. He describes their enjoyment in seeing reruns of *The Great Train Robbery* and *The Jazz Singer* in the university theater. He discusses the growth of their tomato plants. He chronicles their visit to the home of one of Rosalyn former mentors, Duane Roller, who had relocated from Hunter to Wabash College, and expresses their gratitude for Dr. and Mrs. Roller's hospitality and the professional camaraderie shown to them.

The letters document Aaron's interest in the development of the B-29 bomber and his familiarity with developments in aeronautical physics. It was an interest driven by desire for protection of civilization and culture—especially Jewish, the most endangered at that time—and it continued through the nuclear age and the Cold War. Aaron's interest in war machines reached its apotheosis in what would become his son Benjamin's later fascination and intricate knowledge of fighting planes and all manner of high-tech weaponry. Above all, Aaron was devoted to family, and devotion to family was embedded in the values of Jewish life and the religious tradition. This can be read in every line of his cards and letters home, from his plans for his parents' visits to Champaign (complete with train schedules and descriptions of the stations in Chicago and Urbana) to his sharing Red Spot ration coupons so that everyone could have sufficient American cheese, to his relating political developments in Italy and North Africa to the well being of the family. In snapshots from those days Aaron is a remarkably handsome young man in excellent physical condition, very lean, as revealed in the beach shots, but fit, smiling broadly, frequently playing chess, or writing equations on a blackboard for students at Illinois, studying torah, or embracing a loved one.

In a postscript, a typical reference to Ros:

I must tell you about my brave Rosie. Saturday we went walking to Crystal Lake Park. They have a nice playground there and I enjoyed myself on the trapeze, etc. But Ros was too afraid of the height to go on the

Shoot-The-Chute! After all the little boys and girls convinced her that it was safe, she finally went on the little one. My hero!

Rosalyn had broken off the relationship with Sherman just before going to Illinois. First it was the "Big C," that he wouldn't make more of a commitment, but once she was headed in another direction, away from Sherman, she began to see that Sherman didn't fit into her program. He was too headstrong, too wrapped up in his own career. Rosalyn needed someone who could understand her science and her total devotion to her science and who would support her efforts to launch and maintain a major career.

For Rosalyn Sussman, racing toward her Ph.D. in physics, a woman alone in a man's world, that became her ultimate romance. It was the elusive and challenging attraction. Her value was not in the moment—she didn't trust that—it was in the long haul, in choosing a tough problem. She believed in sticking it out to the end, refining and perfecting, then choosing another one and going at it again. She wasn't out for the instant celebration, the epiphany. It was important for her to keep her eyes down the road toward getting her Ph.D. and beyond. The quick rush had let her down: the hikes with Sherman through the Palisades, riding across and back on the Staten Island ferry, sharing a hot dog, these sentimental gestures were things of the past. Now she didn't want hearts and flowers, she wanted a man who could think and talk science, and one who would consider her career to be of paramount importance, at least as important as his own.

In this regard, as singular a person as Rosalyn was, Aaron was an equally rare find. He was a man with all the intellectual equipment to appreciate science and reason, yet whose center was in religion, a nuclear physicist who would support *her* scientific career rather than compete. Oddly enough, it would be a relationship that had roots in a deeply orthodox eastern European Jewish tradition, where the man is concerned with God and spiritual matters and the woman deals with the world. Others had trod this path, but Rosalyn and Aaron would follow it in their own way.

"He had a better background than I had, he had a master's degree in physics, but I was more aggressive. Aaron, being orthodox, couldn't be as competitive as I was." She was prepared to work seven days a week, and at night, and she saw orthodoxy as a professional limitation, observing that of all the prominent Jews in physics, not one was orthodox.

So they studied together and stayed together. Two years later, in April 1943, they spent Passover in Syracuse. At the seder Rosalyn stole the afikoman. In Passover tradition, a piece of matzoh is wrapped in a cloth and hidden. This hidden matzoh is called the afikoman, and the child who finds it may "steal the afikoman" to receive a ransom prize when it is returned to the man of the house. Rosalyn may have disappointed the children by usurping their role, but she had important business to deal with. Those kids didn't have a chance.

When Rosalyn returned the afikoman, Aaron's father, the grand rabbi, the good and saintly man, asked what she would like. "I would like your most prized possession," she answered. "You want my books?" The rabbi asked in amazement.

She took his son, and when she left Illinois she was fully equipped with a degree and a husband. Rosalyn has always considered marriage and family to be essential elements in a woman's life. That is a given, written into the program. She simply had to design a life that would allow her to work harder than anyone else while having a family. A woman has to plan. So a deal was struck, or grew from their deepest needs: She would keep a kosher home, support Aaron's religious convictions and commitments, be an exemplary Jewish wife and daughter-in-law. Aaron, for his part, would make no demands that would impinge upon her work and career. She was clear about that requirement.

For more than fifty years (the duration of their marriage) until Aaron's death, this deal was kept on both sides. Aaron went far beyond keeping out of her way; he pointed her in the right direction, introduced her to the field where she would make her mark, and was her devoted helper, cheerleader, and greatest admirer. Rosalyn was always Aaron's hero.

Rosalyn and Aaron had a marriage that was atypical in that

it was not an arrangement designed primarily to advance the needs and aspirations of the male partner. Her "professional marriage" was similar in that regard.

Rosalyn Yalow is a careful student of women in science, their difficulties, and the strategies for success. She is frequently linked to Madam Marie Curie. Dubbed "A Madam Curie from the Bronx"[2] in newspaper headlines, she hosted the PBS television series on the life of Curie. For her, Marie Curie was the ideal: a great scientist, wife, and mother. And then, of course, after the death of her husband and scientific partner, there was Curie's rise to independent recognition and her involvement with a married man.

Marie and Pierre Curie so loved radium that Marie kept some in a test tube glowing by her bedside and Pierre kept some in his pocket to show friends. This was the element Marie had discovered that is so radioactive that it glows with a bluish light and a few grams can produce five hundred calories of heat each day for a thousand years. In 1906, three years after receiving the Nobel Prize in physics along with his wife and Professor Henri Becquerel, Pierre Curie's skull was crushed when, weakened by work and his exposure to radium, he fell under the wheels of a horsedrawn wagon. He was 48 years old. Marie Curie demonstrated little emotion in public, but she poured her heart out in the pages of a little notebook that she filled with love letters to Pierre. While grieving deeply, she actively rejected the role of the broken widow and went back to work within two weeks.

Pierre and Marie Curie had made the decision not to patent their method of extracting radium salts from ore because they felt that scientists should not seek profit from their discoveries. Marie, who might have been wealthy, was thus quite poor, but refused the offer of money from friends. Within one month the University of Paris offered her a position as an assistant lecturer at a yearly salary of ten thousand francs. On May 1, 1906, she became the first female professor at the Sorbonne. The university had only been in operation for 650 years. In 1911, she began an affair with a long-time friend and scientific colleague. Paul Langevin had been a student of Pierre Curie. He was an important physicist, and a handsome, dashing man with a failing marriage.

When a drawer in his desk was forced open and his wife came into possession of letters purported to be love letters written by Paul and Marie, she sued for divorce. The right-wing French press made Marie into a Polish whore, probably Jewish, who had stolen a French woman's husband. It was a sensation that shook the University of Paris and the French government, and it nearly drove Marie from France. This, along with her radical politics, made Marie a very controversial figure, and, in addition to her great acclaim, she became the the subject of great scorn. The scandal ended the love affair, which was never acknowledged by the couple, and in the end Langevin returned to his wife.

In 1934, at the age of sixty-seven, Marie died of leukemia, as had a number of those who had worked with radium in her laboratory. Her institute had done nothing to study the health hazards of radium, although there was abundant evidence of its danger. A decade before her death a dentist in New York had reported that young women employed to paint radium on watch faces so they would glow in the dark were dying of lip and tongue cancers because they would lick the paintbrushes to produce a fine point.

Yalow struggles with the questions and contradictions that continue to confront American women who are driven to enter the professional preserves of men. But she confronts these issues in isolation; she has no community of women scientists. She relies upon her own ideas and what she thinks others believe. Certainly, in recent years she could have developed ties with women scientists, but she had gone so far by herself, through the years when she was virtually alone, that she had not developed the skills to reach out to other women, and she didn't know that she needed them. And the form to which life's hammer had shaped her might not fit well among others.

The only beacons Yalow found to guide her were Curie and Quimby:

> In our country we had Edith Quimby. Europe had more women in the field. It may have been the longer history, the importance of Marie Curie, that her daughter became important, and there were several other women

who became important. So that Europe had more of a
tradition of women in science than we had. And it may
be because of the death of Pierre Curie that Marie
became the leader, whereas Edith Quimby worked
since World War I with Fiella so she never was the
leader; he was the leader.

Pierre died early so she wasn't much more than a
graduate student when he died. I think that it was his
early death that made a big difference. She lived another twenty years, and she trained many young scientists. *Where would she stand if he had not died?* I think the
way in which world science went, she would have had
trouble being a scientist in a man's world, but by the
time he died she was already pushed up, so that she
had her opportunity. And then, her being a leader
made it possible for her daughter and subsequently
other women to grow. Now what would have happened if he had not died? I don't know. That's a question we can't answer.

But Marie Curie was a role model for women in
European science, so that in European science women
went ahead faster than in American science. The only
field they pushed in American science was in nuclear
medicine, partly because Edith Quimby was Failla's
associate and Edith was more accepting of women. It's
interesting that Edith Quimby was married to an important physicist and never had children. And the
question I always ask: Is it that she couldn't have children, or did she decide that in order to go ahead in the
field it was better not have children? I wasn't that close
to have discussed that with her.

Rosalyn Yalow needed a plan and she needed luck. It was
luck that brought her together with Sol Berson, and it is clear that
neither would have achieved alone what they accomplished together. Yet she believes that she was luckier than Sol, that she
needed him more, because, as a woman and a nonphysician, she
needed a male physician to lead the way and protect her. She

feels she was luckier than Sol and needed him more, even though he probably would have never gone into research at all if it hadn't been for her. But in Yalow's experience even Edith Quimby had worked under a man, Dr. G. Failla, who was the point man, the one everyone knew outside the lab.

As a fundamental article of culture, male chauvinism can be found in too many people—even in those who are disadvantaged by its gross and subtle arguments and injustices. Despite the fact that Yalow placed Berson first, and especially after she won the Nobel Prize, never failing to recognize his genius, making this clear in her Nobel speech, renaming her laboratory for him so that his name would appear on every publication, she has been nonetheless vilified for taking too much credit, for not making herself scarce or completely disappearing. Men and women who know this history, who understand that the Nobel Prize cannot be awarded posthumously, who know how Yalow and Berson worked and accept that she is a great scientist, still seem to blame her, as though with Berson dead she should have refused the prize.

"Sure she's a great scientist," says one of her "professional children," someone who worked in the lab in the earliest days. "But you knew them both, if one of them had to get the prize, who do you think it should have been? And how do you like the way she wears that little replica around her neck?"

The Nobel medallion replica Yalow occasionally wears as a necklace causes considerable displeasure, particularly among male scientists and physicians who assume that Yalow had it made for purposes of self-aggrandizement. Of course, no one has the bad taste to confront her regarding this rare piece of jewelry, one of the only pieces she wears (Fig. 19). She is not a jewelry type. In fact, the replica was a gift from Professor Rolf Luft of the Karolinska Institute. Luft served on the Nobel Committee for eighteen years and was the chair during the period Yalow was selected. When he retired from the committee he had two small replica medallions made as necklaces and presented one to his wife and one to Yalow. When I related the true story to the man who made the comments quoted above, he said, "Oh well, you know what I mean."

Figure 19. Rosalyn Yalow wearing the replica of her Nobel Prize.

And yet, one thing Yalow doesn't want is a feminist movement. While maintaining that there had to be an actual war for her to get a Ph.D. and a job in physics, she says that the war gave women opportunities, not a feminist movement, and if the opportunities dwindled after the war, she feels that it was because "women didn't want them." She ascribes the positive changes that have come in recent years to the fact that it is easier to run a house, while sometimes claiming simultaneously that it is more difficult because good maids are in short supply. She thinks that the feminist movement is a "mistake" because she believes that it encourages women not to get married or have children and because it emphasizes that women should work independently of men or be bosses over men.

The three women who have won Nobel Prizes in science since Yalow have been unmarried and childless. Yalow regards this as incomplete, unfortunate, wrong, certainly in the sense that such talented women should reproduce, and to her that means marriage, and a life with men.[3] She views her life as proof that women can be successful by working in collaboration with men while having children and raising them well. If it hadn't been for certain men in her life, she feels that she never would have achieved what she did. Until men can have children, she insists, there will be differences and problems for women regarding work:

> In those days maids were very easy and good to come by, maids were very competent. My maid, Helen Archer, who I had for sixteen years, if it wasn't for the prejudice against blacks, she would have been a successful person in her own right. She was very bright. And my mother came over every day. My mother lived at Tremont Avenue in the Bronx, a long bus ride, but she came every day. The kids loved Helen and my mother. Aaron thought it was great. He had gone back to teaching at Cooper Union. He really wasn't an investigator, but he was very pleased that I was. So, if I had not married a physicist who understood what I was

doing I might have had more trouble. But it worked fine. I really had a great situation. I had a maid who was terrific and who lived in. I had my mother who came every day. I had a husband who was a physicist, who had worked in medical physics, and who understood what I was doing. I had Sol who was very understanding. I lived a mile away from work, so it was easy to go back and forth, and so it was absolutely ideal. I had planned it that way, but a lot of it was luck. I had all these things.

It would be hard to get another Helen. Someone who is that bright, who would stay with you for a number of years, take care of the kids, who would let you travel, let you not come home at night if necessary. So a lot of the social situation has changed since I was bringing up kids. Bringing up kids shouldn't only be the woman's responsibility.

I can point to my daughter, who is doing very well, in part because she has a husband who is very accepting of her activities. He does his writing at home. I don't know what he writes, maybe something about computers, but he's home more than she is. That's unusual. She doesn't think of me as a role model. I just think she thinks it can be done. She set up her home across the country. I don't think if you ask her, she would say it was to get away from me. I don't think she sees me as dominating. When she went to graduate school she went where the best graduate schools are, and they aren't in New York.

Do I enjoy being a grandmother? I think it's important for bright women to get married and have children. I think it's a serious mistake for bright women either not to get married. . . . The three women Nobel laureates after me are not married, and I think that they're missing something. For the most part, men who become Nobel laureates are married and have children. I think that women who become laureates should also be married and have children. After all, Marie Curie's daughter became a laureate.

My mother and Helen were, in a sense, doing the things that mothers usually do. My children didn't feel that they were losing out on the personal things that happen in the home. And I can say that my daughter is married and has two children and her relationship in her family is like mine, because it felt to her that it was the right thing to do. Marie Curie did the same thing for her daughter.

"The feminist icon need not, after all, be a feminist herself," writes Brenda Wineapple, in her discussion of a lost essay of Gertrude Stein's.[4] Wineapple discovered the essay while researching *Sister Brother*, her dual biography of Stein and her brother Leo. The statement could apply to Yalow as well as Stein, but the isolation of New York Jewish women in the male world of science and medicine had different outcomes for Stein and Yalow. In her essay, "Degeneration in American Women," written shortly after she had failed her graduation examinations and was refused her M.D. degree at Johns Hopkins, Stein wrote, "The only serious business of life in which (women) cannot be outclassed by the male is that of child bearing."

In 1901, the 27-year-old Gertrude Stein, who would go on to become a celebrated writer and a central figure in avant garde intellectual circles, was acutely aware of the discrimination that she was receiving both as a woman and as a Jew. She had worked through four years of Johns Hopkins University School of Medicine, but at the very end she seems to have been unable to take the last step and enter the profession. Stein's medical school career had gone well until the last exam, which she failed, but it seems that her interest in medicine and her resolve to obtain her degree were finally crushed, and she abandoned her plan to repeat her exams during the following year. Instead, she joined her brother in Paris, but not before decrying the modern woman's "lack of respect for the matrimonial and maternal ideal," and writing that. "the incessant strain and stress that the modern woman endeavoring to know all things, do all things and enjoy all things, must of necessity lead to weakness and inadequacy of the genitalia."

Stein had adopted a male outlook, and she joined the ranks of many who feared the rise of the immigrant masses through their high rates of reproduction, calling for women of middle and upper class status to preserve society with the products of their conception. Despite the fact that "Degeneration in American Women" was never published, Wineapple marshals evidence to support her opinion that Stein continued to believe that "most women should do what they did best, and which men did not do at all—bear babies." "Of course," Stein wrote, "it is not meant that there are not a few women in every generation who are exceptions to the rule."

Yalow avoids the question of the relative intellectual abilities of women and men by insisting that "everyone with ability should have an equal chance." But she embraces the idea that intelligent women, intellectually gifted women, should reproduce.

There is a kinship between Rosalyn Yalow and the Gertrude Stein of "Degeneration in American Women." It is in the buried pain, submerged like a hidden river of tears. However, Yalow would insist on beating men at their own game. Instead of giving herself an exemption as a wife and mother, she would insist on perfection there as well. A sign on the wall of her office reads, "Whatever women do they must do twice as well as men to be thought half as good. Luckily this is not difficult."

It's a great line, but at this point in the struggle for equality, there is the irony of the woman as superman, the painful necessity to size up against the failures of male culture. Perhaps we'll reach a day when we'll look beyond simple comparisons of men and women to the unique perspectives that individuals can offer.

8

Lab Rats Tango in the Bronx: Berson and Yalow

Dr. Solomon Berson was joined with me in
this scientific adventure and together we
gave birth to and nurtured through its
infancy radioimmunoassay, a powerful tool
for the determination of virtually any
substance of biologic interest.
ROSALYN SUSSMAN YALOW, PH.D.
1977 Nobel Speech

When I read the papers of Ms. Yalow and
Mr. Berson I was struck, and from that
moment I felt like someone who has
bought a ticket to the next town and finds
himself flying to the stars.[1]
GABRIEL ROSSELIN, M.D.
Director, Centre de Recherches
Paris Saint Antoine

$\mathcal{T}$he turning of the years got harder. On January 3, 1997, at 7:30 P.M., I was leaving my apartment when Benjamin Yalow called to say his mother had fallen in their kitchen and was lying on the floor. It was two years, almost to the day, since George Rifkin had found her in a coma on the living room floor, and four years since her first stroke. This time Benjamin was downstairs in his apartment when he heard her fall. He found her on her left side, the good side, and I suggested that she not be moved. My wife, Bette, was waiting downstairs in the car and we went directly to Tibbett Avenue. When we arrived Rosalyn was lying where she had fallen. Benjamin had gotten a pillow for her head, and she lay there uncomplaining, denying pain, and moving each of her extremities in response to questions. But I found that she had considerable pain on moving her left hip and the leg was externally rotated—sure signs of a hip fracture.

She had been sitting at the kitchen table where she always sat and had gotten up to prepare for bed. Somehow, her feet became tangled and she went down, striking her head on the refrigerator and landing on the hip. Maybe she should have been wearing her ankle brace to support the right foot, which tended to drop a bit, but she never wore it and objected to any suggestion that she put it on. She was never an obedient patient. Having her own ideas about treatment, she tended to browbeat her physicians or shop around until she found someone who would let her have her way.

Her first stroke might have been avoided if she hadn't resisted anticoagulation, the use of drugs to prevent blood clot formation, after she developed atrial fibrillation. Atrial fibrillation is an irregular heartbeat in which the atria, the small upper chambers of the heart, contract ineffectively allowing the formation of clots that may embolize to the brain or elsewhere in the body. But Rosalyn didn't want to be anticoagulated and she never second-guessed that decision.

Rosalyn's health insurance was now through her position as Solomon Berson Distinguished Professor-at-Large at the Mount Sinai School of Medicine. Thus when Hatzollah, the volunteer Jewish ambulance service, arrived we asked that she be taken there. Since she was in no immediate danger they agreed to go to Manhattan. While they were preparing to move her, one of the young men with Hatzollah said he knew Dr. Yalow, that he had taken her to the hospital on January 1, 1995. Benjamin, Bette, and I exchanged glances. I had spent some time back in 1995 looking for this fellow, but was told that Hatzollah lacked funds to keep records of their calls and so they were unable to tell me who had picked her up the time she had been dumped. "What happened at the first place you took her?" I asked. "You don't want to know," he said, shaking his head sadly. "Besides, it's the Sabbath and I shouldn't be talking about that." His not wanting to talk about what had happened back then suggested there had been some unpleasantness before they were forced to move on to Montefiore with their patient.

The men from Hatzollah were skilled and caring in moving Rosalyn from the kitchen floor onto their stretcher and into the ambulance. At Mount Sinai, they rolled her into the Emergency Room and transferred her to a stretcher in the narrow bay where she would be evaluated. It was Friday evening, a busy time, and the room was run efficiently by the head nurse, but they were short staffed—a likely leaner and meaner requirement of managed care. We were told that the only x-ray technician on duty was off doing portable films. It would be a long wait, at least a few hours before taking x-rays.

Just then my old friend Jack Dalton, a radiotherapist at Mount Sinai, spotted us and offered to help. Jack was just passing through the E.R. on his way to visit a patient. Although he wasn't working, he took care of everything so that within minutes Rosalyn had been x-rayed and we were looking at the films. "She will have to fight for her life with a break like that and a stroke on the other side," Jack said. We talked about how she had fought for everything she had ever wanted, and about how her future would be determined by her desire to continue living.

There was her work before there was Sol, and after he was gone there was still the work. Yet it is fair, even necessary for the sake of accuracy, to say that she and Sol and the work were one, that they and their work were a thing apart, a world unto themselves. Without that there is no understanding, nothing but scandalous misrepresentation of a woman and a man whose minds merged in the days and nights of work and travel, and whose identities merged in the minds of others. The work was like a furnace they built and tended. It would become hot with ideas and new ways of learning life's secrets. While it was not holy or sacred, it served the core of their intellectual being, taking precedence over everything else. Here complex thoughts were burned down to essential ash, to their purity, and raw materials were fashioned into tools. Such disparate items as hormones, isotopes, guinea pig antiserum, starch gel, and bits of finely ground charcoal were concentrated, separated, incubated, and transformed for their purposes. They could warm themselves by the fire, and others came to be warmed and to make something to take home. Their hearth was small, and it bore no resemblance in design, funding, or personnel to the research empires of today. The memory of their modest place serves to question whether today's bureaucratic procedure and institutionally directed research may hide and suppress as much talent and imagination as they facilitate.

The work first grew from the circumstance of the availability of radioisotopes, but soon it was from the coming together of the right two people: the one with no background or knowledge of biology or medicine and the other with nothing of research or radioisotopes. But something just clicked, and it came alive, and they worked it with intensity beyond passion, with little regard for themselves or its effects upon those around them, unaware of the questions of others. From the beginning there were questions from outside regarding who was the real master of the flame, regarding life beyond the work, questions that would outlive Yalow and Berson, but that did not exist for them. And it was unlikely, incredible, that two such unprepared people should burst forth with such productivity.

From the University of Illinois Yalow had published three papers with Goldhaber and a paper with Aaron and Goldhaber. When she began as a consultant at the Bronx V.A., she published about a dozen papers in the few years before Berson joined her. It was a good start, sound work using various isotopes to study the circulation of the blood in muscle and skin and the function of the thyroid gland, but she had yet to make her mark. As for Berson, it is fair to say that before they joined forces, he was quite unknown. He, too, had published a few papers, mostly as a junior author on clinical studies done during his residency at the Bronx V.A., some with the chief of medicine. Everyone who met him, those who got to know him even superficially, were of the strong opinion that he was of superior intellect. This perhaps had something to do with charisma and eloquence, in addition to his intelligence. But he had not yet discovered anything. The first sign of brilliance in the laboratory came only after their teaming together, and they were both the sort that spent long, long hours in the lab, and whose minds were always there. They were what research scientists call lab rats.

The Radioisotope Unit of the Bronx Veterans Administration Hospital was initiated in 1947 by Dr. Bernard Roswit, chief of radiotherapy. Little was done before Yalow joined as a part-time consultant in December of that year (Fig. 20). She was then moonlighting from her position in the Physics Department of Hunter College, and she was learning the ropes, getting the feel of biology and medicine, working her way into the kinds of studies for which radioisotopes were being employed. She was excited, foreseeing that "radioisotopes would provide the torch to light the way in investigative medicine." Everyone didn't share that view, however. The first internist with whom she worked quit in 1950 after a six-month stint in the unit, saying, "there is insufficient stimulus and work in my present capacity to warrant pursuing it on a full-time basis."

Yalow recognized this to be an opportunity and snatched it. Rather than waiting for the chain of command to find a new man for her to work under, the young physicist, still just a consultant and a marginal person in a large and growing institution, went

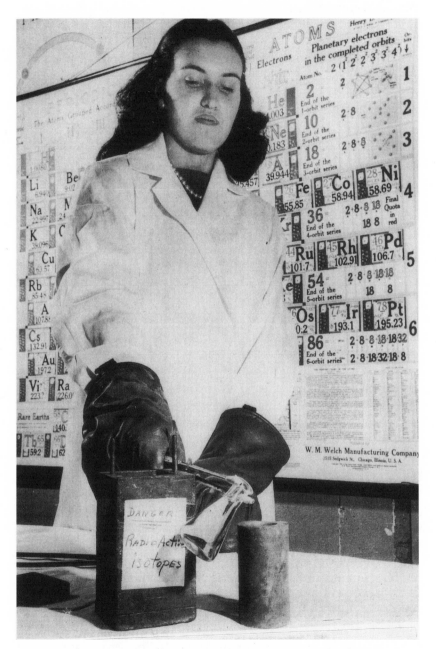

Figure 20. Rosalyn Yalow preparing the "atomic cocktail," 1948.

out and found him herself. Some well-established physicians were being considered for the post, but they did not have what she wanted.

There was considerable chutzpah at play here; she would not only have to work with the man chosen, but quite certainly he would be made her boss. And it was not simply that she wanted to choose her boss, it was bigger than that. It was her future and, as she saw it, the future of radioisotopes in medicine.

What she did might have caused trouble for her and for the fledgling Radioisotope Unit except that she proceeded in the most open and forthright fashion. She had gained the respect and confidence of Dr. Roswit, who, after working with her for several years, understood that she was someone beyond petty manipulations, that she was serious, high-minded, and got things done. Roswit was also aware that Yalow already envisioned a Radioisotope Service that would be independent and not part of the Radiology Department's Radiotherapy Service.

It is hard to imagine, in this era of downsizing, reduced expectation, turf protection, and power struggles, how individuals could take the high road and support the advancement of new initiatives that would open opportunities for others, even if it meant giving something up. At that time, there was enough opportunity and funding to go around. The Bronx V.A. was developing rapidly, with a brilliance and idealism unleashed by the recent victory over racism and fascism. A medical center should be a place of hope, a place that is progressing and improving, intellectually, ethically, scientifically, and humanistically. Without that there is no magic, no passion for the work. There is bureaucratically imposed "quality assurance," or what we now must refer to as "continuous quality improvement," as commissions and institutions pretend that with fewer and more poorly trained personnel everything improves. There are pieces of paper that are filled out properly, but real quality is hard to come by. At that time and place, people took pride in their own accomplishments as well as in those around them. They fed each other, nurturing the growth of the institution, like a campaign.

As in World War II, everyone pitched in for the right reasons. Rosalyn Yalow's loyalty and devotion to the Bronx V.A., and to the V.A. system, is shared by many others. There she and Berson sat on a research committee that reviewed all of the research going on within the hospital. Everyone on the committee worked hard, reviewing research proposals and grant applications. All the committee members did their best to help the researchers to strengthen their work. A lot of people were ready to cooperate and to rethink their prejudices at the end of World War II.

That was the Bronx V.A. Hospital of the mid-1940s and 1950s, as it is remembered by many who worked there and in the book *Ring The Night Bell* by Paul B. Magnuson.[2] Magnuson was the chief medical director of the Veterans Administration from 1948 through 1951 and, more than anyone, he was responsible for transforming what had been old soldiers' and sailors' homes into a progressive health care system. Magnuson, an orthopedic surgeon from Chicago, freed the Veterans Administration from the red tape and bureaucracy in which it had become mired, and established the deans committee system that linked Veterans Administration hospitals to local medical schools. It was his vision to have close interaction between clinical medicine and research and to fashion a career development program that went on to produce a major fraction of the nation's leaders in academic medicine.

It would all too soon be torn apart as our national contradictions came bubbling to the surface and unpopular wars were fought by increasing numbers and proportions of minority grunts. It was that growing, optimistic, the-future-is-ours V.A. Yalow remembers, because it gave her so much. It is the source of her undying loyalty to that institution. At that time, when Yalow told Roswit she would seek help from the Chief of Medicine to find a partner with whom she could seize the moment to enter the new era in nuclear medicine, Roswit gave her the green light. He supported her effort because this would help him accomplish his own goals. Moreover, the Radiology Department had nearly a dozen young men of great ability doing innovative work. These men, who would go on to become the leaders of their fields, were not threatened by Yalow or anyone else because they had ability and opportunity.

She went to the chief of medicine, sure of what she needed and where she wanted to go, and he was not surprised because they had already met. Her focused intelligence was obvious in her precision of language and in her reasoned confrontation on substantive issues. In her efforts to understand biology and medicine, she had attended his conferences and asked questions. There she'd be: a young woman physicist who stuck out and brought a quantitative approach to everything—an "open-the-mouth-and-count-the-teeth" experimental approach to medicine. He wasn't surprised to learn she wanted to build an independent Radioisotope Service. Many people at the V.A. had big ideas but also the ability to back them up. They were young men who in their war experience had not been fettered by bureaucracy and had run field hospitals and base hospitals and were as experienced as he. Here was a young woman in a male bastion. He was surprised at her horse sense, that she knew how to work the system, and that she was looking for a boss. He was impressed with her confidence.

The Bronx V.A. was an imposing place for a young woman to march into and declare that she would set a course toward new horizons. Yalow was still coming over part-time from Hunter College, a one-minute drive south around the Kingsbridge Armory. The old armory was an immense brick fortress where tanks and artillery pieces were stored and military police in full dress could be seen guarding the doors and gates. The V.A. stood at the top of the great Kingsbridge Hill, on the highest ground in New York City, commanding views of the Harlem River and Manhattan to the west, and to the south it towered above New York University's campus on the Heights with its Hall of Fame, an impressive columnade of the busts of great men. The V.A. campus stretched from Fordham Road to Kingsbridge Road, and it was surrounded by a massive iron fence. It had a military atmosphere with its guard house at the Kingsbridge Road entrance through which all employees and visitors had to pass and be checked in and out. Only a few years before Yalow arrived, many of the personnel were on active duty, wore army uniforms, were addressed by rank, and were drilled on the great lawns that stretched up the hill and to the right as one entered the main gate.

At that time the grounds were carefully manicured and the sweeping lawns with their magnificent views were dotted with the largest and most beautiful weeping copper beech trees in North America. Up the main drive to the left was a fine baseball field with stands for spectators. The main hospital building loomed up on the highest ground, a massive brick and stone structure facing the endless view to the west. The road wound beyond a large glass-enclosed building that housed a swimming pool and gym, where in winter the windows were etched with steam, while in summer the panels opened to let in the fresh air. Further down the road were research buildings, dormitories, a chapel with great stained glass windows, motor pools, and all around there were beautiful walks through groves of trees, bushes, and flower gardens.

In the 1980s they ripped all that down to build cheap and smaller new buildings, supposedly more efficient, but hopelessly ugly. In spite of conservationists who chained themselves to the trunks, the weeping copper beeches were cut down, which completed the barren and empty look of today. But the remembrance of past grandeur should be tempered by the fact that Yalow, with all of her confidence, strode into a V.A. where there were few, if any, women in professional service, where nearly all the patients were men, and she had not even a thought of rising to be chief of her planned Radioisotope Service. There were virtually no minority professionals in any capacity, and attempts were made to restrict the numbers of Jews accepted for the coveted positions as internal medicine residents.

At that time Columbia's College of Physicians and Surgeons and the Cornell Medical School dominated the medical scene in New York. They took few Jews, few minorities of any group, and few women as medical students. The senior faculty and administration were almost exclusively white Christian men. The Jews had Mount Sinai Hospital, The Brooklyn Jewish Hospital, Montefiore, Beth Israel, and other community hospitals, but still they had no medical school to support their academic pursuits. When World War II ended and many young physicians with great experience but little formal training mustered out of the military, the V.A. offered them good salaries and the possibility of continued employment after the training period. Leading academic institutions paid little to physicians in training, and some even required tuition.

In 1946 the Bronx V.A. took a young Jewish physician as their new chief of medicine and quickly this was recognized as an opportunity for Jews with talent and academic aspirations. It wasn't a medical school, but the new chief encouraged research, and it quickly became a strong training center, so it was as close as many Jews might get to academia. As the Department of Medicine grew in stature, the quality of the young residents working in the department became extraordinary.

Berson was one among many who went on to distinguish themselves—many were Jews—and although they sought women and blacks, there were few seeking positions because so few were admitted to medical school then. Even two decades later, when I graduated from a New York state-supported medical school in a class of nearly 200 students, fewer than ten percent of the class were women, and the only black student was a woman from Panama. As the Department of Medicine became stronger at the V.A., the influence of the medical schools was exercised through a dean's committee made up of the most prestigious senior members of the Departments of Medicine at Columbia, Cornell, and New York University medical schools. The members of the dean's committee were known to everyone in medicine. They wrote and edited the leading textbooks. They edited journals, chaired departments, ran the academies and the professional societies. They came to the V.A. to participate in the growing research opportunities, to extend the power of their home institutions.

The committee members participated in the process of choosing the V.A.'s new medical residents but not all of them were sympathetic to the open attitudes that had taken over in the Department of Medicine. One member, a jovial fellow, quite liberal in comparison with the others, and like the others, among the most powerful men in American medicine, was fond of greeting the candidacy of the few women applicants by remarking, "If she's good looking, what is she doing in medicine? And if she's not good looking, who wants her?"

Another, the most powerful of all, was known to resent the emergence of Jews in the department. Finally, when considering a Jewish candidate, he strongly indicated that he thought there were already enough Jews in the department. This resulted in others insisting that the candidate be accepted anyway. Bad blood then developed between the committee member and the chief of medicine. The selection process became more of a struggle. The anti-Semitic committee member stopped attending the meetings and sent someone in his place. But the Department of Medicine continued to accept Jews and took at least two black residents in the years leading up to 1954.

In 1954, during the McCarthy era, the FBI arrived and began investigating the V.A.'s Department of Medicine. The investigation sent shock waves of fear and anxiety that traveled well beyond the Bronx V.A. Hospital. Medical institutions took precautions to prevent being considered as liberal targets. Positions tightened regarding who and what was acceptable. The chief was advised to provide information concerning members of the department. He was told what information was required, but instead he warned those who were at risk. After they quickly secured employment elsewhere, he refused to cooperate with the investigation and was fired. Everyone loved him, but for years he couldn't find work, and no one would risk even sharing office space with him.

So much for the unadulterated glory of the old days. Many of us find it easy to see the past through a lens that filters trouble, and more difficult to remember hard times. Both could be said of the V.A. at that crossroads in time. Nonetheless, in 1950 the chief of medicine at the Bronx V.A. had responded to Rosalyn Yalow's request by introducing her to Solomon Berson, his very best graduate resident. Berson was winding up a bad experience in which he had gone into private practice with a long-time friend. He had high ideals. He was a perfectionist; he simply wasn't cut out for the compromise and economics of private medical practice. In any case, it didn't work out and he secured a position in a Boston hospital.

Berson and the chief of medicine had become good friends. They had many common interests in medicine, music, history, and art, and they enjoyed each other's company and conversation, although the chief had several times cautioned Berson in his written evaluations. The chief urged Berson to consider tempering his quick and sharp approach to people who could not keep up with his blinding speed and deep insight into medical and scientific matters. Berson treasured these remarks and saved the written evaluations. He certainly considered the chief's opinion regarding a bright future in scientific investigation with the young woman physicist and his offer to provide some funds from the Department of Medicine until they could secure other support. But it was Berson's meeting with Yalow that compelled him to forego the job in Boston and begin work in the Radioisotope Unit.

Berson was as impressed and excited with their first meeting as Yalow had been, and by both of their accounts, the partnership went immediately into high gear. Within four years Solomon Berson was the chief of the first independent Radioisotope Service in the Veterans Administration system. What follows is a description of their work as it developed from their early studies of blood volume, extended into the area of iodine and albumin metabolism, then moved to insulin and the peptide hormones. It finally opened, through their work with prostaglandins and viruses, into a vast arena of substances and scientific issues as the world scientific community learned from them and applied their methods and approaches to their own work.

Their first paper was published in *Science*. Even that is noteworthy, as this is one of the most exclusive scientific journals, and most investigators do not get to publish in its pages. To be selected, a manuscript must be judged both sound and of major scientific importance. Yalow and Berson's paper appeared in July 1951 and was the first in a long and illustrious series of papers which they published in *Science*, *Nature*, and *The Journal of Clinical Investigation*. The work was entitled, "The use of K^{42}-tagged erythrocytes in blood volume determinations," by Rosalyn S. Yalow and Solomon A. Berson. She was the first author, the senior author of the work, although he was considered the boss from the start. But titles, official or honorific, had no importance in deciding the seniority of authorship on their publications.

They believed that authorship should be determined only by each individual's real contributions to the work rather than by rank, and they adhered to that principle.

Since the time of Galen, the Greek physician who discovered and wrote about the importance of the circulation of the blood in the second century A.D., among the most fundamental questions in medicine have been those regarding the volume of blood in the vessels and its distribution within the vascular compartment and other body spaces. Since the blood brings vital nutrients and regulatory messages in the form of hormones and other chemicals to all of the body's tissues, and since the blood also removes waste, with the urine and other bodily fluids arising as filtrates of blood, knowledge of the waxing and waning of the blood volume can explain a great deal about the state of an individual's health. It is much like studying the flow of river waters in gauging the health of a continent. Alterations in blood volume and its distribution in the veins and arteries and other spaces and tissues of the body occur during normal physiologic processes such as menstrual cycle, or with dehydration, hemorrhage, or in heart disease, kidney disease, liver disease, and in virtually every abnormal circumstance.

Early attempts to measure blood volume involved exsanguination of condemned criminals by opening their jugular veins and allowing as much blood as possible to collect in a bucket or other container. This, of course, was done in bygone days and produced inaccurate and irreproducible results. Clearly, the method has little beneficial application at the bedside, certainly not for the subjects. And while a variety of less ghastly techniques had been employed to study the question, there was still considerable dispute regarding issues relating to blood volume in health and disease when radioisotopes became available in the late 1940s and early 1950s.

Among the first applications of radioisotopes in medicine was their use in obtaining more accurate estimations of blood volume. The more recent methods, including radioisotopic studies, have all used the principle of tracer dilution in which a detectable label (radioactive material or dye) is introduced into the bloodstream. After allowing sufficient time for uniform mixing throughout the vascular compartment, a sample of blood is taken to measure the concentration of the label. Through such a method, if five million units of label are put into the circulation and the concentration in the blood sample is subsequently found to be 1000 units per milliliter (ml) of blood, the apparent volume of the circulating blood is 5000 ml, or 5 liters (5×10^6 Units$/1 \times 10^3$ Units/ml $= 5 \times 10^3$ ml).

It is obvious that a suitable label for this purpose, one that can be repeatedly used in human subjects, should be harmless, and it should remain within the vascular compartment for a period of time sufficient to allow uniform mixing without being destroyed. If the label leaks out of the blood vessels or is destroyed within the circulating blood volume, then its concentration in the sample specimen will be lower than it would be if it were retained intact, and a falsely high value for the blood volume will result. If mixing is not uniform, then the sample specimen will not be representative of the entire compartment and falsely high or low values for the blood volume will be obtained. To extend the analogy of rivers: If we wanted to use the dilution principle to measure the volume of the Mississippi River, we would want to use something that would mix into the river water but not get lost into the land or the Gulf of Mexico, and it should not poison the water.

The labels that can be used to measure the volume of blood within the vessels can travel with the red blood cells or with the liquid blood plasma. Prior to the introduction of radioisotopic labels, carbon monoxide, foreign red blood cells, Evans blue dye T-1824, and other substances were used. Carbon monoxide combines rapidly with hemoglobin and thus travels with the red cells, but it leaks from the bloodstream and combines with the muscle protein, myoglobin, in muscle cells. Therefore, this method gave falsely high values for blood volume. When a relatively small volume of red blood cells of a different type are transfused into a subject's bloodstream, the concentration of these foreign cells in a subsequent sample specimen can be determined by precipitating the subject's red cells by antibody agglutination (making them stick together and settle to the bottom in a test tube) and counting the remaining "labeled" red cells. This method fell out of favor because of the theoretical possibility of transmitting disease along with the transfused red cells. In addition, because subjects would develop antibody to the foreign red cells and in subsequent tests they would be destroyed within the vascular compartment. The Evans blue dye combines firmly with albumin in the blood plasma, providing a relatively good measurement of the plasma space.

When Berson and Yalow entered the field in 1950 there was a lot of confusion because red cell labels and labels that traveled with the plasma proteins provided different values for blood volume. The finding that higher values for total blood volume were obtained using the Evans blue method when compared with the labeled red cell methods suggested that the relative volume of red cells in the peripheral blood taken as samples for the measurements is greater than that in the more central great vessels of the body. So, for example, if you used logs dumped into the headwaters of the Mississippi as your label and then determined the volume by the number of logs per million gallons of water, your result would be larger if the logs accumulated near the banks and you took your sample in the middle of the river. Two iron isotopes, ^{55}Fe and ^{59}Fe, had generally been used as red cell labels but they had to be incorporated into red cells by feeding radioactive iron to donors who would then donate their radioactive red cells for the studies. The obvious disadvantages in this method included exposure of the donor to radioactivity, albeit trace amounts, and exposure of the recipient to foreign blood products.

It should be pointed out that at this time, and during most of the Golden Era of American medical research, no written consent was obtained from the subjects in medical experiments as is demanded today. In any case, Yalow and Berson chose to develop methods in which they labeled the subject's own red blood cells in vitro, that is, by incubating them in a test tube with trace amounts of radioisotopes. They then reintroduced the cells, which now contained minute amounts of radioactive isotopes, into the same subject's circulation. This avoided exposure to foreign blood products and exposed subjects to small amounts of radiation.

With an imaginative approach to the set of problems posed by the use of red cell and plasma labels, and mindful of the question of varying concentrations of red cells in blood from the periphery versus the central regions of the circulation, they performed studies using methods that avoided the points of prior dispute. They made blood volume determinations in human subjects using both red cell and albumin labels simultaneously, and they assayed whole blood rather than plasma or red blood cells.[3] After completing a comprehensive set of studies, Berson and Yalow published their findings in *The Journal of Clinical Investigation*, this time with Berson's name first. This paper is regarded as a major contribution toward resolving the confusion concerning appropriate methods for studying the critical issues of blood volume alterations in health and disease. Their conclusion, that albumin tagged with [131]I (a radioactive isotope of iodine) is a satisfactory material for the estimation of circulating plasma volume and that it has advantages over red cell labels and Evans blue dye, along with their careful consideration of what happens to labeled materials in the circulation during the early mixing phase and over the course of more prolonged periods, established in this area the foundation for subsequent observations and advances.

As just noted, the work with blood volume determination, like much of Berson and Yalow's early work, involved injection of minute amounts of radioactivity into the bloodstream of human subjects. The reader may be aware of the fact that although the Nuremberg doctors' trials took place in the December 1946, and the Nuremberg Code of Ethics, with its first principle, "The voluntary consent of the human subject is essential," came directly at the conclusion of the trials, the consent of human subjects was rarely obtained in the United States until the late 1960s. No one was likely damaged by the tiny amount of radiation injected by Yalow and Berson, but radiation experiments were being conducted elsewhere by U.S. government experimenters for the precise purpose of observing what damage could be done.

President Clinton's Advisory Committee on Human Radiation Experiments (ACHRE) was appointed in April 1995 to examine data relating to extensive U.S. government experiments in which Americans were injected or fed radioactive elements including plutonium, uranium, and radon to see what damage might occur. Pregnant women were given radioactive iron. None of these people had given their consent. Most were never told of the experiments, and some had actually refused but were made subjects without their knowledge. These experiments, carried out many years after the promulgation of the Nuremberg Code, violated all ten principles designed to protect human subjects.[4]

In 1961 Harvard's medical school was faced with a dilemma.[5] In order to obtain military research grants it was asked to comply with the Nuremberg Code. But Harvard did not like the first principle: "The voluntary consent of the human subject is absolutely essential." The administrative board at Harvard concluded that the Nuremberg Code is "not necessarily pertinent to or adequate for the conduct of medical research in the United States. . . . Faith and trust serve as the primary basis of the subject's consent. Moreover, being asked to sign a somewhat formal paper is likely to provoke inquiry in the subject, who can but wonder at the need for so much protocol." This attitude typified the approach of the research community at that time.

Despite the fact that the Nuremberg trials made it clear that the Germans had modeled their forced sterilization and eugenics programs after our own, despite the fact that the American Eugenics Society vigorously endorsed the German Sterilization Law of 1933 that allowed involuntary sterilization of the blind, the deaf, alcoholics, and all sorts of other "unclean" individuals, despite many well documented atrocities committed by physicians in the U.S., and despite the fact that the judges who tried the case and wrote the code meant their analyses and principles to apply to past, present, and future circumstances in all places, American medicine recognized no relevance of the Nuremberg trials or the code to the practice of medicine or the conduct of research in the United States.

While this was to change in the late 1960s with the introduction of Institutional Review Boards for the Protection of Human Subjects (IRBs), local bodies that include researchers and lay members of the community that must consider and approve all experiments involving human subjects, the roots of the cavalier and even self-righteous attitude of American medical researchers went back at least to the Nuremberg trials.

The prosecution's chief expert witness at the trials, Andrew C. Ivy, M.D., came from the heart of the American medical establishment to ground zero of this attempt to consider fundamental ethical issues.[6] But Ivy did little to advance the rights of human subjects as he perjured himself with his testimony insisting on the ethical nature of human experimentation in the United States. And while Ivy would later become involved in a bogus cancer cure, he was also a great physiologist who had discovered the hormone cholecystokinin.

The German defense lawyers argued that forced experimentation on prisoners had occurred in the U.S. just as it had under the Germans. Because he knew that he would be asked about the ethics of prison research at the trial, Ivy, who was from Chicago, had hastily recruited Illinois' Governor Dwight H. Green to appoint him chair of a committee to examine the ethics of malaria research carried out on Illinois prisoners during the war.

At the trial Ivy testified that the Green Committee had debated issues regarding the use of prisoner volunteers, and that the committee had found no coercion occurred in Illinois. He read the conclusions of the Green Committee into the trial record. But the Green Committee had never met, nor had there been any consultation between members, or discussions of any kind.

A meticulous analysis of the early work of Berson and Yalow indicates that the amount of radioactivity they injected into human subjects was trivial, less than is now used in various diagnostic tests. Yet it remains true that Berson and Yalow, like the majority of medical investigators of that time, ignored the Nuremberg Code and the principle of informed consent. In recent years, with the settlement of cases brought against the government by people who had been injected with radioactivity for the purpose of determining what damage it might cause, Yalow was interviewed for her reaction. No case had been brought against her or anyone who had worked with very low levels of radioactivity. Nonetheless, while saying little about the experiments in question because she had little information regarding them, she was quite frank in discussing the fact that she, too, had been involved in experiments in which written consent had not been obtained.

While working with the problem of blood volume determination, Yalow and Berson were simultaneously working in the areas of thyroid physiology, protein metabolism, and radiation chemistry. They described the damage to a molecule of protein, like serum albumin, caused by the energy of radioactive decay when it is labeled with an unstable isotope like ^{131}I. Berson and Yalow called this phenomenon "decay catastrophe" because the radioactive isotopes, like little time bombs going off within the folded strands of amino acids, eventually caused catastrophic damage to the proteins into which they had been incorporated.

They studied ways of drawing water from the body tissues into the bloodstream when the circulation has collapsed due to excessive bleeding and established the superiority of albumin to globin as a plasma expander for the treatment of low blood volume in shock.

They studied the economy of albumin metabolism in patients with heart failure, and the reduced rate of albumin degradation in those losing albumin through the kidney. But their first really major contribution was their study of how the thyroid gland and the kidneys remove iodine from the blood. This study was published in the prestigious *Journal of Clinical Investigation* in February 1952, and it established the measurement of iodine clearance by the thyroid gland as a valid parameter of our physiology.[7]

The thyroid gland influences many body tissues, controlling their metabolism, almost like turning the gas up or down under a pot on your stove. The thyroid makes its hormone, thyroxine, by inserting iodine atoms into the amino acid tyrosine (pronounced tie-row-seen). It is therefore intimately involved in the body's economy of iodine, which is primarily concerned with producing thyroid hormone. If the thyroid gland doesn't take iodine from the blood, it can't make thyroxine and the body's metabolic rate may fall. If it removes too much, it may make excessive thyroxine and the metabolic rate may be too high. Thyroid function had been studied using various methods of estimating the iodine-accumulating capacity of the gland. The amount of radioactive iodine taken up by the thyroid one hour and twenty-four hours after oral ingestion of ^{131}I, the radioactive iodine uptake test, and measurements of urinary excretion of ingested iodide had provided valuable tools for the diagnosis of over- and underactivity of the gland. Still, problems persisted in interpreting the results in at least ten percent of patients. And in patients with abnormal kidney function the data derived from these methods were confusing.

Berson and Yalow developed a method of determining the quantity of blood cleared of iodine by the thyroid gland per unit time. Their method is based on an observed relationship of relative constancy between the patient's body weight and the space of ^{131}I dilution (or the volume of body fluid into which the isotope is diluted) during the first half hour following intravenous administration of the isotope. The clearance rates (expressed as the volume of blood from which iodine is completely removed each minute) are readily determined in a single thirty-five minute sitting from the measurement of radioactivity over the gland in the neck and in a single urine specimen. This provided a relatively simple and quick determination of the activity of a person's thyroid gland.

As she had done for other studies, Yalow designed the instrument used to measure radioactivity over the thyroid gland. Yalow and Berson's thyroid clearance rate is independent of a variety of extraneous factors such as the rate of renal clearance (the volume of blood from which the kidneys have removed iodine in a minute's time), and it is the most direct and reliable index of the iodine-accumulating function of the thyroid gland. It is still the only test using radioactive iodine that is a physiologically sound analysis of thyroid function. The other tests used to evaluate the gland are also based on their methods because they are radioimmunoassays (RIAs) of thyroidal and related hormones, including: thyroxine (T_4), the major hormone of the thyroid gland; triiodothyronine (T_3), the biologically active metabolite of thyroxine; thyroid stimulating hormone (TSH), the hormone from the anterior pituitary gland that stimulates thyroid hormone secretion; and thyrotropin releasing factor (TRF), the hormone from the hypothalamic area of the brain that releases TSH from the anterior pituitary gland.

When their paper appeared in the *Journal of Clinical Investigation* it was immediately recognized for the brilliance of its conception and for the sophisticated mathematical analysis that would become a hallmark of their work. Soon a note arrived from the eminent thyroid expert, F. R. Keating, who congratulated Berson for his accomplishment and said, "I regard it as the most important contribution to the problem of diagnostic tracer procedures which has as yet appeared." Keating's note made no mention of Yalow. Nonetheless, they were delighted. While they would continue to contribute in the areas of thyroid hormone and albumin metabolism, to describe the alterations that occur when proteins are labeled with radioactive isotopes, their attention had already turned to insulin.

Berson had completed an internal medicine residency but had no special training in endocrinology, the medical subspecialty concerned with the endocrine glands and their hormones. The endocrine glands include the pituitary, thyroid, parathyroid, adrenals, ovaries, and testes, as well as the islets of Langerhans in the pancreas where insulin and glucagon are made. The hormonal secretions of these glands, and also the other specialized cells throughout the body, help to regulate what Claude Bernard, the great French physiologist, called the *milieu organique interieur*, or the internal environment of the body. The most common endocrine disorders are under- and overactivities of the thyroid gland and diabetes mellitus, which results from an absolute or relative lack of insulin secretion. Yalow's knowledge of diabetes and insulin was limited to the fact that Aaron, who became diabetic in 1932, was alive only because insulin had become available a few years earlier. Yalow says that Aaron's dependence upon insulin may have increased her interest in the hormone, but it had nothing to do with the initiation or pursuit of the insulin studies. Nonetheless, they would soon open the field of insulin metabolism, initiate the most productive ideas about diabetes, and create a new era for endocrinology.

Among the disorders of the endocrine glands, diabetes affects the greatest number of people. And among the peptide hormones, insulin is the most interesting, and is uniquely essential. A peptide is simply a sequence of amino acids. There are about fifty amino acids, which can be likened to beads of different shapes and colors, and so there are myriad possible peptides, as one might assemble countless different necklaces by varying the sequence in which the beads are strung. A relatively short sequence is called a peptide, and longer strings of amino acids are called proteins.

Diabetes was known to the ancients, and we tend to think of the discovery of hormones as ancient history, but it was in the first decade of this century—less than fifty years before Yalow and Berson began their work with insulin—that the concept of hormones and the first peptide hormone was discovered. It came out of the general question of how the complex activities of digestion are integrated: What was the organization, or choreography, of the exquisitely coordinated secretory functions of the stomach, the pancreas, the gallbladder, and other digestive organs?

The story of hormones really began in New England, about one hundred years before secretin, the first of many, was discovered in London in 1903. Even before that came a classic story of American science. In 1806, a wealthy farmer's son refused his father's offer of land in Lebanon, Connecticut, and instead took about one hundred dollars in gold and a good mare and began wending his way north and west until he settled in the town of Champlain, on the New York shore of Lake Champlain. There he worked as a teacher and, because teachers didn't make much money, he also worked as a clerk in a dry goods store. After about a year he somehow got the notion of becoming a doctor, and so he took the ferry across the lake to Vermont and apprenticed himself to a Dr. Benjamin Chandler. In two years he was Dr. William Beaumont, and he joined the Army Medical Service. We will gloss over the part about how he got in trouble with a superior, nearly fought a duel, quit the army, started a practice in Plattsburgh, New York, then rejoined the Army Medical Service in 1820 and wound up at Fort Mackinac on the northern peninsula of Michigan. There, on June 6, 1822, he was summoned to treat

Alexis St. Martin, a 19-year-old French Canadian trapper who had been wounded at close range by a shotgun blast.

The shot had blown out a portion of St. Martin's abdominal wall below the left breast and caused a perforation of the anterior wall of the stomach. It took a year for the wound to heal, but the aperture in the abdominal wall never closed. By moving the flap of skin that covered the rent, Beaumont could see inside and actually view all of the activities occurring within St. Martin's stomach. For years Beaumont, by his own account "a simple Army surgeon," chased and cajoled the reluctant St. Martin to study the motions, secretions, fluxes of mucosal blood flow, and digestive activities of the living stomach. Several times Beaumont hired detectives to track St. Martin down, finally getting him an Army commission so that he could keep him close at hand. In 1833 Beaumont published *Experiments and Observations on the Gastric Juice and the Physiology of Digestion*. The book was a sensation, the first piece of good Yankee science, and it challenged physiologists to consider the mechanisms through which the complex digestive processes were regulated.

Stimulated in part by Beaumont's work, in 1897 the great Russian physiologist Ivan Pavlov published *Lectures on the Work of the Digestive Glands*. Pavlov dominated the field of physiology, and in 1904 won the Nobel Prize for his work on digestive secretions. His doctrine of "nervism" sought to explain all of homeostasis, and certainly the regulation of the secretory activities of digestive glands, in terms of the nerves that innervate these organs. But before Pavlov received his prize, two brothers-in-law, William Bayliss and Ernest Starling, discovered an entirely new mechanism of control.

Working in London on "(their) great afternoon" of January 16, 1902, they severed all the nerves to a dog's pancreas and found they were able to control precisely the secretion of water and bicarbonate coming from the gland's main duct by injecting doses of a chemical messenger into a leg vein. Pavlov had shown that a dog's pancreas begins to secrete water and bicarbonate the instant gastric acid enters the first few centimeters of the duodenum. So Bayliss and Starling prepared the chemical messenger by taking bits of the mucosal surface lining the dog's duodenum and boiling them in acid. And with the injection of their extract, the secretory activity of the gland could be regulated in the absence of any nerves by the action of the chemical messengers contained within it. Moreover, by the inactivation of their extract through the application of the proteolytic enzyme trypsin, which is capable of breaking down proteins containing negatively charged amino acids, they knew the messenger to be a protein. They called this protein secretin, and they fully expected that other such chemical messengers would be discovered. The central paradigm of their newfound mechanism of control was that a chemical messenger could be made in one tissue and released to travel through the bloodstream to find and regulate the activities of a distant target tissue. On that great afternoon, Bayliss and Starling had suddenly understood something about life that had not been known before. They gave the term hormone, from the Greek, *horman*, "to set in motion," to the class of chemical messengers that act through this paradigm. Within a year a fellow named Edkins, working in London along the lines set down by Bayliss and Starling, discovered the second hormone, gastrin, which regulates the stomach's secretion of acid. It was the dawn of endocrinology.

In 1921 the Canadians Frederick Banting and Charles Best extracted insulin from the pancreas in a form that was capable of controlling diabetes in a dog. In a short time bovine (cow) and porcine (pig) insulins were available to treat human diabetics, and the previously fatal juvenile, or Type I, diabetes could be controlled. An untold number of people, mostly young, had died from this disease, and the discovery provided nothing short of a miracle life-saver. Banting shared the 1923 Nobel Prize for medicine or physiology with J. J. R. Macleod, who was the chief of the laboratory where Banting and Best were working at the University of Toronto. Best was only a lab assistant, an undergraduate medical student, so he got no prize. Banting shared his prize money with Best, and they worked together at the Banting and Best Department of Medical Research in Toronto, where Best went on to discover the vitamin choline and the enzyme histaminase, which breaks down histamine, an important amine found in many tissues of the body, and he was the first to use anti-coagulants for the treatment of blood clots.

While Type I diabetes clearly resulted from a loss of the pancreas' ability to make and secrete insulin, the hormone that lowers the blood sugar, the Type II (adult onset) diabetic had ample pancreatic insulin and released the hormone into the bloodstream in response to the usual provocations, like the ingestion of sugar. So if Type II diabetics have plenty of insulin, and if the insulin is able to lower blood sugar, and if it is released to the bloodstream appropriately, why do Type II diabetics have high blood sugar? Why are they diabetic?

We cannot live without insulin, nothing will suffice for its absence, only the small protein hormone will do; it is essential. Other peptide hormones are crucial, but they are only relatively essential, like adrenocorticotropic hormone (ACTH) or parathyroid hormone (PTH). In the absence of ACTH (the pituitary gland's hormone that stimulates the cortex, or outer rim, of the adrenal glands that sit on the upper poles of the kidneys), cortisol, the secretion of its target organ, will do nicely. Similarly, without PTH, which regulates calcium metabolism, treatment with vitamin D and calcium will allow normal life. But only insulin can replace insulin. Among other things, like its fascinating arrangement of two peptide chains connected by two sulfur-containing bridges, and the frequency and complexity of diabetic states, this essential nature of the insulin molecule gives it a special panache. Everyone who worked with Berson and Yalow came to appreciate that each of the many hormones has its special personality. Some are pesty and difficult to work with. Some are rugged and forgiving. Some are prominent and some are obscure. Insulin is a star. Berson and Yalow were on the right track.

In 1952, I. Arthur Mirsky published his lecture from the Laurentian Hormone Conference entitled "The Etiology of Diabetes Mellitus in Man." Mirsky hypothesized that adult-onset diabetes (Type II) might not be due to a deficiency of insulin secretion but rather to abnormally rapid degradation of insulin by an insulin-metabolizing enzyme in the liver.[8] If this idea was correct the rate of insulin disappearance from the bloodstream would be faster in maturity-onset diabetics than in juvenile diabetics (Type I) and normal subjects. Highly purified insulin was available from the Eli Lilly Company and radioiodinated insulin-[131]I (insulin into which the radioactive isotope of iodine, ^{131}I, has been incorporated) could be produced in the laboratory by modification of the methods of other workers, or bought from Abbott Laboratories. By testing the Mirsky hypothesis, they would be probing the center of the most important questions in endocrinology. Their prior work with albumin, iodine, and thyroxine had prepared them to think about the metabolism of circulating hormonal proteins and radioactive iodine. They had developed facility with the iodination and electrophoretic techniques (methods for the incorporation of iodine into proteins, and for the separation of mixtures of proteins into their individual components) that would be necessary, and in 1954 they were ready to go.

Here, at the point where Berson and Yalow were about to begin their most productive studies that would lead them, not by design, but through a process of following their imaginations and the flow of their data to the birth of radioimmunoassay, I believe it is important to consider that they had neither grants, mandate, nor commitment to go in any particular direction. They had no requirement to satisfy the specific expectations of any supervising agency. Without this freedom they probably would not have conceived or birthed their method. It also should be appreciated that Berson and Yalow had more to do than research. They had to earn their keep by running a clinical nuclear medicine service in which they provided the full gamut of lung, brain, liver, thyroid, and bone scans, and a thyroid clinic.

Today's medical investigator competes for government funding by filling out forms designed to allow a group of peers to consider what the investigator plans to do or has partially completed. The peers must see the research plans as a logical extension of what is known in the field. It's a competitive process in which only about ten percent of applications are funded, and it is at least questionable that the system brings out the best in the applicants or the panels of peers, called study sections.

An alternate route to funding has the investigator respond to a request for proposals (RFP) in which an agency, like the National Institutes of Health, suggests a line of investigation and the investigator convinces a group of peers that she/he is best suited to proceed in that direction. I think that the theoretical and operational problems in such a system should be evident to any intelligent person who considers the situation, and they are at least as serious as you would predict. Old boys' networks manage the pools of money like lions around the last drink on the plain, and once a spot at the edge of the water is achieved there is great pressure to keep it, to produce something that will allow the others to tolerate your presence for another funding cycle. It is a culture of scarcity, a survival of the fittest in which fitness may not translate into scientific excellence.

In the best of times, research funding is prudently profligate and directions are reasonably free. Bread is cast upon the waters and most of those who are competent get a chance to work. In worse times, when only the very best research can be funded, great caution and the idea that a group of peers can select the best research can be stifling, and it can end in flimflam and outright fraud. When the pie shrinks, those who get the most are not necessarily the best, but they are increasingly defined in those terms. And the culture of scarcity, resulting from the relatively small investment our government directs to biomedical research, has resulted in more of our researchers working for the pharmaceutical industry where efforts are goal and product oriented, and where contracts are signed that stipulate that findings may not be published without the drug company's explicit permission. Let us not review the many sordid incidents of thwarted academic freedom, scientific fraud, and economic exploitation that have been presented as isolated events and are clearly the growing product of this situation.

To mention just one, we need not go further afield than the synthetic thyroid hormone, Synthroid, whose manufacturer, Knoll Pharmaceutical Company, as reported in the *New York Times*, purportedly suppressed the publication of studies done at the University of California at San Francisco. These studies demonstrated that the cheaper generic products were equally effective.[9] With at least an estimated $350 million per year at stake, the company allegedly coerced the investigators who had signed a contract giving the company authority over publication, bullied the university, and has been accused of buying out the American Thyroid Association.

Finally, seven years after the conclusion of the study, when the company relented and allowed publication of the findings, an accompanying editorial in the *Journal of the American Medical Association* was critical of Knoll, the university, and the American Thyroid Association. In a letter published in the same edition of the journal, the president of Knoll apologized for blocking publication of the paper. But this is not the subject of this book. Still, an alternative approach to science and research, represented by Berson and Yalow and others of the same dying tradition, is part of our subject and should be understood by today's citizens, if only to be clear about what we have sacrificed.

"We were completely free to develop in our own fashion," Yalow says. "Our Radioisotope Service enjoyed the confidence and support of the Veterans Administration, locally and in central office; the laboratory was funded to the full extent of our requests without a need ever to submit a research grant proposal." Berson and Yalow never had a research grant, and furthermore Yalow insists that she never would have been able to obtain one because the process, in which one must describe what one is going to do as though it has already been done, is fundamentally unacceptable. It is an undisputed fact that Berson and Yalow ran their operation at a fraction of the cost of their contemporaries and prided themselves on the smallness of their "mom and pop shop"—a real contrast to the empire builders of today. If today's science requires some massive operations, it is still clear that the current system of funding is making careers in science less tenable, especially for newcomers, few of whom can obtain and maintain sufficient funding for their work and salaries.

In Yalow and Berson's first study of the metabolism of radioactive insulin in humans, they injected radioactive insulin (insulin-^{131}I) into control subjects who had never been treated with insulin or had received insulin injections for less than one month, and into study subjects who had received insulin injections for many months or years. The control subjects included normal healthy volunteers and hospitalized patients, both diabetic (many maturity-onset, or Type II, diabetics are not treated with insulin) and nondiabetic. The study subjects included fifteen diabetic subjects who had received insulin from three months to seventeen years, and one schizophrenic patient who had received insulin shock treatment for six weeks. Doses of 0.1 to 7.0 units of insulin containing 15 to 200 uc of ^{131}I were administered intravenously, and urine collections and blood samples were taken thereafter. Processing and analyzing the urine and blood samples was tedious and time consuming. Assays of radioactivity were carried out on urine, plasma, and packed red blood cells, and on the filtrates and washed precipitates of plasma treated with cold trichloroacetic acid (TCA) to precipitate proteins.

It was not possible simply to inject radioactive insulin and then count the radioactivity in blood samples taken at successive time intervals because as the radioactive insulin is metabolized the ^{131}I is released and returned to the plasma. Thus, at any given time the total radioactivity in a sample consists of some proportion of both intact insulin-^{131}I and free ^{131}I. (The TCA precipitates the protein in plasma while allowing the ^{131}I to remain in solution, and so the radioactivity in the precipitates was assumed to represent intact, unmetabolized insulin.) The TCA acts something like a fish net, allowing the small free ^{131}I to go through the netting while trapping the larger protein-bound ^{131}I.

When Berson and Yalow plotted their data so that TCA precipitable radioactivity (intact insulin-^{131}I) in plasma was shown as a function of time following the administration of insulin-^{131}I, they found that the rate of disappearance of insulin from the plasma was not dependent upon whether the patient was diabetic, but on whether the subject had been treated with insulin for more than a few weeks. There was a rapid disappearance of insulin in diabetics and nondiabetics who had not been treated with insulin. Insulin disappeared more slowly from the plasma of patients who had been treated with insulin, either for the treatment of diabetes or as shock therapy for schizophrenia.

At this point most investigators would have been satisfied. They had determined that the Mirsky hypothesis was wrong; insulin did not disappear more rapidly from the plasma of maturity-onset diabetics. But Yalow and Berson were not at all satisfied. The Mirsky hypothesis was no longer of interest, but they were intrigued with their findings and with the methods of characterizing the radioactivity in the plasma samples. Why did insulin disappear more slowly from the plasma of subjects treated with insulin for at least a number of weeks? Was the insulin changed in some way in these patients? Could they examine the radioactivity that they found in these plasma samples to better define what it was attached to?

They would sit in their office or in a small conference room with a few of the young fellows training in the lab, and the speculations and ideas for new approaches or inventive methods would fly between them so that the air would become charged with energy until they would burst out to the laboratory to try something new. Working out technical problems or coming to the answer of a portion of a central question might take weeks, even months of work. They would attack the tedium by actually performing the physical work with glee. Although they had some technical help, no one spent more time than they did in the cold rooms doing electrophoretic separations at four degrees, or centrifuging and washing hundreds of protein precipitates, or changing thousands of test tubes in radiation counters, all the while talking, especially to each other, about the ionic strength of the buffer, or the saturation of binding sites on the filter paper, or the question of whether the insulin was bound to a serum protein.

They came early and stayed late. They talked more to each other than to anyone else, and they had an inner sanctum, an office with one door that opened into a laboratory. The door was almost always open but that was their private place. As noted before, their two big desks were pushed together so that they faced each other across a large surface cluttered with books and papers, more cluttered on his side. It was rather dark in there. They had fine old chemical scales for weighing chloramine T and sodium metabisulfite for the iodination of peptides, which they liked to do themselves in a kind of ritual in the iodination room under the iodination hood, handing the little vials of chemicals back and forth, rubber pipetting tubes dangling from their mouths, whispering through their teeth: "twenty microliters of phosphate buffer, right, two microliters of insulin, right, five microliters of [131]I—you know we can get ^{125}I now and with its sixty day half-life we'll only have to iodinate once each month—ten microliters chloramine T, here it is, OK, and twenty microliters sodium metabisulfate. Finished. Tell Manny I made the starch gels last night so he can purify this right now. That way the assay can be set up tonight and separated on Wednesday before we leave for Washington."

To approach their scientific problems Berson and Yalow invented a new method of electrophoresis (a technique for separating and purifying proteins and other chemicals, based upon their relative mobilities when driven through a supporting medium, i.e., a gel or a paper strip, by an electric current). They called it paper chromatoelectrophoresis. It is a process in which "free" insulin-^{131}I bound to the site of application on a filter paper strip, which was soaked in a buffer solution and stretched horizontally across vertical plastic supports, the ends of the paper dipping down 10 cm into the buffer vessels and a constant current running between positive and negative electrodes. The method was fast and accurate, separating molecules along the paper like rocks of different sizes and shapes rolling down a mountainside. The plasma proteins migrated across the paper strips driven by the current and the evaporation of the buffer as the strips were exposed to the air in the cold room, and they separated out as gamma, beta, alpha 2, alpha 1 globulins, and albumin, spreading across the paper according to their charges as the current and the air drove them for hours. Then it was time to go in again and stand in the glow of the fluorescent lights at four degrees for another thirty minutes, take off the finished strips and put on new ones, in groups of twenty, hundreds of them, with the only break from the tedium being the accidental touching of the electrodes and the 200 volts going through your body, the shock running through your arms and slamming into the back of your head. On to the drying of the strips in ovens, and the counting of the radioactivity on the paper with the strip scanner until it was clear: The radioactivity in the plasma of insulin-treated patients didn't bind at the site of application like "free" insulin; it moved across the paper with the gamma globulins. So in fact, after months of struggle, Yalow and Berson found that the TCA precipitable insulin-^{131}I in the plasma of insulin treated subjects was changed. It was bound to a large protein, a gamma globulin. It was as though the smaller radiolabeled insulin-^{131}I molecules were being picked up and carried by the bigger gamma globulin molecules.

They immediately asked themselves: Could the gamma globulin be an antibody? Antibodies are gamma globulins produced by the immune system in response to repeated injection of foreign proteins. The treated subjects were repeatedly injected with beef or pork insulins, which are small proteins and foreign to the human body. Could it be that they developed antibody to insulin? If that were the case it would mean that some important principles of classical immunology would have to be reconsidered, and that they had discovered a new method of using radioactivity to study immunologic reactions. And so they restudied a subject who had been receiving insulin for only a few weeks when they had begun their studies. At that time the radioactivity in his plasma samples had bound to the paper. However, by the time they had made their observation about the gamma globulin he had been taking insulin for many months. So when they restudied this subject, the radioactivity moved with the gamma globulins, it was insulin-^{131}I bound to an insulin-binding antibody, they were almost sure. They confirmed their findings with ultracentrifugation experiments in which the insulin-^{131}I in the serum of insulin-treated subjects sedimented with the globulins, but in the serum of control subjects it sedimented at a slower rate than serum albumin. They were sure. This proved that when people are repeatedly injected with beef or pork insulin they develop antibodies that bind insulin. The insulin, which is bound to the much larger gamma globulin molecules like a baby held in its mother's arms, is retained in the bloodstream, sequestered, sheltered from metabolic degradation, and unavailable to participate in the normal activity of lowering the blood sugar.

Insulin is a relatively small protein with about fifty amino acids and a molecular weight of only 6000 daltons (a dalton is a unit of atomic weight, with each amino acid weighing something over one hundred daltons; albumin, for example is 69,000, gamma globulin is 170,000 daltons), and at that time, 1955, it was believed that only large proteins could be antigenic. (In this context, antigenicity refers to a molecule's ability to stimulate antibody production when it is injected into an animal to which that molecule is foreign.) There had been a few prior suggestions that insulin could stimulate antibody responses, and Berson and Yalow cited these in their manuscript. However, this was the first real proof that a small protein could stimulate an immunologic response, and the scientific establishment, which like other establishments tends to be rather conservative, perhaps a bit dogmatic, was not prepared to accept the finding. Their paper was rejected by *Science* and by the *Journal of Clinical Investigation*. The reviewers, and the journal editors, including leading authorities in the field of immunology, would not allow the insulin-binding globulin to be called an antibody. After an argument waged through back and forth correspondence with editors and anonymous peer reviewers, the editor-in-chief wrote:

> I regret that the revision of your paper entitled "Insulin-I[131] Metabolism in Human Subjects: Demonstration of Insulin Transporting Antibody in the Circulation of Insulin Treated Subjects" is not acceptable for publication in *The Journal of Clinical Investigation*. . .
>
> The second major criticism relates to the dogmatic conclusion set forth which are not warranted by the data. The experts in this field have been particularly emphatic in rejecting your positive statement that the "conclusion that the globulin responsible for insulin binding is an acquired antibody appears to be inescapable." They believe that you have not demonstrated an antigen–antibody reaction on the basis of adequate criteria, nor that you have definitely proved that a globulin is responsible for insulin binding, nor that insulin is an antigen.[10]

Berson and Yalow felt strongly that their data provided absolute proof of an antigen–antibody reaction between insulin and insulin-binding antibodies. They had shown that in response to repeated injections of foreign (pig or cow) insulin, subjects began to produce a gamma globulin that bound specifically to insulin. It looked like an insulin-binding antibody, it walked like an insulin-binding antibody, it talked like an insulin-binding antibody, so they considered it an insulin-binding antibody. The expert peer-reviewers and the editors disagreed, simply because insulin was thought to be smaller than some undetermined critical molecular size believed to confer the property of antigenicity. The struggle to get their paper published and their failure to convince editors and reviewers of what they regarded as obvious caused them to regard many reviewers and editors as "dumbbells." Finally, in a compromise with the editors, the paper was published in the *Journal of Clinical Investigation*, but only after they omitted "insulin transporting antibody" from the title. Nonetheless, they were able to use the term "insulin antibody" within the text of the paper. This was a compromise they could live with. Although the brouhaha delayed the publication of their paper by only a few months, they were angry and disappointed with the process.

The publication of their paper, "Insulin-I^{131} Metabolism in Human Subjects: Demonstration of Insulin Binding Globulin in the Circulation of Insulin-Treated Subjects," put the issue to rest as it was readily apparent to those without vested interest that the binding protein was indeed an antibody.[11] Within a short time their observations were confirmed by others and the same journal published their next paper entitled, "Ethanol Fractionation of Plasma and Electrophoretic Identification of Insulin-Binding Antibody." The use of the term insulin-binding antibody in the title was a triumph, a clear sign that the significance of their finding was now acceptable to even the most dogmatic critics. More than twenty years later, after Yalow had included a copy of the journal's rejection letter in her Nobel speech, a young woman approached me at a scientific meeting and, with sincere emotion, asked if I could intercede with Dr. Yalow to prevent her from continuing to call attention to her father's decision regarding the 1956 paper. Yalow never mentioned it in public again.

It is now well appreciated that peptides much smaller than insulin, even those of only a few amino acids, can be antigenic.

This means that our immune system can recognize and respond to even the smallest molecules in protecting us from foreign invasion or in producing protective antibody in response to vaccination with tiny antigens.

In studying the interaction of insulin with insulin-binding antibody, Berson and Yalow were the first to use radioisotopic techniques for the study of the primary reaction of antigen with antibody. In so doing, they provided a window into the previously invisible world of antigen–antibody reactions that take place in solution, without the formation of the obvious clumps of precipitated material that form when large conglomerates of antigen and antibody form and fall out of solution, looking like grains of salt or fluffy flakes or crumbs. Soluble antigen–antibody complexes, as opposed to those that spontaneously precipitate out of solution, are invisible, and therefore were more difficult to detect and study prior to the publication of these methods. They were well aware of this and the argument over globulin versus antibody was not simply a matter of semantics. Prior to the introduction of their ideas and methods scientists were essentially restricted in the analysis of the reactions between antigens and antibodies to those that produced visible precipitation of antigen–antibody complexes as a line in a gel, or other visible methods like the clumping of red blood cells. With the older precipitin line method a clear agar gel is poured in a Petri dish, about one quarter of an inch thick. When it hardens, a little hole is punched out in the center surrounded by several additional holes. If a solution containing sufficient antibody molecules is placed in the center hole, and antigen-containing solutions are placed in the surrounding holes, the antigen and antibody molecules will diffuse through the gel, moving toward each other. Where they meet they will form a visible line of precipitated antigen–antibody complexes in the form of a small grayish arch. It is a crude method that requires a great deal of antigen and antibody to precipitate in order for visible lines to form in the gel. Berson and Yalow initiated a revolution in theoretical immunology. Their data indicated that the energy requirements for antigen–antibody reactions had to be reconsidered, that the equilibrium constants for the antigen–antibody reaction can be as great as 10^{14} liters per mole, a value up to 10^8 greater than the highest value predicted by Linus Pauling's theory of 1940.

Their crucial paper (entitled "Insulin-I^{131} Metabolism in Human Subjects: Demonstration of Insulin Binding Globulin in the Circulation of Insulin-Treated Subjects") appeared in the *Journal of Clinical Investigation* in February of 1956 and is a classic in the scientific literature. It is twenty pages long, with lots of data, sixteen figures, and two tables. In this way it differs in style from the papers of today. These data would now be published in a series of many publications, each one dealing with a small portion of the work. And buried in this paper is the finding that provided the basis for the radioimmunoassay of insulin: the observation that the binding of insulin-^{131}I to a fixed concentration of antibody is a quantitative function of the amount of insulin present. In other words, if you were to put some insulin-binding antibody into a test tube along with just a bit of insulin-^{131}I, all of the labled insulin would be bound to the antibody molecules. But if you did it again, this time adding unlabled insulin, some of the insulin-^{131}I would be prevented from binding to the antibody because some of the antibody's binding sites would be occupied by the unlabeled insulin. And the number of unbound insulin-^{131}I molecules would be in direct proportion to the number of unlabeled insulin molecules you had added. Berson and Yalow understood this before they wrote what they always called "the 1956 paper," and from that time forward they worked to develop a practical method for measuring insulin based upon this observation.

It took Yalow and Berson several years of work, including detailed studies and mathematical models of the quantitative aspects of the reaction between insulin and antibody, and evaluation of the species specificity of available antisera that they had raised in guinea pigs and rabbits, before theoretical concepts of the RIA method could be translated into measurements of circulating insulin. They honed the technique with measurements of beef and other animal insulins using antibody in the plasma of their human subjects. Finally, in their 1959 paper that appeared in *Nature* ("Assay of Plasma Insulin in Human Subjects by Immunological Methods"[12]), they were measuring the insulin in human blood.

RIA—Berson and Yalow's crowning glory—is simple in principle. The concentration of the unknown unlabeled antigen, such as the insulin in your blood, is obtained by studying your blood's ability to displace the binding of radioactively labeled insulin to insulin-binding antibody. We compare the ability of a small quantity of your blood to inhibit the binding of insulin-^{131}I to insulin binding antibody with the inhibitory effect of known standards. Thus, if a small volume of your blood inhibits the binding of radioactive insulin to antibody to the same extent as 10 pg (pg = picogram, 10^{-12} grams) of a standard insulin preparation obtained from a manufacturer, then your little sample of blood contained 10 pg of insulin.

The most remarkable thing about RIA is its sensitivity. It can measure unbelievably low concentrations of all sorts of substances. This sensitivity is essential for the measurement of peptide hormones because they circulate in the blood at incredibly low concentrations. And the RIA method has all of the specificity inherent in the precise reaction of an antigen with its specific antibody. The insulin antibody will find and bind and measure only the insulin among the myriad substances, many in billion-fold higher concentrations, which are present in your blood sample. It is also inexpensive to do, and it is nearly as easy and quick to assay thousands of samples as just one or two. RIA was a breakthrough approach.

In 1960 Yalow and Berson published a paper in the *Journal of Clinical Investigation* ("Immunoassay of Endogenous Plasma Insulin in Man") where for the first time they described the pattern and quantity of insulin released in response to ingestion of sugar.[13] The paper included data for normal subjects, Type II diabetics, and patients with a variety of other disorders. This long paper contains many important discoveries, but the most striking is the finding that Type II diabetics, while having lost the first rapid upstroke of insulin release in response to rising blood sugar, nonetheless release more insulin and have higher plasma insulin concentrations during the hours after ingesting glucose.

This observation that Type II diabetics frequently release more insulin than normal people, so that while they have high blood sugar they also have high insulin levels, led to the realization that Type II diabetics are resistant to the action of their own insulin. In other words, while Type I diabetics have high blood sugar levels because they have little or no insulin, most Type II diabetics have high blood sugar levels despite secreting excessive amounts of insulin. Somehow, the insulin-requiring cells of their bodies, like the muscle and liver cells, resist the action of insulin. And the concept of insulin resistance has been one of the most important and productive ideas in the understanding of the diabetic state.

RIA was first applied to the measurement of insulin and then to the other peptide hormones, primarily by the young researchers who came to work with Berson and Yalow. It was adapted to measure all manner of substances, including vitamins, thyroid hormones, steroids, prostaglandins, biologic amines, drugs, cyclic nucleotides, enzymes, tumor antigens, serum proteins, viruses, and many others. Berson and Yalow consistently and tirelessly broadcast the message of RIA's nearly limitless applicability, and in addition to helping others to extend the method to a variety of substances, their assay for the hepatitis B virus brought RIA to the study and practice of infectious diseases in a way that has saved countless lives and that had not been considered before (Fig. 21).

Finally, the basic principles of RIA were adapted for other types of competitive binding assays. Nonantibody binding substances, like the natural vitamin B_{12} binder in stomach secretions, called intrinsic factor, was used to make assays for vitamin B_{12}. And membrane receptors, the specialized molecules that specifically bind hormones and other substances to the surfaces of cells, can be measured using adaptations of the RIA principle.[14] Nonradioactive labels, like enzyme markers, can be used in place of radioisotopes. In the end, it doesn't matter what kind of label you use to make a tracer for the material you want to measure, and the specific binder need not be an antibody, so that many imaginative innovations have been developed based upon the fundamental RIA concept.

RIA was Berson and Yalow's baby. When it grew up and everyone wanted to embrace it, Berson and Yalow continued to

Figure 21. Solomon Berson with Rosalyn Yalow holding the check for the First Eli Lilly Award of the American Diabetes Association, 1957.

define its conceptual and technical integrity and to protect it from those who might distort its origins or limit its applicability. Very quickly, Dr. Roger Unger, a brilliant endocrinologist, made his own RIA for glucagon, a pancreatic hormone that balances insulin's glucose lowering effect and helps maintain blood sugar above the level that would cause damage to the brain and other tissues. And Dr. Sheldon Rothenberg, working in Berson and Yalow's laboratory, developed a competitive radioassay for vitamin B_{12} using radioactive cobalt[57] as the label for B_{12}, and intrinsic factor, the native B_{12} binding molecule from the stomach, in place of an antibody.[15] Others were quickly developing competitive radioassays using the same principles, and, especially after Berson died, a few even began to campaign with the notion that they had been first.

Clearly, many scientists felt that a Nobel Prize should be given for the discovery of a method that had revolutionized medicine and biomedical science. Yet with everything Berson and Yalow had accomplished, Yalow's chances were in doubt. Berson was dead and no surviving member of a scientific team had ever received a Nobel.

9

Mother

I think she was a pretty wonderful mom.
ELANNA YALOW, PH.D.
There was the family in the lab and the
family at home. I'm not saying the family
in the lab was more important.
BENJAMIN YALOW

*S*he was in pain, but it wasn't the pain in her hip that was hard, it was the pain of keeping on and knowing that the struggle to rehabilitate could do no more than recover to an unsatisfactory level. Several days were wasted as she lay with the broken hip. She had fallen on a Friday evening, and the neurologist wanted an MRI of her brain to see if the fall had been caused by another stroke. So no surgery was planned before the scan could be done on Monday. And the scan was not done until Tuesday, just minutes before she was taken to the operating room to repair her hip.

After the surgery she wasn't herself. She wouldn't eat, and she answered all questions with a wave of the good left hand saying, "whatever you want."

"Would you like the newspaper?"

"Whatever you want."

"Would you like the TV turned on?"

"Whatever you want."

I knew what she wanted, and we discussed it whenever we were alone. She insisted that she had thought it out and would not change her mind: She had lived a wonderful life, her children were independent and did not need her, she would leave it to me to take care of the matter.

She had no hobbies, no diversions. There had been nothing but the work, and that was over. A week after the operation, while she was being visited by her oldest friends, Herb and Natalie Zagor, she asked for help to find "a brown bag with pills that Gene had left for me." They looked everywhere, they asked the nurse for help, but there was no brown bag.

She was spending most of the days and nights sleeping and dreaming. She could not remember what the dreams were about. The question arose of an infection in the operative wound, the possibility of having to operate again. She waved her hand. "Whatever you want."

It is not possible to consider a female scientist without regarding her motherhood—her relationship to children and family—or its absence (Fig. 22). The female scientist will usually insist that her struggle and her sacrifice be acknowledged. There need be no other reason than to explain how she accomplished what so few have done. Rosalyn, who tends to deemphasize the difficulties she experienced as a woman, nonetheless brings it up first in any discussion of her career, or of women in science, and she is proud of her 1987 Outstanding Mother Award from the National Mother's Day Committee.

In a society that prides itself on being modern, even today women still must fit a career around the demands of childrearing and homemaking. Most academic institutions provide inadequate facilities for child care, especially in the early years. Those with preschool programs generally don't start until the child is three, so the family must deal with the infant to three-year-old on its own. When the child enters kindergarten communities may lack sufficient after-school situations. Benjamin Yalow was born in 1952 and Elanna was born two years later, so Rosalyn Yalow had her children right in the midst of the busiest and most important years of her career. She got help at home from her mother and her maid, but she accepted the idea that the responsibility for organizing the home and childrearing belonged to her and not Aaron. It is of particular interest that Rosalyn's daughter, Elanna, is in the business of running daycare facilities.

In my experience, including several years on the board of a cooperative daycare center on the upper west side of Manhattan and as a founder of a cooperative after-school center more than a decade ago, responsibility for child care, even in families with high sensitivity to the issue, generally resides with the mother. I believe that much of the emerging change in attitudes regarding family and gender roles was washed away in the social backlash of the eighties and nineties and with the fear for job security and financial stability that is being injected into the middle class ethos by a rapidly changing and less secure relationship to employ-

Figure 22. Rosalyn Yalow with Benjamin and Elanna in Florida.

ment. People have much less confidence regarding their ability to find and keep satisfying and financially sound positions in science and medicine. I see medical students and graduate students in science who are fearful of the future. This pushes them into more traditional roles; they take a job with a big group practice, or they go to work for a giant drug company. I hear older established people who know what's going on say how much harder it is for young people today than it was when they entered science and medicine. Opportunities for meaningful careers are narrowing as in various other sectors of the job market. This is not an atmosphere for bold change and advancement in the effort to provide equal opportunity.

Maybe we would rather not know some things, like Einstein's fatherhood. Perhaps careful analysis of traditional fatherhood is hard to face. Fatherhood is often an avoided topic in books about male scientists. So it was something of a shock when several books published during the past year, after so many books and articles about Einstein, delved into his unfortunate family relationships and his absolute neglect of his daughter. Certainly, John Rigden's biography of the great physicist I. I. Rabi, *Rabi: Scientist and Citizen*, a fine book about a great scientist and humanitarian, has nary a word about Rabi's wife, Helen, or about their family.

For years the Rabis would come to the Yalow seder on Passover. Once they were joined by Isaac Bashevis Singer and his wife. There was always a lively group at the Yalow seder (Fig. 23). I would drive the upper west siders to the Bronx. From the ride up and back from Riverside Drive in Manhattan, I learned that there was plenty to say about Rabi's family, but the biographer and his subject, both male physicists, didn't think it important enough to include. Perhaps a passage from Rabi's biography may explain:

> The same man who saw physics as a way to touch God saw it also as a way closed to women. Rabi thought most women temperamentally unsuited for great physics: "I'm afraid there's no use quarreling with it, that's the way it is." He never had a woman postdoctoral or graduate student; he typically did not support the candidacy of women for faculty positions in his department.

Much has been written about the recent acceptance of women as equal participants in the "system" of science. It is certainly true that the relative numbers of Ph.D. and M.D. degrees awarded to women have been rising. But the data indicate that gender parity in salaries has not been achieved, and there is nothing like gender parity in rates of promotion or acquisition of tenure. What is frequently referred to as the "puzzling difference in scientific productivity," generally measured in terms of numbers of papers published, cannot be truly puzzling in the face of the continued inequities, and the fact that the daily work of parenthood and homemaking are most often placed on women alone. Nonethe-

Figure 23. I. I. Rabi, I. B. Singer, and Rosalyn Yalow at the Yalow seder, 1984.

less, while women scientists publish an average of 2.3 papers a year to 2.8 for men, the citation rate (or the number of times a paper is referred to in another published work—a recognized indication of the paper's impact) is higher for papers by women (24.4 per paper for women versus 14.4 for men).[1]

Mildred Dresselhaus, with four children, president of the American Association for the Advancement of Science, past president of the American Physical Society, treasurer of the National Academy of Sciences, Distinguished Professor at MIT, had seven graduate students receive Ph.D.s the year she was president of the American Physical Society. "Ros had this influence on me," she points out.[2]

> We have to do excellent work in our research and teaching. To make it possible for women to succeed later we have to take on some of these administrative roles. And if we do it we have to do it well because otherwise the next person will not be asked. For whatever reason Ros didn't move in that direction. She could have, but she didn't. So I did that. I was the first tenured women faculty member of the engineering school at MIT. So we don't go back that far. It was my role to provide some leadership here. It had to be done, and with a small investment in time I had some impact. Now the younger people are doing it, and I appreciate that.

These are the Jackie Robinsons of women in science. They had to hit home runs in the lab and slide home with dinner. They had to stand out to get any recognition. If they had to turn a cheek or two, well, Rosalyn can turn a slap into a handshake, until she gets you where she wants you, then she can get in your face, just like Jackie. She can be an uppity woman. But the toll on that road is high, and Jackie died young.

Rosalyn Yalow wanted her daughter to be a physician or perhaps a research scientist, like Marie Curie's daughter, Irene Joliot-Curie, who succeeded her mother as director of the Radium Institute in Paris and shared the 1935 Nobel Prize in chemistry with her husband, Frederic Joliot-Curie. The Joliot-Curie team produced artificial radioactive substances, a direct continuation of her mother's work. But it was not to be for the Yalows. Elanna was every bit as strong-willed and determined to go her own way as her mother. She has a Ph.D. in educational psychology and is the president of a large corporation that establishes and maintains daycare facilities across the country. It's an interesting business for a woman whose mother regards childcare as the key issue for women in science. Elanna is a beautiful woman and an athlete. She is very much involved with her work and her family. She laughs easily, and she holds and expresses conflicting feelings without confusion or fear of contradiction.

Yalow regards her son, Benjamin, as a genius. "He's much smarter than I am," she says, taking pride in his ability in mathematics and physics. Yet, if anything, she seems perplexed by his career in computers, which she calls "machinkies," a derogatory diminutive for machines, and by his preeminence in science fiction fandom. It was the uniqueness of his personality, his unorthodox psychology, that may have left her confused about his interests and directions. While her relationships with her children are normal in their complexity, it is striking that she refuses to recognize any difficulty or ambiguity in them.

Rosalyn Yalow did the things that most mothers do for their kids—she cooked dinners, took them on vacations, held birthday parties, she was concerned—and she feels that her children paid no price for the demands of her scientific career. She is glad that Benjamin lives at home now that Aaron is gone and she needs his help. With regard to Elanna she denies having had any conflict, always stressing how similar they are in being strong women with supportive husbands. But Elanna has the ability to hold and express her conflicts, differences, and resentments, while at the same time honoring, respecting, and loving her mother. I believe that this ability is much more available to women than men, and it is something that, to a male observer, seems to characterize mother–daughter relationships. When Elanna speaks of her mother, she can express all of her feelings, complete with ambivalence and contradiction, but in the end, tears well up, and she says, "I love my mother, and I respect her."[3]

I think that when I was growing up I thought she was the perfect mother, because I was independent and, either because she had no choice, or because she believed in it, she allowed me my independence. Probably through junior high school it was fine because I didn't want to do anything that she didn't want me to do, so there was no source of conflict. It worked out fine. She could give me the freedom to do what I wanted to do. She just wasn't physically around. I would come home from school and there was nobody there, although I do remember her coming home with the shopping, and she was very dutiful, and I have no memories of trauma or neglect. She traveled a lot, like I do, and I missed her, like my kids miss me, but she would always bring back a present. But that's my mom; she does everything physical very well, and what I believe now is that the emotion was lacking.

Even years later, when I moved out to California, she would come out to visit me four times a year. It could be awful; it could be two days where we didn't say a word to each other, or fighting, and if she had another trip planned in six weeks she'd come out and visit me. She needed to feel that she had a great relationship with me, she wanted that very badly, for herself and for me. But sometimes those visits were truly painful, the silence, the tension, sometimes because the interrelationships were negative, sometimes because there were none. But she never failed to come the next time.

I was much closer to her than I was to my father. I was very distant from my father because of religion. He and I had almost no relationship because I was not religious, and he was so religious. I think my mother created a distance between us, without meaning to, because her way of dealing with my father, and certainly where it came to religion, was not to tell him anything. From an early age I was trained to do what I wanted and not tell him anything. I don't think I ever closed that gap with my dad. So she wasn't around, and I think she didn't want to know things either, because then she wouldn't have to deal with them.

When I got into high school I was a product of the Sixties. I started wearing clothes she didn't like and hanging around with people she didn't like. She has no idea of what I did, but what she could see from the surface she didn't like. Actually, I think I hurt her feelings once and it shocked me because it was the first time I clearly saw that she was being totally irrational. Her rule was that you could do whatever you wanted as long as it didn't hurt you or anyone else, and she violated that rule, and that was, as I remember, a turning point. She could not explain why that rule had to be violated. She just wanted me to do something. But she had created me, and she had given me too much freedom to suddenly turn it off, and that was the first of many episodes where I wanted to do something and she didn't want me to do it. She didn't like the way I dressed, she didn't like my friends, but they were not harming me or anyone else, so by her own rules there was no reason I couldn't be doing what I wanted, but she insisted. So from that time on, I don't think we've ever been close, and for a long period there was anger, and then the anger dissipated to apathy and distance, and even though she was very proud of me and represented me in the most positive terms to every human with whom she came in contact, she did quite the opposite with me. This continued, and when I became an adult, she didn't like the fact that I wasn't going into medicine, at least I should go into law, and I should socialize with the kinds of people that she judged as worthy.

She never really tried to understand what I was doing professionally. So even though I was successful in doing traditional things, getting my doctorate, forging ahead with my career, she didn't value it. She didn't do the kinds of things that parents are supposed to do to make their kids believe that they value what their kids are doing, even if they couldn't care less. I'm sure a lot of parents don't understand what their children do, but they have some interest just because it's their kids that are doing it, and they get some intrinsic joy out of that. I don't think my mother gets any intrinsic joy out of me. She likes the idea of me, very much, and she loves me very much, and she would do anything for me. I know all of that, but it's not that just being around me gives her pleasure. I think that for a lot of parents just being around their kids, knowing that their kids are happy, gives them pleasure. It's not like that for her. I have never acknowledged that that bothers me, because I'm so used to it.

Now I look back and wonder what it was like to have been a kid in that environment, to have had that level of disinterest and lack of approval. I see it with my kids when my mom's been around them. When her first grandson was a little guy, like one year old and just running around, she said, "I'm sure he'll be more interesting when he learns to read." That attitude just made a gap between us.

I don't see someone who struggles with things. She has clearly said that she has made no mistakes in her life, has no regrets, and would do nothing different. And if you suggest that something she did caused something negative to happen, she says that at the time she made the right decision. You can't argue with her. She is certain that things are as she believes them to be, and she is unwilling to look at them from another perspective. The fact that her family isn't perfect makes it like everyone else's, but she can't accept that.

I don't know if she started off a little more balanced, more typical of how people are, and she had to adopt that to get through to what she did, or if she had that view of the world from the beginning and that's what got her where she went. She was already formed that way when I was a little girl, so I don't know. I left home pretty young, and I don't think that I knew that she was that way until later, when I reflected back on things she had done.

I think that the earliest forms of her denial was

when she was drinking a lot and I had already left the house. It was clear that she was drinking heavily, and there was no acknowledgement of that. My brother and father were scared to even discuss it with her. That was when I was in high school, and we were pretty estranged by then, and I had pretty much checked out of the house.

When I was fifteen I was a vegetarian, so I didn't take any meals at the house, by then we were pretty distant from each other. She was completely dismissive of all my friends. She never remembered their names, not even my boyfriends' names, because they weren't at the very top of the class. It was Science High School. They were basically all Jewish, and all smart, but they were not at the top academically, and so she never remembered a thing I told her about them, so I stopped talking to her.

My high school boyfriend's dad was a tailor, and she hated that, because it was not the class she wanted for me. He had made some clothes for me, and if I would wear any of that she would be furious. One time we were going to see my dad's family in Brooklyn, and family meant everything to my dad, and she didn't like what I was wearing because it was a coat that my boyfriend's father had made for me. Well, she said that we couldn't go if I wore that coat. So I said, OK I'm not going. And my poor dad said, "Ros please! Elanna please!," trying to get one of us to give in. I wasn't going to give in to her for my dad, even though I felt really badly for my dad. It wasn't like we were going to see her mom. She put my dad in the middle, and he was very much stuck in the middle.

It was so different from what just a few years before I had viewed as her image. We had some huge fights about clothes. I didn't care about clothes. I was just wearing the uniform of the day, and I had gotten that from her, not to value clothes, and I think that was a very good value. She didn't value clothes, or how you looked, just your contribution to society. But then I saw that it did matter to her, she did care what you looked like, not just your goodness, or how you treat people. I was doing OK in school but it wasn't good enough because I didn't have the career path she wanted, and she was dismissive, and couldn't understand why anyone would want to do that. It was something other people would do, not what her daughter would do.

The argument phase didn't last that long because I went my own way. By the time I was fifteen I was a junior in high school and I was never home on the weekends. My dad was orthodox so I couldn't do anything in the house, so I had to sneak out of the house, and I couldn't tell him what I was doing, and she didn't want to know what I was doing. By the time I was in junior high school I was doing what kids in the sixties did, hanging out, talking, nothing radical, but certainly not just studying and planning for the future. I couldn't discuss how I was spending my time with her, she would have considered it wasting time, and she made it pretty clear that she didn't want to know. I don't know whether she can't accept that other people are human or that she's human.

Still, in the end, I think she was a pretty wonderful mom. I think our problems are part of normal problems, and I respect what she is, and I came out good enough. My problems have nothing to do with her, and on balance I got more from her than I was damaged by her. Certainly, I got the feeling that a woman can do anything.

But my brother had a hard time. I really love my brother. He's a little odd, but he's a really good guy. We can talk about anything. Growing up with him as my older brother was very healthy for me because he was so different, and everybody knew it. He was frequently ridiculed, and I think that it made me more compassionate for people who are different, because he was. He always wore his bow tie, and everybody made fun of him for that, and he went through so much abuse as a kid growing up. People would say, "you're the younger sister of that guy?!"

We had natural sibling rivalry growing up, but my mom kind of played us against each other, in a natural way, like parents do. She would always say, "why can't you be smart like your brother? Why don't you do as well as he does in school? You're really not as good, your scores aren't as high." I really got a lot of that, and my brother got "your sister is so much more socially adapted, she can talk to people," but I think that's normal parent stuff, well meaning.

I was distanced. They had science in common and I didn't. They'd be doing physics problems and debating science, but my mother was always right and always telling them she was right. All my brother and my father wanted was a chance to talk about stuff, so they would get into some ridiculous debate, because they just liked to debate, and she would say this is nonsense, this is the way it is, and she would stop the debate. So a lot of their relationship would go on when she wasn't around.

My brother and my father would worry about everything, about every little thing. To me it was like fighting for some dignity, because my mom wouldn't give them any dignity at all. She always told them how things should be. She was so demeaning to my father, just completely emasculating, and gave him nothing even though she came to need him. Although he was clearly very strong in the family, she was demeaning to him all the time when I was growing up. I was angry with her for that, and I was angry with my dad because he seemed weak. It wasn't until many years later that I understood the choices he had made, and I respect those choices now. In a lot of the fighting I did with my mother he clearly would be on my side, or he would say my mother was being unreasonable, as much as he was permitted to say, that she was being unreasonable.

I would say, "then why am I fighting? I'm just a kid. Why don't you go out there and tell her she's wrong and fight the battle for me?" But nobody ever fought the battle for me, and I took the easy way out and left. It wasn't an easy situation for my father, but he made the best of it because there were good parts as well. But I remember him trying to kiss her and she just turning her cheek. I remember him struggling through the pain because he understood, and he loved her.

But I think my father loved me and loved the family so much that he could have accepted me whatever I was, and one of the saddest things for him in his life was that I never let him see that. I have no doubt that he would have accepted my lack of religion, my friends, whatever I might have done, although it would have been painful, he would have accepted me as I was. In the early years, because he was so weak, I didn't understand all the goodness that was inside him.

I sometimes thought that Sol was the strong man that she didn't have with my father. I liked Sol, he was always very nice to me. I always wondered if they were having an affair, and I wondered about that more as I got older, because I tried to understand his wife Mimi's anger toward my mother. That was something that was never spoken about or considered. Nobody in my family would ever bring that up, but at some point I just wondered if it was some part of their relationship. She never talked about the sexist side of things, or the controlling side, but once I saw him really yelling at her. When he left and went to Mount Sinai, I knew that it was hard on her. But the way she presented it was classic for her, it was that he was making a bad decision, not that he was leaving her, but that he was making a bad decision. She showed no sign of personal hurt or rejection, just that he was making a bad decision. I don't know if she actually feels things at the time and then very quickly rewrites the episode, or if she denies it even at the point that it occurs.

But she might have helped me, just as a mother helping her child with the traumas in my first marriage, if she had shared something with me, and it might have been other relationships that she could have had, or that she had just considered but didn't go through with. She might have shared something of her relationships, or the lack of them, to have helped me to put my problems in some context other than making it all that it was my problem and that I couldn't handle anything and I was making all these mistakes and stupid decisions. She could have done that for me, but I know it's hard for anybody. When she won the Nobel Prize one of the first things I wondered was if she would mellow out. Could she relax? If anything, she went the other way, she became even more certain that everything she thought was right.

The first time I met Benjamin Yalow he was twenty years old. It was at about two in the afternoon on a day when I had been working in the Bronx V.A. for only a few weeks. Rosalyn asked me to come to her office to see him. There he was in great pain with his neck twisted hard to the right and his eyes rolled up looking at the ceiling. His lips were slightly blue and he was struggling for breath. "Has he been taking compazine?" I asked. "Yes," Rosalyn answered.

I thought that he was in the midst of an oculogyric crisis, a severe, if uncommon side effect of compazine, one of the phenothiazine drugs, like thorazine, but more often used to control nausea and vomiting than for psychiatric disorders. I ran off to the medical wards, desperate to get a dose of benadryl for intravenous injection. When I got to the ward, I realized that as a Mount Sinai gastroenterology fellow who had been working exclusively in the V.A. research laboratory for only a few weeks, the nurses would not know me. I had no clinical privileges at the Bronx V.A. Hospital. Still, I accosted the first nurse I saw, and showed her my Mount Sinai identification. I explained in an agitated fashion that I was a physician and that I needed bena-dryl for intravenous administration immediately because some-one in a laboratory was having a severe toxic reaction to com-pazine. Without a word the nurse ran off and came back with two vials of benadryl. One vial given by slow intravenous push was sufficient to relax Benjamin's neck and eyes, and to completely reverse the frightening experience within minutes. He was soon quite composed, and related that he generally collapses and has a seizure when approached with a syringe and needle. Then he looked at his mother, and in a voice that revealed his pleasure at being right, but with no trace of bitterness, said, "So you see, it wasn't hysteria after all."

About an hour earlier Benjamin had been working at the computer center at Columbia University. He had felt something serious coming on and called his mother, who had suggested that it was simply nerves, some form of psychological agitation, but she jumped in her car and went immediately to his office. When she got to his side he was well into the crisis. Still, she thought that it was some manifestation of an emotional disorder. Instead of taking him to an emergency room she had brought him to her office.

There were other young physicians in the laboratory, who had been there far longer than I, and my clinical skills were unknown to Rosalyn. Because she knew my father well, she assumed that I was the appropriate person to consult. After the crisis was over, I asked why Benjamin was taking compazine. Phobias, I was told. I then spent an hour interviewing Benjamin alone. At the end of that time I told him that, while not a psychi-atrist, I could see no reason for him to be taking medication for "needle phobia," his extreme fear of hypodermic needles. In any case, compazine was not an appropriate medication for him to take. I advised Rosalyn of this, and later discussed the event with Sol Berson, who had prescribed the compazine. That was twenty-five years ago. To this day Benjamin has taken no medication for psychiatric disorder, nor has he displayed any manifestation of significant psychiatric illness.

"There were two families," says Benjamin Yalow.[4] "There was the family in the lab and the family at home. I'm not saying that the family in the lab was more important."

My grandfather would come over on weekends, and if I was good, and I was always good, we would walk up the hill to the candy store on the corner, a real candy store with fountains, and I would get a soda . . . I was about six when he died. After he died my grandmother's younger sister Sue moved in. She had never married and was supposed to have been the sick one. She retired from her bookkeeping job because she was supposed to die, and sixty years later she did die from complications from a hip operation. My grandmother, Clara (it was grandma and grandpa on my mother's side and the Yiddish equivalents, Bube and Zade [pronounced bub-e and zad-e] on my father's side), she was very warm and outgoing, she broke her hip when she was about ninety and it slowed her down for about three days. But really, I don't know much about family history because nobody ever talked about it.

I went to a Yeshiva (a Jewish school) through fifth grade. They put me in first grade but after one day they decided that it was demoralizing for the other kids because they were teaching them the alphabet or something and I was sitting in the back of the room reading The *New York Times*, so they put me in second grade. They might have tried to move me faster than that but they decided that the age gap would get too big. I guess that I was older than my mother was at the equivalent grade level. She would have been fifteen when she graduated from high school, just about to turn sixteen. I had already turned sixteen, essentially comparable grade levels, but I don't think anybody wanted me to get too much younger relative to my peers at school. I socialized as little as possible because when you're in second grade and it's time for recess, if you're the kid who doesn't want to go out to play but would just as soon sit in the corner and catch up on reading, that isn't what second graders are supposed to do. I switched to public school because I was pushing ahead too fast on the secular side of my education and my parents wanted me to get into the advanced classes that they had in public school, to get used to the public school environment, and eventually into the Bronx High School of Science. In those days you went to public school for the education. In those days Bronx Science trumped everything. I continued my Hebrew school education with a private tutor.

My mother got involved with religious Jewish life when she married my father. They worked out a compromise that seemed to make both of them happy: he was clearly far more orthodox than she was, and effectively they negotiated their way around it. This house still is a kosher house. It always will be. It would be unthinkable any other way. Friday nights there was candle lighting and there would be everything. It was an orthodox Jewish house. In some sense she made more accommodation to him. But if she went up to the lab on Saturday, if she broke the Sabbath, it was not made an issue. And if she drove there, it was not an easy situation to live with. [Sabbath teaching forbids doing work of any kind and driving a car falls under that category.] And if my sister is not observant, and if I am substantially less observant than my father was ... He was one of those rare individuals who could live in both worlds, religious and secular, and to find an orthodox scientist—and he was a scientist and a teacher, one of the finest teachers—it's rare. He helped her with her work. I won't say it was the same partnership she had with Sol, it was a very different partnership. But that professional partnership was very much there, but of course, no one knew it.

She was, for as long as I can remember, driven by her career. This didn't mean that she wasn't there when we needed her to be. She worked a five-minute drive from the house. She could be here in an instant if we needed her to be, but she was going to go ahead and do science. She essentially had two families: there was the one she had married into and raised, the biological and marriage family, and there was the scientific family. It was very clear . . . I won't say that it was very clear that the scientific family was more important because it was clear that if the biologic one absolutely needed it she was always there. But in the day to day aspects it was clear that the scientific one was the one in which she spent the predominant fraction of her time, which is different from the most important. She made it very clear that we were the most important. But that was where she was spending most of her time. Those two are not even vaguely the same statement. And we all took advantage of that. I used to go into the lab as a kid. My sister spent a summer there as a technician. It's where a lot of our childhood pets came from. She didn't like to sacrifice animals and we ended up with a lot of guinea pigs and rabbits around here.

For years the scientific family was her and Sol and whoever happened to be drifting by at the time and as the ring of contacts expanded. But the scientific family became her and Sol against the rest of the world. Sol was probably the most impressive man I ever met. He was just so incredibly smart, incredibly talented. He could go from random facts to conclusions, skipping the intermediate steps, faster than I've ever seen anybody else do. And more than just in science. He would come over and help me with the violin in ways that my violin teacher just couldn't do. He was not only a brilliant chess player but he could teach it, just an incredibly quick and facile man, and he did everything with flare. He was wonderful. For years the two families were close. We played together and toured together, and everybody got along. My parent's friends, the Zagors, and their kids grew up with us. Their daughter

Harriet and Wendy Berson, Sol's older daughter, became great friends and went off to Europe together. When Wendy died, right after Sol died, she just keeled over in a department store of a ruptured brain aneurysm. Jeff Kelman, Sol's nephew, met Harriet Zagor at the funeral, and now they're married and live in Washington. I thought of it as an extended family.

One of my mother's regrets was the estrangement of Mimi Berson. I don't know what happened, but right after Sol died, there was an estrangement, and the feeling I get is that my mother doesn't know why. But Berson and Yalow were like one person, and I don't know what happened. I thought it was great because it meant that I had an extra father, I mean I had an extra father, my mother has two other halves, one is my real father and the other is Sol, but so, from my viewpoint it was a great thing. From my father's viewpoint it was a great thing. I remember him being so happy when I said "look, you're not able to teach me chess any more. I'm enough better than you that I'm just not learning any more. But Sol is being great, he's teaching me now." And he said, "Wonderful! Great!" He was utterly thrilled by it. But the estrangement happened so fast and so hard that there was no time to talk to Miriam and say, "What's going on here? We've been friends for decades, why aren't we even on speaking terms anymore?" My mother was hurt enormously. Clearly Mimi must have been terribly hurt by something.

But my father was absolutely thrilled by everything that my mother did. He just gloried in it. He knew that he had married the most wonderful woman in the world. He was just always madly in love with her. He said many times that the very first time he saw her he fell in love with her. He stayed that way for fifty years until the day he died. She talked about it less but she felt the same way. It was utterly clear that this was one of the happiest partnerships—for better or for worse, in sickness or in health, they really did mean it. You couldn't have asked for a better partnership. Of course they occasionally fought, but nothing significant, never major.

Of course, having fights with her is generally nonproductive, because she's always right. The amount of evidence that it takes for her to change her mind is staggering. Effectively, getting into an argument with her is futile: You just can't win, you just cant win, because she's just never wrong. This is a slight exaggeration. If you accumulate enough evidence to prove your point absolutely, and nail it down absolutely solidly, yeah you can win. But that requires that it be about a scientific thing where there is a way of proving beyond any possible doubt, so you can't win. Now, the reason that this isn't intolerable is that in fact most of the time she is right. The way she can get away with being impossible to have her mind changed is the fact that she is probably right, so that in the end, she will turn out to be right. But it's real tough in the middle there.

She wasn't that way with Sol. She subordinated herself to Sol. But when you're really functioning as a team you don't worry about whose in charge. She was different with Sol than with anybody else. They were two very integrated pieces of the same person.

I was probably closer to my father [than my mother]. She has no sense of humor. None, zero, zilch. I can't imagine her ever telling a joke. My father, on the other hand, was the worst punster that I have ever had the pleasure of knowing. So that my father and I could share some aspect in ways that my mother and I simply could not do. My father and I were night people, and we would stay up together when she had already sacked out. I look like him, I sound like him. It's scary. I look at pictures of him when he was my age, and if it weren't for the fact that they are black and white and I know I wasn't there at the time, I would swear it was me.

I don't think they had any formal expectations for me as long as I was doing my best, and was happy, and thought I was doing the right thing. There might have been some minor undertone of disappointment when I was lured away from physics by computers, but it was very well controlled. It was clear that I was going to be very good at computers, and maybe not as good at physics.

I'm the uneducated one in the family. I mean, I've got two Ph.D.s for parents, and my baby sister has a Ph.D. and an M.B.A. I'm the one that isn't Dr. Yalow. It doesn't mean anything. I started out in grad school working toward my doctorate, and I got bored and not learning enough and so I stopped. They both said, "Are you sure that's what you want to do?" I said "yes," and they said "OK." Were they happy when my sister got her degrees? Of course! But they showed no inclination to criticize me. They only expected me to go out and do my best, however good or bad that was would be fine. They taught me that determination and hard work were essential, no matter how smart you were. I admit I was a bit slow in learning that lesson. I had absolutely never had to work in school until I got to Science [The Bronx High School of Science]. At Science everybody was smart and you had to work to cut it. The best decision they made was to make sure that I ended up in a school where I wasn't the smartest kid in the class. Both my parents were clear that you had to work hard, give back to society, and be a good human being.

Elanna was far more rebellious. In her teens she and my parents just. . . . I won't say didn't get along, but it was a strained relationship, especially between her and my mother. My father was more accepting. But she and my mother just seemed to disagree about, I won't say everything, but it was a lot of things. They just weren't getting along. My sister was going to go her way come hell or high water. It was the usual teenage rebellion stage but rebellion and my mother do not get along that well, and my sister is as stubborn as her mother. My sister saw my mother more as a distant figure and she was more conscious of my mother not being home. I certainly wouldn't call it estrangement, or bitter disagreement, or anything like that, but there was certainly more tension in there. By her late teen years, she wasn't really home that much. She went to Stony Brook and then out to California. As she grew older, she and my mother figured out ways to accommodate each other. And as far as being grandparents, it's nice for my mother, but for my father it was ecstasy.

In terms of what I do, essentially, I need to answer the same kinds of questions, within a much smaller field, the science fiction community, that my mother has had to do in the larger community of science, or for that matter, within the world in general, because the world in general recognizes Nobel Prizes. It doesn't recognize or care what happens to ten or twenty thousand science fiction fans. But to my vague horror, I have discovered over the last decades that I occupy a relatively prominent position within the community. It's great because it's a wonderful community. Out of the thousands of people who are at the larger conventions, I know the most active ones, and it's a good selection mechanism because they're the most interesting. But, of course, I'm never completely able to be just me, I tend to be "Ben Yalow, icon," which is a rather awesome responsibility. It's not easy having to be Ben Yalow all the time. It means that if I give advice, I can't just give off the cuff advice. If I give a suggestion I always have to think, is this likely to be misinterpreted, is somebody going to say, oh, he said so, therefore it has to be gospel. It's a tough sort of responsibility and I do my best to try to live up to it. But it's tricky, it's a tough balancing act, and to a certain extent I have been able to look at what my mother does and to see how somebody else who also can't go shooting off with off the cuff pronouncements because somebody will say that Nobel laureate Rosalyn Yalow says bumpity, bumpity, bump, and it's the same kind of a thing.

How we got to where we got is by entirely different pathways. She generally tended to work as a solo or as a two man act. I don't work that way. If I have to go out and work in a solo role, fine, I'll do it, but I'm most effective surrounded by a team. I think that my talent is to identify who will work together well as a team and try to build teams. I don't care whose name goes up in lights. So in that sense it's a very different kind of thing, but nonetheless it's still a similar kind of issue. Now some of the Ros and Sol issues, at least that some people perceived are things that I view as issues. One of the unfortunate things of being Ben Yalow noted icon is that the people who I'm working with don't get the credit that I think they should. I'm not the superstar. I'm just a player as part of the integrated team. I'm not the one who necessarily should be getting the credit. It goes to the collective. If anything, I'm much too ruthless in that I try to build strong teams to set up and run the best possible science fiction conventions. I go out to find people who are smarter, cleverer, more talented than I am. So they deserve to get the credit as much as I do, and I always worry that people will think that they are just Ben Yalow's sidekick. It's a real problem. I feel that in some sense I interfere with the recognition that these people deserve. Far too many people take a look and say "Ben Yalow and sidekick, or Ben Yalow and team," or whatever. . .

It's been more of a problem for the last couple of years because for most of the big ones, the Worldcons, the largest international conventions of science fiction fans, I've often been teamed up with the same people. We work very well together. We team up brilliantly. They have zillions of talents that I don't have and I do some things better than they do. It makes the team far better than any of us working solo. But to the extent that I have an international reputation, and certainly a very significant national one before we got to spend much time together, and the others only had a regional one, it was Ben Yalow and sidekicks. But no! It's a combination. I really worry that they don't get the recognition they deserve. These people are absolutely first rate, some of the finest talents to come down the pike in many years. People say "Ben must be carrying them." No. I'm not carrying this team. This team is functioning as a team. And we're close personally as well as professionally. I can rely on them to take over when I can't be there.

At the 1995 Worldcon, we worked separately. It was in Glasgow. I was off being chairman's advisor and the others were running various divisions and other roles. They proved that they are major players in their own right. I don't know if it will convince everyone, I'm hoping it will help. I don't know how to make it clear that they are not Ben Yalow's sidekicks. It goes back to: was my mother just Sol's sidekick? No. Was Sol as good as everybody says he was. Yes.

Benjamin is extremely busy within the world of science fiction fandom. Nearly every weekend he travels to meetings and conventions. They are in Boston, Seattle, Los Angeles, Austin, San Antonio, Europe. He often plays a central role in these events. He edits collections of fannish science fiction essays. He has many friends in the science fiction world, and they are very good friends. Benjamin is a very good friend, with deep and sincere interests in people. Like others within science fiction fandom he jokingly calls those on the outside "mundanes." He has romantic relationships with women from the science fiction community. These have tended to be a bit geographically challenging, including women living on other continents. But with e-mail, telephone, and frequent flyer miles, this appears only to enhance the experience. Nonetheless, he limits himself to dating women within science fiction fandom, and when asked why he says with a sly smile, "Mixed marriages don't work."

Recently, some journalists came up from Washington to interview Rosalyn for a book on Jewish mothers. Benjamin stood by in the background as they interviewed his mother in the house on Tibbett Avenue. He would make sure everything would go smoothly. He would take down any necessary contact information, give directions back to the highway, whatever was needed. When the interview was over the photographer asked if she would like a picture with Benjamin. "No," she said. "I want it of me alone."

"That's my mom," Benjamin smiled. It was a proud smile. He has an aficionado's appreciation of his mother's lack of sentimentality. Still, he sometimes draws the parallels between his mother and his "baby sister," and wonders about his correspondence with Allie. "I haven't committed suicide yet," he says with a big smile.

Why neither Elanna or Benjamin went into research is a question that presents itself, especially in the face of Rosalyn's expressed correspondence with Marie Curie. As mentioned before, Marie's daughter, Irene Joliot-Curie, took over her mother's work and shared a Nobel Prize with her husband, Frederic. Just as quickly, the answer that comes is that Rosalyn's children must have instinctively avoided such direct competition with their mother. Any comparison between Yalow and Curie might include the facts that they both worked with radioactivity, that they were married to physicists, that they came to greater prominence with the death of their male partners, forced themselves into exclusive bastions of male privilege, became controversial figures, and that their lives and careers illustrate salient issues concerning gender, ambition, and society. But beyond those interesting similarities, they and their families are as different as any individuals and families living in different countries and in different times might be.

Elanna, while similar to her mother in terms of assertiveness, self-confidence, and the ability to work hard and achieve, is, nonetheless, very distinct in regard to her interests. She is more people-oriented, more concerned with her relationships than is her mother. While she has a high-powered position as the president of her company, a job that requires a great deal of time and travel, she is far more centered in her home and family than was her mother. Elanna's devotion to her husband, Terry, and their young sons is more in the style of her father. Her choice of working at establishing childcare facilities might be seen by some as tacit criticism of her mother for not being a full-time mom, but it is more clearly a vote of confidence for her mother in enabling her to undertake a truly challenging career. Her childhood experience and her adult reflection on life in her mother's home seem to have guided her to a way of life that is both professionally rewarding and personally comfortable and fulfilling. This would appear to be one of the great advantages of her youth. Her parents were indeed role models, and her experiences were positive enough for her to have the advantage of using them both as positive and negative influences, to accept and reject aspects of her parents roles, and to continue to evolve.

Like her mother, she was twenty-three and in graduate school when she first married. But she married a young man who was a Christian. Rosalyn felt that this would be terribly difficult for Aaron, and it seemed that she was right, so Elanna pushed her fiancee to convert to Judaism. He did convert, and the marriage did not last long. But her second husband, Terry, isn't Jewish either, and they have a wonderful marriage. I suspect that after her prior experience, Elanna was not so influenced by her parents' needs with regard to her own life, nor would she push someone that way again.

As a powerful younger sister, Elanna invites comparison with her mother in relation to their respective older brothers, Benjamin and Allie. Here, too, the similarities may be intriguing, but they end close to the surface. Rosalyn and Elanna have Ph.D.s and rose to powerful positions, while their older brothers did not. But Elanna and Benjamin are very close, openly sharing their love and admiration for each other. Benjamin, as opposed to Allie, did not seek to get away from home. He is in his forties and has not yet married. Perhaps it is most telling that Benjamin, with his undergraduate degree in physics and his deep interests and talent in science and mathematics, was drawn to science fiction as his passion. Here he can exercise his interest in science without competing in the same arena with his mother—who has no interest in science fiction—or his father for that matter. And science fiction gives full vent to the imagination. It allows full speculation on ideas, while still retaining the feeling of scientific rigor. In that sense, it is the ultimate cutting edge, and it is freedom. So Benjamin, who at first glance might appear to have been totally dominated by his parents, really developed his own very different life and interests. His passion for science fiction, sports, and music, especially all styles of popular music, are completely distinct from the experience of his parents. While he has always lived at home, his social life and his rich inner experience has been foreign, even unknown to his parents, and it is a more artistic and expressive realm than theirs.

Very little has been written by or about mothers in scientific careers. There is a real need, especially for young people, to understand the barriers that still stand squarely in front of women. A daughter cannot become a scientist and a mother with the same effort and talent that allow a son to become a scientist and father. In addition to the strictly educational and professional problems faced by Rosalyn along her career path, there were even more deeply rooted issues regarding womanhood, and motherhood, and these loomed large and shaped her. Manhood and fatherhood can be defined in relatively narrow terms with respect to general obligations and specific responsibilities, especially within the context of a demanding career. A man with a successful career is generally excused if he doesn't pay close attention to the everyday activities of his kids, or if he doesn't clean, cook, or make sure that those things are taken care of. If he doesn't look so good, if he gains weight, if he spills cocktail sauce on his ties, he is forgiven. A woman can never do quite enough. It is worst of all if she can't do enough in her own eyes. Yalow had to do everything. She had to believe that everything was taken care of, or at least that everyone else could believe that she had taken care of everything. Her kneidel (matzoh balls) had to be light, her charoses (nuts and apple ground in spices and wine) had to be sweet and pungent, her credentials as a balabusta (an efficient housewife) unquestioned. Her headline had to be, "She Cooks, She Cleans, She Wins The Nobel Prize." Yalow feels that some other great women scientists didn't do enough in terms of a

Figure 24. Rosalyn Yalow with Elanna and Benjamin, 1975.

woman's obligation to become a wife and mother. There is no mercy and no end on that road. Was Yalow a good enough mother? Is her home clean enough? Does she dress well? Should Benjamin be married and in a successful career? Is Elanna close enough to her mother?

Being a mother was an essential part of Rosalyn Yalow's plan for her life, and she insists that motherhood should fit into the lives of other women with careers in science. The data with respect to women in science indicate that this is very difficult. Society does not provide facilities and services to allow women with families to pursue scientific careers without the need for superhuman efforts. Nonetheless, if Yalow represents an important case study, the lessons her career must teach are about the difficulty and the possibility of becoming a successful scientist and a successful mother. Her children are warm, compassionate, productive people. They love, honor, and respect their mother, even with their criticisms, and in spite of the price they may have paid (Fig. 24).

10

Professional Mother

One of the lessons I learnt in the laboratory was that of impeccable integrity and honesty. . . . In addition, an outstanding feature of working with both Sol and Ros is the credit and the public praise they gave to their fellows.

SEYMOUR GLICK, M.D.
Ben-Gurion University of the Negev
Beer Sheva, Israel

All of us loved them, and we knew they cared about us.[1]

ENOCH GORDIS, M.D.
Director, National Institute on Alcohol Abuse and Alcoholism

Once, just before I was about to give an important talk, she came up to me and criticized my work. She was trying to rattle me.[2]

JESSE ROTH, M.D.

$\mathcal{R}$osalyn Yalow lay atop Mount Sinai Hospital's beautiful new tower, on ward 11 west, where the walls are lined with dark wood and everything is the best, but she was sinking. The January 1995 stroke had left her with impairment on the right side and a feeling that there was little left for her to do, and now the broken left hip seemed the last straw. Benjamin spent his evening hours on the phone. It was well known that her situation was grim. Her friends and relatives called me to share their concerns and to ask if more could be done because they felt she was falling so fast. Those of her professional children who went to the hospital were shocked. One said, "She made many careers, she created industries, her work helped so many people, saved lives. . . . It hurts to see her this way. In Japan she would be considered a national treasure; here she will be soon forgotten." Another said, "She'll never walk again, and she doesn't look like she will ever leave the hospital." The Veterans Administration was preparing to discontinue her secretarial support.

Rosalyn Yalow has always insisted upon the term "professional children" for the people who came to her laboratory in the early stages of their careers and accomplished there the formative work that launched them to a successful future. It is a term that implies a great deal, for it is more, and certainly different, from mentor. The term mingles pride, maternalism, dominance, even love, in the insistence that she is the "mother." If the relationship is not rejected, there is an implied right to examine it, to consider her professional maternity, and even to rebel. She claimed the role of mother rather than the more traditional boss, and in a real sense there is an obligation to inspect her mother knot—the nature of the bond, its tightness, the nature of its obligations.

A few have rejected the relationship out of hand after leaving the laboratory disappointed, even bitter, because they had come with high hopes and failed to build a foundation for their future work. Some found that they were drawn out of research after leaving her lab. They are not her scientific children because their careers became entirely clinical, but they still retain important observations about her from a different perspective. There are people, like Mildred Dresselhaus, who worked in completely distinct fields but who were inspired and encouraged by Yalow. And Dresselhaus' view is unique because her relationship with Yalow predates the Berson partnership, and, of course, because she is a woman.

"I saw the emotional side of Ros Yalow," Dresselhaus says. Of the women whom Yalow has mentored, she made the greatest impression on Dresselhaus.

> When I was a young student just entering physics and giving my first papers at the American Physical society, I remember her walking into the audience, often carrying a little shopping bag, I don't know what was in it, but there was this woman with a shopping bag, and she had Aaron with her, and they would sit right in the front so I would see them and listen to my little contributed talk. When it was all over she would encourage me, say how well I was doing. She didn't have to do that. I didn't expect it. I was just amazed and overwhelmed. She had a very strong maternal feeling about the people she was associated with. She felt that way about her students, all of us. At the same time, she felt that as a professional she had to provide an image of a stern scientist who was really interested in what she was doing. But she cared about the people who she was associated with far beyond the call of duty. I would always write to her whenever I achieved something. She would appreciate it, and she had a lot to do with my success.
>
> There are so few women Nobel laureates, and they are very, very special role models. And Ros has built those shoes very, very well. She reaches out to the

public, only the Nobelists can do a certain aspect of
that, and it's important to have a few women doing
that. She's been pitching even though her health hasn't
been so good, and I appreciate that. It's important that
science does that. She talks in simple terms that anyone
can understand about the nuclear issues, and she takes
anybody on, unrelentingly, and she doesn't let anybody
bamboozle her, and it's always the facts, never personal.

There is a group of people who have the stamp of Berson and
Yalow upon their careers. They acknowledge their debt, and that
kinship was expressed at the dedication of the Solomon Berson
Research Laboratory in 1972. It was also expressed in the Festschrift (festive scientific event honoring a major scientific figure
who is retiring) that we held in 1991 for Rosalyn on the occasion of
her seventieth birthday and her retirement from research.

These children are scattered across the country and the
world. They have made their own contributions to science and
medicine, and Yalow takes pride and a measure of credit for their
success. "He is one of my professional children," she will say
when the name of one of them comes up in conversation or if one
is speaking at a meeting. It has all of the flavor of the matriarch,
the dominant mother who is responsible, who is the source.

The earliest of the children were nearly the same age as
Yalow and Berson themselves. Sidney Schreiber and Marcus
Rothschild, who were among the first, went into nuclear medicine. They continued to work together in the area of albumin
metabolism, became leading authorities in that field, and developed the nuclear medicine service at the Manhattan V.A. Hospital. Arthur Bauman, who was at the Bronx V.A. in the early days,
worked in albumin metabolism along with Rothschild. Bauman
left and went into clinical endocrinology, but he was an author on
the famous 1956 "insulin-binding globulin" paper. His son, William, became a second-generation "child" when he joined Yalow
two decades later. Enoch Gordis, the director of the National Institute on Alcohol Abuse and Alcoholism was there in 1958–1959.

In 1962 Sheldon Rothenberg, now professor of medicine and
chief of hematology and oncology at SUNY Health Science Center at Brooklyn, worked in the lab nights and weekends while

completing his internal medicine residency at the Bronx V.A. Rothenberg, working with the guidance of Berson and Yalow, developed the first assays for the essential vitamins B_{12} and folate, but he worked so independently that their names do not appear on the publications that came out of their lab. Still, Rothenberg says that his time in Berson and Yalow's lab was the most exciting period of his scientific life.

Johanna Pallotta, the endocrinologist at Boston's Beth Israel Hospital, was there in the mid-1960s. Gabriel Rosselin was there in 1965–1966 and returned to Paris where he continues to work on the development of the insulin-secreting beta cells of the pancreas. In the late 1960s Stanley Goldsmith worked in the lab before going on to become chief of nuclear medicine at Mount Sinai and a leading figure in nuclear medicine. Carlo Patrono began his work on prostaglandins in the Bronx and returned to Rome to become a leader in the area of eicosanoid biosynthesis and metabolism.

In 1969–1970 John Walsh worked with the intestinal hormone gastrin in the Bronx before going to the University of California at Los Angeles. He became one of the world's authorities in the area of gastrointestinal hormones. While with Yalow and Berson, Walsh also was instrumental in developing the first radioimmunoassay for a virus. This assay, for hepatitis B virus, was a real breakthrough in the field of infectious diseases and for the prevention of post-transfusion hepatitis, the debilitating and frequently lethal liver infections that can occur when blood from an infected donor is transfused into a recipient.

In 1970, Goran Nilsson worked with Yalow and Berson and then returned to Sweden to work with gastrin and the regulation of gastric acid secretion. N. Kochupillai came from New Delhi in the 1970s to learn methods for studying nutritional iodine deficiency and endemic goiter. He returned to India and made a great contribution to the prevention of neonatal iodine deficiency and endemic cretinism. Later there were John Eng and Robert Greenstein, who continue their work on gastrointestinal hormones at the Bronx V.A.

But the Berson and Yalow offspring who were closely associated with them in their classic and most productive period are

Jesse Roth and Seymour Glick. They became a team within a team, and their brilliance rivaled that of their masters. Roth and Glick met each other when they arrived as fellows in July 1961. Together they worked out the RIA for the pituitary gland's growth hormone and then discovered the natural fluctuations in the secretion of this essential hormone that controls the growth of our skeletal structure and tissues and contributes to our response to stress such as low blood sugar. After leaving the Bronx V.A. they each went on to great careers as physician-scientists. They are individuals whose ideas regarding the morality and ethics of science and medicine continue to be heard and respected and who have built important institutions and nurtured important scientific concepts and careers.

A research laboratory is characterized by the people who work there; they create the environment, particularly those at the top. But the people who develop their skills in the laboratory and then go on to independent careers both form and are formed by the laboratory where they were trained. Their professional personalities, memories, and careers are living testimony to the quality of the soil in which they were cultivated. It is well known that in the early days of the Radioisotope Service at the Bronx V.A., Berson and Yalow were not interested in having research fellows training in their lab. Any number of people have observed that Yalow would have been happy to have been alone with Berson so that they might concentrate exclusively on their work. Nonetheless, the histories of several key figures who came to the lab include the observation that it was Yalow who convinced Berson to take them on.

"I met Sol before I met Ros," Sheldon Rothenberg remembers:[3]

> It was in the summer of 1959. When I got to the Bronx V.A., where I was to do a final year of residency to become eligible to take the Boards in Internal Medicine, I heard that there were two people doing research in nuclear medicine, and I decided that this was an important new area. I asked Julius Wolff, who had taken over for Dr. Straus as chief of medicine, if I could work

with them and he said that I should go down to their lab and ask. I'm sure that he thought that they would say no, because at that time they weren't taking people. So, in July, I found Sol wearing a spring coat in the cold room of the lab. I said that I wanted to work in the lab, and he said that they only took people who would not disturb them. I said that I only wanted to learn the techniques, that I wouldn't get involved in their research. He said, look, my associate is away, but when she gets back, if you can talk her into it, you can stay. I got the feeling that I wasn't going to be successful. When she got back I knocked on her door, they shared the same office, but he was at rounds. So I said I had talked with Dr. Berson, and that he wasn't enthusiastic, but he said that if it was alright with you I could come into the lab. And we talked about my background and my interest in internal medicine, and some of their papers which I had been reading. And she said, let me talk it over with Dr. Berson. And she called me to say that I could come into the lab on the condition that I don't bother them.

So I started in late August, very excited, and Ros taught me how to use a slide rule again, and she taught me how to do the thyroid studies, and the Schilling tests for radioactive vitamin B_{12} absorption, and radioactive chromium red blood cell survival studies. After about six weeks I could do all that and I was getting restless. Just then Sol said, "Aren't you interested in doing a little research?" "Of course," I said "I'd love it." He said, "we're working on insulin, why don't you open a refrigerator and find something you'd like to work with." Well, that day I was doing a Schilling test, and I was pipetting vitamin B_{12} labeled with cobalt[57], and I said to myself, what they're doing with the insulin (their paper with insulin and insulin antibody was already published in the *Journal of Clinical Investigation*, and they were already working with the assay for insulin) I might do with B_{12} using intrinsic factor, the natural B_{12} binder found in the stomach's gastric juice, instead of antibody. So I went to them with the idea, and they said, "It sounds good, see if you can do it." About a week or two after I started working with it, and I was addressing them as Dr. Berson and Dr. Yalow, they stopped that and said, "It's Sol and Ros, that's the way our laboratory runs." It took me a while to get used to it, but after a while I did.

So I started with intrinsic factor from the stomachs of their rabbits. But I couldn't separate the free vitamin B_{12} from the vitamin B_{12} bound to the intrinsic factor molecules, and, after weeks of trying, I was going out of my mind. One day I went into them, they were in their office, and I told them how frustrated I was, that I was thinking of going back to my stethoscope. Ros said, "Just relax, we will find a way." And Sol said, "There's a method of separating proteins from glucose. It's used in the Somogyi method of measuring glucose. It's a zinc sulfate method, with barium hydroxide. Why don't you get that method and try it?" So I went to the library to find the Somogyi method. It was published in 1936, and that was it. It was fantastic! You add zinc sulfate, and you precipitate it with barium hydroxide. You get a white precipitate. The free B_{12} is in the supernate, and the bound B_{12} is in the precipitate. There was a method for separating bound from free! I got a standard curve, and we had a celebration. That's how I spent the year. I would work until 10 or 11 o'clock at night. They would be there.

Just being around them, I was awed, but it was ambivalent for me. I would come home and tell my wife, "They're too smart, I don't belong there." On the other hand, I waited to go in the next day because it was so exciting. And then, after one year, I went into a hematology fellowship at Long Island Jewish Hospital, but that was a mistake, because something happened there that was not good. I should have stayed at the Bronx V.A. and finished the work with B_{12} there, because when I finished the work during my hematology fellowship I took it to Sol and Ros. They went over it in their meticulous way, and they made suggestions, and they helped me to write the paper. It was my first paper, and, of course, they were my mentors in this work, but they felt that it was mine, and they didn't feel that their names should appear on the paper. In fact, when I wrote the first draft of the paper it was "Rothenberg, Berson, and Yalow" until they said that it was my work and I should be the sole author. But when I showed the paper to the supervisor of my hematology fellowship, just as a courtesy, he wanted his name on it. So I said that I would ask Dr. Berson and Dr. Yalow what they thought, and he said that he didn't care what they thought, that he was my supervisor and he wanted his name on the paper. Well, Ros and Sol said, it's your work, our names should not be on the paper, and certainly his name should not be on it. So I went to the Chief of Medicine at Long Island Jewish to act as a mediator, and it was decided that my supervisor's name should not be included.

Rothenberg remembers that he had a much easier time relating to Ros than to Sol, especially at the beginning of his tenure in the lab. She was always available, always willing to help, while with Sol he had to wait for the opportune time. Sol needed more privacy. Some days he would be in the office playing the violin, but Ros was always available. She always understood and was ready with suggestions and guidance. Still, Sol was a man and a physician. When Rothenberg needed help and advice with his career he would go to Sol, and it was Sol who could pick up the phone and call his old friend Rachmeil Levine, the chairman of medicine at New York Medical College, and say he had a smart young physician named Rothenberg who needed a job, and that was it: job landed.

"Jesse and Sy arrived at the lab together the year after I left," says Rothenberg. "I should have stayed longer."

Seymour Glick, with his thoughtful, flowing, and delightfully humorous speech, his full red beard, has six children (two daughters and four sons) and thirty-one grandchildren. He was the first chairman of the Department of Medicine at the Ben–Gurion University of the Negev in Beer Sheva, Israel. He went on to serve the school as Dean, and now is Gussie Krupp Professor of Internal Medicine. In addition to his scientific work, his essays on the morality of medicine and the ethics of scientific research have appeared in the *New England Journal of Medicine* and other leading publications. He is loved and respected for his humanity, intelligence, warmth, and wit. These characteristics were apparent, along with his genuine humility, even as a young man.

Jesse Roth must be six-feet, five-inches tall. He is very handsome, and he fills any space he enters with his cheer, his personal magnetism, and a riveting elegance of speech that captures attention. Give him a blackboard and a piece of chalk and no one will ever leave the classroom or the largest convention center auditorium. He discovered "big insulin," the insulin molecule that comes off the pancreatic beta cell's synthetic apparatus before it is finally processed into the smaller and more active form that is secreted into the bloodstream. He became the chief of the Diabetes Section of the National Institutes of Health, and there, working with his fellows and helping them on to their own important careers, he elucidated a variety of mechanisms that produce unusual forms of diabetic disease. He was a central figure in the early conceptual and technical work with hormone receptors, the very special molecules in the outer membranes of cells that bind specific hormones from the bloodstream and initiate the processes through which hormone action is mediated. Hormone receptors were a mere concept when Roth began working with them. Now the complex structures of these molecules are known, genes that control their production have been cloned, and, just as RIA had done, hormone receptors have provided the next revolutionary breakthrough in the study of how biological systems, like you, receive and relay the signals that regulate their activities. Roth is currently Raymond and Anna Lublin Professor of Medicine and Director of the Division of Geriatric Medicine and Gerontology at the Johns Hopkins University School of Medicine in Baltimore.

"I really stumbled into the laboratory," Glick remembers. "I had no idea where I was going, or why I was going there." He had trained in internal medicine at Yale and at Mount Sinai, and he had developed an interest in diabetes. He became a clinical fellow in diabetes, working in the laboratory at the Jewish Chronic Disease Hospital in 1960 and doing independent research, when Dr. Sherley Weisenfeld suggested that he go up to the Bronx V.A. to work with Berson and Yalow.

I didn't know Berson and Yalow from a hole in the wall, and I didn't know what I was getting into, but I met Sol when he came to the Jewish Chronic Disease Hospital, and I said that it was something that I would try. I knew that they were measuring insulin, but it was dumb luck, that's what it amounted to. I wasn't even sure I wanted to go into research. Then I met Jesse Roth independently. He was looking for a fellowship—I think that he was at Barnes Hospital in St. Louis at the time—but he came to visit me in East Flatbush. He had agreed to work in the lab at the Bronx V.A. We became friends and decided that we would work together. We went up to see Sol and Ros to discuss what we would work on. I remember Sol said, and most of our interactions were with Sol, anyway, he said that they had a project working out an RIA for growth hormone but that by the time we would arrive it would all be worked out, no problem. He said that we should put the growth hormone project down on the paper work and we would see what was happening in the lab when we got there. When we got there nothing had been solved for the growth hormone assay. Berson and Yalow were going to be away for the summer, and before Jesse and I were to begin I went up to the Bronx for a day in July 1961, and I just followed him around in the lab. It was like following a whirlwind. I was getting tired and hungry, and I remember that nobody ever wanted to eat. So at about 1 or 2 o'clock I said to Charley Iversen, who was a lab technician there, "listen, when do they eat around here?" It turned out that Berson and Yalow went into their office and had lunch and later took some coffee and cookies. Well, they gave me some growth hormone and showed me how to iodinate [incorporate iodine into the structure of a hormone], and then they took off for a conference in Europe together.

For two months Jesse and I were going crazy. When I think of the radiation exposure that we had in those days! We used to use chloroform extraction and we used 50 millicuries of radioactive iodine and stand there and shake it all covered with caps and gowns. But then Jesse and I came across the Hunter and Greenwood method for iodination and that improved things. So we began to work on the problem of growth hormone immunoassay, and we worked, and we worked, and we worked. One thing about the laboratory was that they really let us do our thing. They were never on our backs. When we had a problem we would go to them. Every once in a while there were storm winds in the laboratory. As Jesse used to say, we both had very domineering fathers and so we knew how to handle domineering fathers. When things got hot we just closed the door, and we never got into bad graces with Berson or Yalow. Once we contaminated a scintillation counter with radioactive iodine, the major sin that you could commit in the laboratory, and we had to clean it out. But we really didn't make any progress with the growth hormone assay for a long time. We tried everything, but we couldn't get off the ground, for nearly a year we struggled. And then Ros went away for the summer, and that was a disaster, because when Ros went away Sol didn't have anybody to work with. And so he came and helped us. He was going to solve the problem. So we worked the whole summer with him and we still didn't solve the problem. And, thank God, she came back and he went back into their little private lab with her, and we finally solved the problem ourselves.

He was the person we consulted with most of the time. It was very interesting. He had this mishagos [pronounced mish-ah-gos; Yiddish for craziness] for mathematics, and he was going to teach us differential equations. He made his own notes—no books were good enough—he wrote us handwritten notes and for three hours twice a week we had a machine gun lecture on differential equations. Then we had to spend a week trying to figure it out at home. Ros sat in and, of course, she knew that stuff. We weren't stupid, but it was very hard for us. Sol thought it was very important and he was determined to make scientists of us. He was the volatile one and she was the stable one. She had her feet on the ground, particularly when it came to institutional politics. He was naive at times, she really knew what the score was, and she would save him at times, like getting rid of some noodnick [jerk]. He was too nice. He would believe people and she wouldn't.

She had this thing about going home and making lunch. She had to show that she could be the good Jewish mother and housewife and simultaneously be a researcher. She would come in early and then go home and make breakfast, and then she would work and go home to make lunch, and then she would be back and work and go home to make supper, and then she would be back and work until three in the morning. It was part of what she felt she had to do. They both worked all hours of the day and night. *They did everything themselves.* It was almost an insane preoccupation. They pasted the paper strips for the electrophoresis themselves. They would stand there and paste the strips together. No one could do it for them. They also had a fetish about not having any grants. They were very frugal; they never wasted a penny. They wanted to run the place on a shoestring and show results.

They were both very smart. It's hard for me to dissect out who did what. It's obvious that he was much smarter than anyone I have ever known. When we first got to work there we developed a very serious inferiority complex. It was devastating. He was so much smarter than anybody, and he had no insight that other people didn't understand what he was saying or were not as smart as he was. He didn't understand that. It took a while but when we met the visitors who came through, all full professors, accomplished, and we saw that they were like us, normal people, and that he was an order or two of magnitude different, we saw that it was not our problem, that we weren't stupid or anything, but that he was some type of creature that was endowed with things that most normal very bright people don't have. His mind was just extraordinary.

She, of course, was also extremely smart. She made great contributions to the work. She was a great scientist, and she also kept him in line and protected him. They had a perfect partnership. She had more of the masculine traits and he had more of the feminine traits. She was very determined. She had to pull herself up. She had to do a lot to prove herself in her life. At that time no Jewish women, no women, made it in physics or medical research. And she was the protector. She protected Sol and she protected us from scientific or other attacks, on our time, on our work. . .

And her husband, Aaron, was a very talented guy, a good scientist in his own right, and he looked up to her as though she was a supernatural creature. He worshiped her. He basked in her honor.

Ros was the rational, pragmatic scientist. She was the driving force. No one can say how they might have done without each other. They worked day and night for decades with each other. She raised hypotheses, presented them, dissected them, said that things were ridiculous when she had to. She was no slouch in any area. No one can say just who did what. But Berson was God to Yalow. She could argue with him, but in the end she deferred to him. And appropriately so.

And when he died she had to prove herself again. Apparently she did. Certainly Berson respected her greatly, he always respected her opinions. I never saw either of them put the other person down in any way. All the discussions were to the subject, an argument was always to the data, never emotional. And they spent more time with each other than they did with their families—days, nights, weekends.

I have no idea whether there was anything more than a work relationship between Ros and Sol, we always thought about it, but I have no idea. Of course, Mimi Berson worshiped Sol too, even more than Ros did. And it was clear that Sol really enjoyed the time he spent with his family. And Mimi, like Aaron, was a very giving person. Very few women would have tolerated the relationship Sol had with Ros.

Well, it's a great story, Berson and Yalow, with a lot for people to think about, I mean in terms of morality and ethics, and what's happening to medicine and medical research. The saddest part is about Jesse Roth. I've never really understood that, the pathogenesis.

They were holed up in the Bronx, outside of the regular commerce of academic and scientific life, in their own cocoon, and they relied on no one outside of their lab. They had no university colleagues to ease their way in the early days when they could have used some help, introductions to the inner circles, a word of acknowledgment here or there. They had burst out of nowhere. Along the way, for a brief period, Berson and Yalow had run into some trouble having their ideas accepted, although even the controversial 1956 *Journal of Clinical Investigation* paper, the one in which they were unable to use the word antibody in the title, was submitted for publication August 22, 1955, and accepted on October 17, 1955, so it was only delayed a few months.

From their relative isolation, they had friends within the scientific community, and there were people they did not trust. There was the good list and the bad list. That's how the world was divided. And if you were on the good list you could do no wrong.

Jesse Roth went from the very top of the good list to the bad list. For years he had been the golden boy. The reasons for this express the values that were part of the environment in Berson and Yalow's laboratory: 1) he had made important discoveries; 2) because his laboratory put out important science for many years, he attracted outstanding people to work with him, and they continued to excel on their own; 3) because he has unique perspectives on scientific issues, and he speaks with a beautiful economy and grace, so that when he discusses a scientific idea and its development, it changes the way you think about it, he forms it in your mind. It's a gift, and you are grateful.

"For a brief period of time," says Jesse Roth, leaning back in a chair made for someone smaller and beginning a laugh that punctuates his sentences and crescendos to the end of his thought,

> You could not call insulin-binding antibody an antibody. You had to call it 'gamma globulin that binds insulin in patients who have received insulin.' And for that sin [the editor who insisted on removing the word antibody from the title of the 1955 paper] has paid dearly! And he didn't originate it, because he wasn't an immunologist. We *still* don't know who . . . *Who* was the immunologist who developed those rigorously high standards that forced [the editor] to be the front man? We have to get a pardon for [the editor]. We would like some Deep Throat to come forth and tell us who the immunologist *was*.

It takes a while for the laughter to clear. He goes on talking about Yalow and Berson:

> The extraordinary impression was the deep sense of commitment to scholarship and research. They really worked very hard. They were almost like a married couple in the sense that the relationship between them was that she would make the lunch all the time, the coffee, and in her deference to Sol, especially on medical matters. But the work was spectacular, very creative, and they burst on the scene from nowhere with this series of papers in *Science* and the *Journal of Clinical Investigation*. It was miraculous, but, of course, the work had roots in what had come before. There had

been a few prior papers about insulin antibodies and they made reference to these in their early papers. Yes, I really look forward to a book about Yalow. She is certainly a pioneer, and there is inadequate history of science being written. Of course, a book about Berson would be fabulous. They were children of immigrants. They grew up in the shadow of the depression, and anti-Semitism was still a very palpable force. By the time we grew up, it cost us a few percent, but it didn't thwart us, whereas they really did suffer.

"I never understood why she. . ." His voice trails off, he doesn't want to discuss the mysterious rift that came between them, but there it is. In any case, Roth is not unlike Yalow in his refusal to gossip. Nor is he a sentimentalist or disposed to hero worship. He is more likely to turn things around and, for example, look at the downside of important scientific advances. He does this even with Berson and Yalow's work. Again, he offers a unique perspective, and one that illustrates how a scientist must retain the flexibility to see new possibilities, even in the face of apparent answers. It is not unlike the process that led Bayliss and Starling to discover hormones, a new mechanism of organ system control, in the face of Pavlov's powerful doctrine of nervism.

"Look, Berson and Yalow made a number of important advances," Roth says, warming to the subject because he simply can't recite a record of past accomplishment without taking a new look.

But these advances both accelerated and retarded scientific progress. Take anti-insulin antibodies. Berson and Yalow proved the existence of anti-insulin antibodies in insulin-treated patients. That was an advance, but it also retarded scientific progress because their powerful presentation delayed the appreciation that individuals ocassionally develop auto-antibodies to the hormone, without ever being treated with insulin. Or take their emphasis on high titer (high concentration) anti-insulin antibodies in understanding extreme insulin resistance. Certainly an advance, but it retarded the understanding of extreme insulin resistance in the absence of anti-insulin antibodies: the appreciation of insulin receptor mutations, and antibodies to the insulin receptor, or circulating factors that reduce the effectiveness of insulin. Their finding that insulin damaged by radiation binds nonspecifically to proteins and surfaces like glass, and their insistence that such binding was due to damage to the hormone, retarded the study of other biologically relevant binding of hormones, like to cell surface receptors, or to specific binding proteins for peptide hormones in blood. Even their measurement of circulating insulin by RIA, the power of that tool, and their dominance in that area, retarded the discovery of insulin-like growth factors (molecules in the blood that act like insulin but are not detected in the insulin RIA because they are not structurally related to insulin and so do not bind to insulin-binding antibody).

No one knows why Jesse jumped lists. Was it something he said? Had Jesse just gotten too big? Was it that Ros thought he had been wrong about something? An imperfection found? Or that he was nobody's child anymore? Perhaps he was threatening, because he placed Berson and Yalow into a larger scientific landscape, one that included the interesting sketch in which the power of their ideas retarded certain important lines of investigation? In any case, Roth came out of Yalow and Berson's lab and went on to become one of the most important and productive endocrinologists of his era (Fig. 25).

"Sometimes I felt that she was competing with some of us," says Johanna Pallotta, her Boston accent flavoring her speech.

And there was no competition there. It's like my son Andrew who is a pitcher now in college, competing with Roger Clemens. There's no game there. I'd say, "Ros, there's really no game here. Cool it!" But she had been very nice to me. It was 1965, and I was terribly confused because I was going to leave New York, and then at the last minute I decided to stay, and Dr. Wolff,

Figure 25. Jesse Roth and his wife, Susan, waiting for the start of Rosalyn Yalow's Nobel lecture, Stockholm, 1977.

the chief of medicine at the V.A. Hospital, had no place for me, and so he said, "Go downstairs and talk to Ros Yalow and Sol Berson, see if they'll take you on." So when I went down there Dr. Berson was a little huffy with me. He said, "what are you doing?" And I said, "I don't know. I think I want to be a cardiologist." And he said, "Well, what are you doing here?" And I said, "Well, I have a new boyfriend (I sounded like a flighty person, I'm sure), and I decided I wanted to stay in New York at the last minute," and he was really laying into me. Ros came to my defense. That was my first meeting with her, which was really nice. And she told him, and I thought that it was a good thing, because she told him in no uncertain terms to lay off me. She said that I was very young, and it was OK to be going through my emotional turmoil. She said, "why don't we give it a whirl, and come down and try it."

She soon realized that I wanted to be a good doctor, that I wanted to go into medicine and not science. And she wanted me to know that it was OK, so she told me that she often thought that she wanted to be a doctor. You know that she knew a lot of medicine, and even when I was in endocrinology up at Yale, I would come down with the records of difficult patients, maybe I was concerned that they might have an insulinoma (a tumor that secretes insulin) and she could look through the record and sort it out and say, you'd better watch out, maybe he's taking chlorpropamide (a medicine that lowers blood sugar), and she'd be right. I mean, she knew a tremendous amount of medicine. It was interesting. And there was a very warm part of her, but at times she could be intimidating.

She is a very dynamic, very complex woman, and her relationships are dynamic and complex. But she's a giving person, and someone you can really respect. I was struck by her integrity, by her insistence that you had to be sure, that you had to do another experiment, even if it meant that someone beat you to publication.

She brought a lot of scientific rigor, she did a lot of the work, but she was less of a mentor than Sol. Of course, Sol was in a better position to do that.

But Ros had such a hard time. I mean, anybody with even a little bit of sensitivity is an outsider, but Ros had it tough. Even Sol, as wonderful as he was, and he was a liberal person, not a conservative like Ros, but even Sol would sometimes exclude her, and she would fight for her place. You know, even after her stroke, I called her on the phone in the rehab hospital and she told me that she was doing better than the other patients. I thought it was sad that she was competing even then. I told my daughter, and she said, "Right on Ros! That's good momma. You shouldn't look upon that as tragic, but as a gift. It's what will get her out of there."

What kind of a professional mother was Yalow? She was the only one in town. She invented the role. Would she have related differently to her professional children if her own children had gone into scientific careers? Who can say. She certainly nurtured the careers of many young people, and the overwhelming majority are very grateful and hold her in the highest esteem. Rosalyn Yalow brought respect to women in science and medical research. She brought the issue of scientific motherhood, the role of women as mentors in science, to a table set only for men. She barged in, and her very existence called attention to the absence of feminine values in scientific work.

Setting herself up as a professional mother was typical of Yalow's audacity and courage, for mothers are open to a good deal of criticism and even abuse, and in the case of a male–female partnership, it might be anticipated that some professional children might honor their father and take their mother for granted. Yalow will not complain, and not because she is a martyr or a doormat, far from it. She continues to force an examination of gender stereotypes. She argues, embarrasses, protects, and hurts. She has fought through setbacks and pain, and picked herself up. She is imperfect. She is a challenge to do better. Her professional children are proud of her.

11

Death

Did Sol and I always get along? Do husbands and wives always get along? No. You have fights and it doesn't mean anything. It was almost like a marital relationship. The fellows were our children.
ROSALYN SUSSMAN YALOW, PH.D., 1996

*E*verything seemed finished, gone, broken down, with only pain, bed sores, fever, and confusion left of the boundless stores of confidence and energy. She, who formerly would bend whatever came to her will, lay helpless, alone, silent in her despair. For even now she would not complain. The broken left hip was pinned in the operating room at Mount Sinai Hospital on January 7, 1997. Everything was going as well as could be expected from a medical point of view. She was receiving excellent care. The hospital staff was warm, understanding, efficient, but she would not respond. She would not answer the phone. She would not eat or suffer to be coaxed by nurses. The only times she showed interest or focus was when she and I were alone and she repeated her insistence that she had had it all, that she was content but finished, that her children didn't need her, that she wanted to go, and that she trusted me to take care of that wish, without telling her, just to do it. I would say that we would talk but that it wasn't the time or the place or the way, and she would close her eyes and fall asleep and upon waking say that all she could do was sleep. She would refuse to begin rehabilitation, and she would refuse to get out of bed to sit in a chair.

Solomon Berson was a small man with sharp features and an animated face. There was a gap between his front teeth that lent mirth and mischievousness to his smile and gave a look of the common man with nothing of the aloofness or the rarified air of the big professor. A generation of physicians and researchers studied that face, looking for it along hospital corridors, at meetings, on rounds, to find in its flashes of expression and emotion the workings of a dazzling mind and a compassionate soul. Berson was everyone's idea of the great physician, moving with assurance and imagination from the bedside to the laboratory bench, from technology to science to philosophy.

Nevertheless, Berson was spinning his wheels at Mount Sinai, unable to build the kind of department he had envisioned. No one would confront him directly because he was a powerful force, a consensus choice for the Nobel, a brilliant, sharp-tongued man. Many of the young physicians and the productive researchers loved him. He always had a few minutes for anyone with a problem relating to their research, or for advice regarding a scientific manuscript, or an opinion about a clinical matter. The young research-minded faculty members were closest to him. They knew he understood their career questions, struggles with thorny scientific problems, differing clinical approaches and orientations, and joy as the research experience deepened their clinical understanding and opened their scientific imaginations. They knew that he believed that the young physician-investigators were the heart of the Department of Medicine faculty, even more important than the men who did big ticket procedures: the cardiologists and gastroenterologists who brought money into the institution with their endoscopies and stress tests. Berson felt that this was the difference between a medical school and a community hospital. Sure, university hospitals like Mount Sinai had to offer the latest in techniques and skills, and Berson respected the people who practiced good clinical medicine. But clinical medicine and techniques could be learned and taught in many good clinical institutions.

Berson believed that the medical school is the major setting, virtually the only place, in which the physician-investigator can have the time, stimulation, collegial interactions, and facilities to nurture an academic career. In the medical school one can pursue research while enmeshed in the clinical issues that drive the imagination and create the sense of immediacy that are the hallmarks of discovery in the clinical sciences.

In 1968 Solomon Berson was the Murray M. Rosenberg Professor and the first chairman of medicine in the newly formed Mount Sinai School of Medicine. He wanted to change the nature of the department from one that was appropriate for a great hospital to a department designed for the needs of a great medical school. Of course, change is always difficult, especially within a strong tradition like Mount Sinai's, and Berson's vision for the Murray M. Rosenberg Department of Medicine was not uniformly understood or appreciated. In a 1970 letter to Mr. Rosenberg, Berson tried to make the case for strengthening the research environment. "It is an unarguable fact," he wrote, "that the reputation of a medical institution in far corners of the earth depends more on the quality of its research than on the quality of its patient care programs. Mount Sinai has had many eminent clinicians and indeed, even some fine researchers. However, whereas Mount Sinai stands preeminent in the former area, the quantity and quality of its research could be improved."[1]

It was Berson at his most diplomatic. He would lobby the benefactors and the members of the board with gentle expressions of his beliefs and ideas for future development. His interactions with the professional administrators were much more difficult and quickly, within a matter of months, deteriorated into mistrust, anger, and finally contempt.

Berson was not interested in money or empire building. He would fight for this vision of the medical school as a place of scholarship and creation, and for the concept that his faculty should be engaged in research and teaching rather than excessive service. In this effort he would refer to the historical perspective of the university. He was a scholar and a zealot, prone to writing long memos to the president-dean (in that era the roles of president and dean were frequently given to one man) about the historical struggles to preserve academic values at universities throughout the world. But in 1968, only months after taking his position at Mount Sinai, he was already in open warfare with the president-dean.

Solomon Berson was a sensitive, thoughtful man, decisive and very direct, without the political skills for behind the scenes manipulation or deception. He was not someone who would take a job for the title and the salary and then go along with whatever program was handed down from on high. He expected that important issues regarding his department and the entire medical center would be discussed in a forthright manner and that his voice would be heard. While he had patience with young people, neophytes, and those who were junior in their experience and understanding, he became quickly frustrated, even angered, when senior people could not understand, pretended not to understand, were deceitful, or were moving on hidden agendas. Berson was fully capable of storming out of meetings if he could not convince administrators to follow his advice, or if he found that they made the important decisions behind closed doors before or after the committee meetings. He was not an organization man, nor a company man, nor necessarily even a "team player." Should his faculty spend their time with clinical service responsibilities in an expanding network of community hospitals with which the administration was affiliating? Or should they be spending that time doing research? To Berson the answer was obvious. Anyone who disagreed was impossible, had faulty values, and was destroying the ability of his department to become a cradle of discovery.

The struggle between Berson and the Mount Sinai administration is a classic study of the creator, with all of the confidence flowing from the success of his creations, caught in the web of a large institution. The institution is propelled by forces in addition to idealism, reason, fairness, and is ruled by men of affairs, not men of science. Berson and the administrators spoke different languages, almost literally. It would be interesting to know their personal responses to his extended memos relating union affiliation contracts to philosophy, culture, and civilization:

> We regard the functions of a medical school and university in quite different ways. . . . I regard the thin spreading of our human rescorces as a real threat to the quality of excellence of Mount Sinai Medicine. To regard further spreading as serving some high-minded community service is to ignore that paper affiliations with monster responsibilities and limited personnel of quality is only to present a false posture of altruism from a position of impotence and inadequacy. Since the Middle Ages, politicians and scholars have been opposing each other on the role of the university. Urban and civic problems of today differ only in appearance from those which beset the University of Paris at the time of Abelard and those afflicting Galileo.

One suspects that they enjoyed his style even less than his content, as the latter could simply be ignored. At its core, the conflict was rooted more in the direction that was being imposed upon clinical and academic medicine by economic forces than in personalities. Academic medicine was increasingly being viewed as an extravagance. Institutions were becoming more business-like, and although the words "for profit" still had the ring of profanity, they were nonetheless the beacon toward which the ship of medicine was sailing.

Yalow regarded Berson's involvement in such arguments as frivolous, wasteful of time and energy, and self-destructive. Whatever she thought of the issues—she tended to agree with Berson's view of the university, and certainly was equally dis-dainful of turning medicine and science into mighty engines of profit—she believed that these issues were moved by forces far beyond Mount Sinai. She knew that Berson would isolate himself and be cut down. In the lab, when Berson went off on what she regarded as a tangent, Yalow could rein him in, get them back on track, but now Berson was on his own.

By December 2, 1968, Berson was refusing to attend all com-mittee meetings with the senior administration. In a memoran-dum to the president-dean he wrote:

> I remind you that until only a few weeks ago I attended committee meetings religiously but had failed to be-come convinced that these were bringing about im-proved communication. . . . We must look to our dean and president to defend the university from being bur-dened with responsibilities that are not university re-sponsibilities, rather than to ourselves to defend the university from the dean and the mayor. . . . The pri-mary responsibilities of a university and its medical school are in teaching and research and in providing a certain intellectual milieu. The care of patients is a secondary function and important to the school only as it contributes to the other functions. . . . The medical school and the university, however, have other unique functions not necessarily connected with the cure of the

medical and social ills of mankind. It probably can be argued that diminishing the number of births will be as valuable as keeping those born alive for a longer period. The "pill" was developed by academic research. Also, the evidence on smokers and cancer, lung disease, etc., was based on research. . . . You cited as an example the way you had to react to a query from the mayor over the phone regarding the willingness of Sinai to take on Metropolitan Hospital while at the same time keeping Elmhurst, and that you had to make a split second decision. If this were really the case, how can one respect a mayor who demands such a quick decision or a dean-president who is willing to make it on an issue concerning the health and welfare of many thousands of citizens? If my attendance at committees will give the president the "courage" to make decisions in such a way, then I must opt for nonattendance since I refuse to be a party to such caprice and cavalier disregard of the need for mature and responsible deliberations about important issues. . . . I therefore must reserve my own forces and energies for attempting to accomplish what I can do within the limits of my prerogatives. What I object to and am frustrated by are the administrative dyspareunia and memo fever that block such attempts and by the necessity for repeated discussion of issues that were thought already to have been settled.

Yalow's response to these struggles was less, "I told you so," and more, "so what else is new?" She could not understand how someone as smart as Berson could get embroiled in fights that he could not win. The problem was that Berson did not have the keen understanding of power that Yalow had developed as a resourceful woman having to function within institutions that were hostile to her very presence. Despite her deference to Berson, which, in part, grew from that same understanding of power relationships, she confronted him directly, and in ways no one else would dare, until he simply stopped telling her what was going on at the medical school.

At the V.A. Berson's passionate intensity had focused entirely on research. Although contrasting in scientific background and style, Yalow's involvement, commitment, directness, and energy equaled his own. Because they had begun their work and progressed so brilliantly as the stars of the developing V.A. research administration, they knew everyone in the V.A. Central Office in Washington. Their ideas were always received with respect, if not reverence, and there was no time or energy wasted in administrative strife. Yalow understood the importance of the history, the uniqueness of their relationship to the V.A. bureaucracy. Berson could not imagine that his relationship to the administrative structure could be so different in a medical school; if he made sense, he felt they would listen and follow. He simply had no experience outside the V.A., and the immense respect and influence he had within the V.A. was poor preparation for entering a different arena. His style, like his ideas, was frank, passionate, immediate, and it rankled. Berson did not know how to play ball outside of his home park.

There is no doubt that Berson disturbed the power structure at Mount Sinai. This was not due to any specific fault of the people at Mount Sinai, it would have been the same elsewhere, perhaps worse. It is also obvious that the administrator's vision of the modern medical center was far closer to what we now have, but it's remarkable, from the perspective of more than a quarter of a century, how clearly the issues were drawn. The administrators, of course, were at the helm, and so it should not be surprising that we have come to where these men were bound.

The Golden Age was over, even if Berson didn't know it, and increasingly the role of a chair of medicine requires a businessman rather than a scientist-scholar-physician. Berson was a poor choice for a chair of medicine in a new medical school. He was navigating toward a beach that was eroding. His ideals were in decline. If few people understood that we would arrive at shores covered with advertising, where money would be absolutely everything, swallowing up the medical schools, the hospitals, the doctors, and that the money would be made by denying care and spitting out the twisted ethic of profit over all, then it only made the sordid trip more sickening to him.

Mount Sinai chose Berson because he brought the best possible academic credibility to a brand new school. He chose to go because he misread the time, and he was not a shrewd reader of institutions or people. Yalow, the outsider, with no illusions about being able to alter the movement toward a profit-driven system, was pained by Berson's dilemma. She had better instincts about the tenor of the times, the nature of institutions, and the character of men, and she said that Berson's entanglement would destroy him. She said it often, and she meant it quite literally. People felt that she was hostile to Mount Sinai, but it was not Mount Sinai or the people there. She had nothing against Mount Sinai. She just knew that chairman of Medicine was not a job for the Sol Berson she knew she cared for so deeply. Everyone—friends, people at Mount Sinai, their many colleagues across the country and throughout the world—thought that she was thinking of herself. They believed that deep down she felt left behind, that Berson was going on to glory while Yalow was stuck at the laboratory bench.

"How many papers have you published, Sol?" The question came from the man who had towered over Mount Sinai until the arrival of the new chairman of medicine. The question was not hostile in its intent, the question did not mean to force a comparison. It was simply part of a feeling-out process, initiating a dialogue in the academic sphere. After all, Berson was from a backwater in the Bronx. He didn't have the traditional background of a chairman of medicine, and it was only the power of his accomplishments that made him a force in the institution. The older man might simply have been surveying.

"I'm ashamed to say that I've published more than one hundred papers," Berson responded.

"I've published 384 papers," said the man, who more than anyone represented Mount Sinai's old guard.

"Well," Berson answered, "I said that I was ashamed at the number of my publications, but the reason is that I haven't made a hundred significant discoveries . . . How many have you made?" Silence. The great colossus had made none that he could mention to Berson. And then Berson elaborated a theoretical ratio relating discoveries of increasing importance to numbers of papers published. The giant of The Mount was compelled to suffer. He learned that Berson could become pugnacious, and he learned to compete on his own ground.

If there were hard feelings among the powerful, among men who were unacquainted with science, people who had risen to power through entrepreneurship, men who feared the simple question, "and what have you discovered?" it was easier to vent them on the other half of the team, the dark presence in the Bronx, the woman who seemed to think that she was better than a great medical center, than on Berson. She had made her feelings known, her criticism of the evolving medical center, the rival that had taken Berson away. She was known for believing that it wasn't good enough, that the atmosphere at an emerging medical school would be tainted with the necessary struggles for hegemony, and that she wouldn't move her laboratory there. These views did not make her a popular presence at Mount Sinai. Her stock there was rather low between 1968, when Berson went there, and 1972, when he died. By that I mean that when her name came up eyes might roll and some less than complimentary reference might be made to her toughness and her dagger-like remarks. She was resented for her refusal to recognize greatness in some of the physician-scientists at Mount Sinai, including, and especially, some who were admired by Berson. Yalow thought that they buttered Berson up and in return he inflated the significance of their efforts and accomplishments.

This was the case with Dr. Dorothy Kreiger, whom Berson had appointed chief of endocrinology. Kreiger was highly cultivated, both intellectually and physically. She was a clever raconteur, carefully clothed, and groomed to perfection. Berson thought highly of Kreiger as a clinical endocrinologist, and he praised her research efforts. He also enjoyed playing the violin at the musicales she organized at her home. Kreiger played the piano rather well, and she could create a dazzling atmosphere for the cogniscenti. Yalow was not among them, and in the face of Kreiger's immense popularity, she found her less than compelling. She took a critical view of Kreiger's research, a rather hard view, and there was some passion there, as Kreiger came to represent Mount Sinai. There was, at Mount Sinai, a general attitude of

"Oh, Ros Yalow . . . she's a tough cookie. I wouldn't want to have to deal with her." And so when I decided to go up to the Bronx V.A. to continue my research in her laboratory, even those who knew that I had my own funding, and that I was then working in an area unrelated to hers, could not resist warning me against the move.

Again, the Mount Sinai people were not different from others who were wary, fearful, even hostile to Yalow. For example, at scientific meetings both Berson and Yalow were capable of going to the microphone during the question and comment session that follows the delivery of a paper and giving instant analysis and criticism of the data just presented. They could both be very direct and forceful. Berson more so than Yalow. In the audience someone next to me might say, "That Berson is a genius! How can he think so fast?" When Yalow did the same thing, my neighbor was more likely to say something like, "That Yalow, what a ball buster! She's just trying to show how smart she is."

It is also true that in 1960, when the Albert Einstein College of Medicine in New York was negotiating with Berson to become its chairman of medicine, Yalow was against the move for roughly the same reasons. She would have opposed anything that took his attention from the work in the lab. She had always done so.

Things didn't improve for Berson at Mount Sinai. He was a charismatic man and people liked him, but there were basic differences regarding the use of space and medical economics for which no amount of personal dynamism could overcome. He fought with the administration over office and laboratory space. They fought over the number of hospital beds allocated to the Department of Medicine. They fought over the number of the department's beds to be allocated for service or "teaching" patients (those without insurance and private attending physicians). They fought over the number of resident physicians and their distribution among the affiliated hospitals, especially the Bronx V.A., where Sol's loyalty to the V.A. would not permit him in any manner to shortchange the V.A. in the traditional manner.

The job was wearing him down. He would page me and we would have lunch in his office. We would talk about gastrointestinal hormones, what I was doing in my gastroenterology training.

In 1971 he began to mention retiring from Mount Sinai and even wrote a memo to the president-dean that showed he was considering retirement from Mount Sinai and returning to the V.A.

In early 1972 the president-dean of Mount Sinai, Dr. George James, suddenly died. He was replaced by Dr. Hans Popper, chairman of the Department of Pathology, and the dean of the Graduate School at Mount Sinai. Popper was a gruff man, very capable in the area of institutional and medical society politics, but he was controversial, especially among those Jewish physicians who were aware of the situation in Germany and Austria during the Nazi period.

Popper had been a protegé of Dr. Hans Eppinger, a leading physician in Vienna, until Popper left Austria in 1938. He revered Eppinger and kept his portrait displayed in his office. In addition, he had encouraged the Falk Foundation of Freiburg to establish an international Eppinger Prize to honor physicians who made contributions to the study of liver diseases. The physicians who had fled Germany and Austria during the Nazi period knew Eppinger had been involved in experiments on prisoners at the Dachau concentration camp, and that he had poisoned himself in 1946 when he was summoned to the Nuremberg war crimes trials. Popper, of course, was well aware of Eppinger's past. In the 1980s, when Dr. Howard Spiro of Yale University learned of the prize, he wrote an editorial in the *Journal of Clinical Gastroenterology* exposing the facts about Eppinger and pointing out that Eppinger's involvement in the Dachau experiments was well known because Spiro had learned about it in 1946 at the time of the suicide. Although many were very disturbed by the prize and its implications, including former recipients like Dr. Baruch Blumberg, the 1976 Nobel laureate in medicine and physiology, Popper defended his loyalty to his old professor. In any case, Popper was a powerful figure, and a master in the rough and tumble of medical institutions. Popper and Berson represented different approaches to institutional issues and they did not feel comfortable with each other. Berson was particularly disturbed by the portrait of Eppinger in Popper's office.

Many at Mount Sinai knew that Popper and Berson didn't get along, and it was known to several of the clinical department chairmen at Mount Sinai that shortly after becoming president and dean, Hans Popper went to Sol Berson's office on Friday, April 9, 1972, to tell him he was relieving him of the chairmanship of the Department of Medicine. That afternoon Berson left New York to attend a scientific meeting in Atlantic City. On Sunday April 11, 1972, he was found dead in his hotel room. The cause of death was a heart attack.

Yalow had said that going to Mount Sinai would kill Berson, though some felt that in her opposition to his leaving the V.A. she was thinking only of herself. The woman who was never wrong turned out, in some strange way, to be right. When he died, she was broken. At the funeral she wept openly, continuously. Her grief was so profound, her emotion so deep and uncharacteristic, that she attracted attention. Her deep sobs and the flood of tears came up from her hidden river of pain and joy, sorrow and ecstasy. It was not that she was crying for Berson that was so notable, it was simply her unprecedented display of deep feeling that attracted so much attention. It was a wonder, and a great relief, to see the depth of feeling moving within her. "Did you see Rosalyn Yalow crying?" everyone asked each other, as if to verify the observation. People searched their memories for the times when Yalow had displayed emotion. No one remembered. But at Berson's funeral, standing in the middle of the funeral home foyer, dressed in black, her shield down, she wept for all the world to see. And a remark to Benjamin was overheard: "Your other father is dead."

With the exception of Berson's own family, Yalow suffered most from his death. Again some said she was thinking only of herself. And again, Yalow was caught in an impossible situation, because the deep feelings for her scientific partner were, of course, woven into the fabric of her own desires and expectations. Berson and Yalow had very rapidly gone from unknowns to the highest level of scientific achievement and recognition, and they were inseparable in the minds of those who knew them and in their work. In this partnership, as opposed to her marriage, the man was the interface with the world, which in the last year or so increasingly had come to mean the subtle, but nonetheless tangible, maneuvering toward a Nobel Prize. It meant showing your face in the right places, keeping the significance of the discovery in the minds of the right people, speaking, writing, receiving awards and memberships in exclusive societies, academies, and editorial boards, interfacing with the scientific world. Much of this activity had been Berson's province, while Yalow kept the lab producing. And suddenly he was gone, and then the tributes, memorials, and outpourings from the scientific community were over. She was a woman alone in that very male world where she could be soon forgotten.

She cried for Berson and his family, and she cried for herself and her family, for the personal and professional losses. While for Yalow there were no questions regarding the boundaries between these elements of her life and of her grief, for others there was confusion, even resentment. Aaron, of course, understood completely and shared her feelings. Aaron alone understood the deep and turbulent currents that carried his wife's heart and soul, her passion to work, discover, to break the molds that held her as a woman, and the extents to which she would go, and the limitations. Aaron understood his wife's feelings for Berson, and how inextricably they were woven into her own driven purpose. Miriam Berson did not understand or sympathize with Yalow's grief, and after the funeral she never again spoke to Yalow.

Rosalyn Yalow never understood the hostility that Miriam Berson expressed by withdrawing and remaining silent after Berson died. When Berson's death was announced in the *New York Times*, Yalow received a great many letters from scientists all over the world expressing their sympathy. Virtually every one wrote of the importance of their work and the unique nature of their partnership. Most of those who knew them well tried to express their understanding of the profound grief they knew Yalow was feeling. One declared that Berson had left "two widows." Professor Oscar Hechter of Northwestern University offered words that were echoed by several: "I think you will have to go on alone and win the Nobel prize that you and Sol should have shared. I think this is a responsibility you owe to Sol and to yourself, and to the world."

There were so many letters for Yalow to answer that she responded to most with the following lines:

The [New York] Times clippings of the death of a great
man are hardly adequate to describe what he meant to
us. Fortunately for him, his death was painless and
probably unknown to him; he died from a massive
coronary.

For his family, his associates and friends and, indeed for all of medicine this is a tragic loss.

Of course, many who knew Berson and Yalow became aware
that Mrs. Berson had estranged herself from Rosalyn Yalow.
Some assumed that this had to do with a love affair, and certainly
there had been speculation regarding such a possibility for many
years. Berson and Yalow were as enmeshed in their professional
lives as two individuals can get. They worked long days and
nights together for twenty years. They were inseparable at scientific meetings and gatherings. They traveled together, and they
were open in their respect and admiration for each other. They
both had a certain high-toned, even old-fashioned formality that,
coupled with the immense respect, even reverence, with which
they were treated, discouraged the sort of personal delving, or
prying, that would be required to open and explore that subject.
So many people, including some family members, wondered, or
assumed, but no one knew.

The fact is that Rosalyn Yalow and Solomon Berson had an
intellectual and scientific marriage, never a love affair. Neither
one wanted that. Neither one would have been able to maintain
such a deception. Certainly, from Yalow's point of view, what she
had with Berson was more significant, more stable, and even
more exciting to her than a sexual relationship. Just to be there
with him, to share the work, to make their way in the world
together, to make his lunch, it was more than enough, more than
anything. Her part of Berson was not available to Miriam anyway, so Yalow never felt that she was taking anything from
Miriam.

Miriam Berson simply did not like Rosalyn. She did not
seem to resent the fact that Yalow and Berson spent so much time
doing important research together. But I believe that she may
have been offended by Yalow's "scientific marriage" to her hus-

band. It was a marriage of minds among individuals for whom the intellectual life was certainly a high order of priority. Moreover, when Berson and Yalow were together, issues and people who had nothing to do with their work seemed diminished. I think that Miriam saw this being driven by Yalow, because Yalow was focused on the science to the exclusion of other things and people. She could not blame her husband, she could not confront him. The specter of the funeral was the last straw, and there was no longer a need to keep up appearances.

When Sol died, in the prime of his life, Miriam Berson's loss was so great, she had loved him so, and her young daughters had been so tragically deprived, that a rival in grief must have seemed quite inappropriate. Then, when Yalow got the Nobel Prize and Berson didn't, there was nothing that could have been done to right that percieved injustice for Miriam. As someone close to Miriam Berson has said, "If Ros Yalow would have gone to the top of the Empire State Building and announced seven times an hour that 'SOL DESERVED IT WITH ME,' it wouldn't have been enough. Miriam would have said, 'why didn't she do it eight times an hour.' " Even Rolf Luft's explanation that Alfred Nobel's will prevented a posthumous award, and that in honoring Yalow, Berson was also honored, and certainly Yalow's own insistence on Berson's preeminence, were never enough.

Solomon Berson's sudden and tragic death ended many things, but Rosalyn Yalow would not let it end her dream of a Nobel Prize.

12

Transfiguration

When Sol died the question was, would a
woman Ph.D. who was a partner in a team
win a Nobel Prize? Had I died there
would have been no question that he
would have gotten the prize.
ROSALYN SUSSMAN YALOW, PH.D., 1996

Ros' discovery with Solomon Berson
changed the course of biomedical research
in an unforgettable way. But the Nobel
Prize had no major impact on Ros' place
among scientists, where Ros will remain a
historic figure and her discovery a
landmark—regardless of any prize.[1]
ROLF LUFT, M.D.
Formerly Chairman of the Nobel Committee
Professor Emeritus of Endocrinology
Karolinska Institute, Stockholm

$\mathcal{I}$t was crisp and clear on the morning of January 22, 1997, when Rosalyn Yalow was loaded into an ambulance at Mount Sinai for the transfer up to the Hebrew Home for the Aged in Riverdale. The Hebrew Home, on the shores of the Hudson River, with sweeping views north to the Tappan Zee Bridge and south past the George Washington Bridge down to New York harbor, is the most beautiful and perhaps finest facility of its kind. It is also just a few minutes from Tibbett Avenue. The plan was for Rosalyn to rehab there until she was able to go home and resume working in her office at the V.A. That was our plan, Benjamin's and mine, while Rosalyn still wasn't saying much about anything, especially about the future. The social workers, physical therapists, and occupational therapists, both at Mount Sinai and the Hebrew Home, had no confidence in this plan. They felt we were "unrealistic," that she would never get back to work, and that she would either have to remain in the Home or return to Tibbett Avenue only with permanent twenty-four-hour home care assistance.

Somehow the brightness of the day and the anxiety of going to a new place energized Rosalyn. She bantered a bit with the young attendant in the back of the ambulance, just a few words about the rough streets, how it hurt her hip when the truck bounced, and she asked how long the fellow had been an emergency medical technician. I was back there too, and the tiny spark I saw on the short trip up the Henry Hudson Parkway was encouraging. I wasn't sure that Rosalyn would make it out of the Hebrew Home, but I felt that any other plan would concede the possibility of her having a reason to go on.

That afternoon we settled her into her new room. Soon we put some familiar pictures up on the wall and brought her a television set, but she showed no interest in these amenities. She didn't want her teeth or her watch. "What will I do here?" she asked.

A few days before his death Solomon Berson wrote the following to Dr. Alexander Marble:

> Thank you very much for the invitation, on behalf of the committee for the Joslin Memorial Lecture of the New England Diabetes Association, for me to give the 1972 lecture. I am delighted with the honor of this invitation and would be pleased to accept provided that the invitation of the lectureship is extended to include also Dr. Rosalyn S. Yalow. I would present the lecture but, since, as you know, *Dr. Yalow and I have been longtime collaborators, neither of us would consider accepting such an honor as this without the other sharing in it* [italics mine].

This statement, and others like it by both Yalow and Berson, along with the facts concerning the development of their partnership, and the observations of virtually everyone who worked in the laboratory, confirms the rather obvious conclusion that Berson and Yalow regarded themselves as equal participants in their collaboration. Nonetheless, when Berson died both their names were removed from nomination for the Nobel Prize. Along with Berson's death, this was nearly an overpowering blow to Yalow.

As noted before, it is important to understand that Alfred Nobel's will stipulates that no one can be awarded the Nobel Prize posthumously. It may be received posthumously when it is awarded to a living person who then dies before the award ceremony. But Berson and Yalow were a team, and suddenly, without Berson, the dream of a Nobel seemed to be over.

Yalow's contention that had she died, Berson would have received the prize directly, while speculative, is most probably correct, although members of the committee do not discuss such matters. Still, Yalow learned that she would have to demonstrate continued productivity on a high level if she were ever to be reconsidered. And then, for the first time, she stumbled, appeared lost, and nearly made a poor career choice.

She called me into her office for a talk. It was a few weeks since Berson's death and she still looked devastated, without moorings. What she said made it clear that she had not yet found her way.

"I am thinking," she said, "of going to medical school in Florida. I feel that it is important to have an M.D. degree, and they will work out a program so that I can have one in two years." I told her that this was not a good idea.

I believe that the thought of medical school was something to grab hold of in a turbulent sea. Simply having an M.D. would not have changed much for Yalow, and after a short time she realized that the only way to solid ground was to start swimming with the strokes she knew. She quickly scrapped the idea and decided to keep doing what she loved, and to hope for the best. But she was looking up from the bottom of an abyss. From a scientific partnership that was most certainly about to be awarded a Nobel, she was now someone, even with the many awards which she had already won, who had to begin again, or certainly to prove herself in some new and amorphous way. She had brought her partner into science, and while he was alive her position as coequal was unquestioned. But after he died, she would have to demonstrate that she was more than just his technician. "She was the muscle," some said, "but he was the brain." It seems ironic that the woman gets to be the muscle in an intellectual partnership with a man, but it is not unprecedented. Yu was thought to be Gutman's muscle, Frieda Robscheit-Robbins was considered to be George Hoyte Whipple's muscle,[2] and the muscle–brain question is less likely to arise in a male–male partnership. Roth and Glick were both brains. Brown and Goldstein, Cournand and Richards, Lee and Yang—these were great male scientific teams, and all brains.

Berson and Yalow were very different personalities. In addition to Berson's male privilege, his M.D., and her clearly expressed admiration for his genius, the contrasting personal characteristics contributed to his seeming dominance of the pair. One thing is clear: Berson regarded Yalow as an equal partner.

Berson, a charismatic man, was able to dazzle with his broad interest and knowledge, his ability to hold his own on the violin within a good amateur chamber music ensemble, his strong chess game, his passion for mathematics, and his smile. He was the natural front man for the team, and he certainly made more of the contacts with journals, professional societies, and colleagues, while she did more of the bench work in the laboratory. He could also be a bit impractical and impatient, while she was down to earth, steady, analytical, certainly less flashy, but his match for quickness and the ability to consider experimental approaches to a problem. Yalow was also far less interested in developing and maintaining social contacts. She was single-minded in her devotion to work, and living so close to the Bronx V.A. Hospital, it was she who regularly worked nights and weekends. Berson lived out in Roslyn, Long Island—at least a forty-five-minute commute. He was devoted to his wife and daughters. He frequently entertained the scientists and physicians who came to New York to visit the laboratory.

In any case, Berson and Yalow's differences were complimentary, and an important ingredient in their immense success. More than one scientist came away from a visit to their lab with the observation that Berson had inspired his interest and understanding of how RIA was creating a new endocrinology, but that sitting at the laboratory bench and working alongside Yalow provided the deepest appreciation and insight regarding what their work was creating.

While Berson also worked at the bench, Yalow's understanding of biological systems and the medical implications of their work was remarkable. Never mind that she never had a course in biology, the depth of her understanding and insight in these areas was stunning even to medical experts. Harold Rifkin, for example, dean of clinical diabetologists, would seek her opinion on issues relating to the use of newer insulin preparations for the treatment of diabetes. And Morton Grossman, an acknowledged leader in the field of gastrointestinal physiology, would consult her with regard to clinical syndromes of gastrointestinal hormone excess.

It wasn't long, perhaps a few months, before Yalow was back to herself, forging ahead, structuring her world to fit her needs. Dr. Robert Silverman, who had done excellent work in sorting out problems relating to the measurement of parathyroid hormone (which regulates the metabolism of calcium and bone formation) left the laboratory to practice endocrinology in Westchester County. She was soon joined by George Gerwirtz, Bruce Schneider, and Roberta Moldow, all exceptionally capable and productive people, as well as a good number of workers from Europe, South America, and Asia. Interesting data began to emerge.

With Gerwirtz, she demonstrated that the changes in the lining of the bronchial air passages in the lungs of smoking dogs and humans result in the secretion of a large form of the pituitary hormone (big ACTH) that stimulates the adrenal glands to secrete corticosteroids. This meant that the cells were becoming less differentiated, and that big ACTH could serve as a marker for this cellular change. With Schneider she showed that insulin labeled with several radioiodine atoms is capable of binding to insulin receptors on the cell membranes of lymphocytes. Some workers had felt that the presence of more than one iodine atom would prevent the labeled insulin from binding to its receptor. This was of practical value in the study of cell surface receptors. With Moldow she mapped the distribution of pituitary ACTH in and around the brain tissue in proximity to the gland.

She began to direct the general attention of the laboratory to the emerging issue of brain peptides, especially the finding of traditional hormonal peptides from peripheral glands and tissues like the pancreas and the intestinal mucosa—hormones like insulin, glucagon, gastrin, cholecystokinin, and secretin—which were, most unexpectedly, now being found in the brain. The finding that the very same molecules act as hormones when secreted from endocrine cells into the bloodstream are also made by brain cells and act as neurotransmitters in the central nervous system was expanding the concept of regulatory peptides. It enhanced the appreciation of the evolutionary development of peptides as a nearly limitless encoding system, like a structural alphabet, that could be applied to a variety of purposes.

She began to write and speak in a different style. It was more animated. It engaged the audience, and seemed more relaxed. Berson had written the first drafts of most of the papers, and he had given virtually all of the invited lectures. For someone of her prominence, she had relatively little experience with writing and speaking. During one of the few occasions when Yalow had given a major address Berson was sitting in the audience with a copy of the text from which she was reading. Later, he complimented her on her delivery, but noted that at one point she had said "these" when she should have said "this." It was partly a joke, for he was her equal as a controlling person, and it is not likely that anyone else could have put up with him as a partner, or that he would have put up with anyone but her. But they had unusual self-confidence, and they needed and understood each other.

Her writing and speaking skills developed very naturally, she didn't appear to work at it, she just did it, and she seemed unaware of the transformation. Always, she spoke of Berson. She wanted his name to be remembered. She would have it on every scientific paper she wrote, and to achieve this she dedicated her laboratory to him. The laboratory dedication was a pivotal career move for Yalow, and it unified her personal and professional involvement with Berson.

The Solomon A. Berson Research Laboratory of the Bronx Veterans Administration Hospital was dedicated on April 4, 1974. The dedication ceremony was a wonderful, fulsome event, missing only the presence of I. Arthur Mirsky, due to illness. I spoke with him on the phone just before the dedication. Mirsky was a courtly and elegant man of the old school. He had continued his research on insulin and other peptide hormones and had remained in close personal and professional contact with Berson and Yalow for more than twenty years. He spoke with warmth and humor about the development of their scientific approaches and techniques, but I was unable to convey to the audience the depth of his emotion regarding his association with both Berson and Yalow.

There was a large and distinguished audience. Dr. M. J. Musser, chief medical director of the Veterans Administration, was there. The professional children paid tribute by giving scientific presentations of their current work. In her opening and concluding remarks Yalow, as always, spoke of Berson in terms of awe and reverence. For her the Berson Laboratory symbolized the reality of the Berson and Yalow legacy, and it announced to the world that Yalow did not die with Berson, that she was still there, still a player. It was a bold stroke, because in calling attention to the Berson Laboratory she invited the possibility of diminishing herself if the lab were to languish. But by then she was ready, and there stood a different Rosalyn Yalow. Now she spoke for herself. Now she represented Berson and Yalow, and more important, there was Yalow without the formidable support of Berson.

For the people who went back to the early days, the Bronx V.A. Hospital staff, the older children, the many colleagues from around the country and the world who had come to know and feel comfortable with the old team, the new Yalow seemed unsettling. She had stepped up and assumed the Berson mantle but she was not Berson. She was certainly in no position to help people the way he had. Yalow's suggestion could not bring a job or a promotion, and as a Ph.D., she could not even belong to the important societies for physician-scientists; she was out of the power loop, and her exclusion made her a living symbol of the "old boys' network." More than that, they had known a Yalow who had cared little and learned less about the social interactions that cement relationships and form networks in any field. In the mom and pop shop she and Berson had run, mom had been more strict, a harder example of the work ethic that had characterized the place, and she was less able to appreciate and connect with the literary interests of this one, that one's knowledge of cubism, or the other's piano talent. Berson had been their main man.

But for most, they came to recognize her fight to go on, her ability to continue to be productive, and that her laboratory was in the thick of some important scientific developments. The Berson Laboratory published important work in the area of parathyroid hormone metabolism. It made advances in understanding that many of the peptide hormones exist in several molecular forms, some smaller and some larger than the traditional molecules that had been well known for years. It was very active in the area of gastrointestinal hormones, and in providing data to show that the gut hormone cholecystokinin could be found in the brain where it functions as a neurotransmitter and relays information from brain cell to brain cell.

Yalow was very much the leader of her laboratory and she was invited to speak at important scientific meetings. In her own voice she wrote and spoke, and she was very good at it. She fought off pretenders, men who believed that with Berson dead they could lay claim to discovering the general methodology of competitive radioassay. She disposed of them gracefully and definitively. In 1975 she was elected to the National Academy of Sciences. Berson had been elected shortly after his death. In 1976 she was the first woman to receive the Albert Lasker Basic Medical Science Award. She became the only person to be given honorary membership in prestigious physician-only research societies. And then, in the early morning of October 13, 1977, before dawn, she received the call she had been waiting for. It was her friend, Rolf Luft, an endocrinologist, a great scientist in his own right, but also the chairman of the Nobel committee. "Good morning Ros," he said, and she knew. "I am calling to inform you that you have been chosen to receive the 1977 Nobel Prize in medicine or physiology." The quest was over. She was overwhelmed with joy and a sense of fulfillment.

It was still dark that morning when my phone rang and I heard Rosalyn say, "I've won." I hesitated, more from being awakened from sleep than from surprise, and she said, "Rolf called. I've won, Gene. Come early, and we will have a little celebration." She was calm, her voice relaxed. She sounded relieved. In prior years she had waited for that call and it hadn't come and she would gird herself for another year of struggle. The Berson Laboratory had published more than sixty scientific papers in the years between 1972 and 1976. Now there was no shouting or crying, just a letting go, like getting off a bucking horse. That morning she gathered together all of the people who had helped her in the early years of her career and who were close enough to come to the Bronx V.A., and she thanked them. She was joyful and proud, speaking of the importance of RIA as the word traveled and more and more people from the V.A. hospital gathered in the lab. Yet she was gracious and humble, and everyone knew they would be welcome at the impromptu celebration going on in the Berson Laboratory, from the hospital director to the technicians in medical media, and the janitor. When the press arrived, we had already finished many bottles of champagne, and Rosalyn had consumed her share. She first introduced Aaron, saying that he had helped and supported her, and then Benjamin, saying that he was much smarter than she, and then Dr. Roswit, explaining that her career had begun under his direction, and even the old chief of medicine who had been fired during the McCarthy era, hugging him and, with her precious tears, thanking him for having trained Berson, and for "bringing him to me." When the cameras rolled she said, "My only regret is that my partner, Dr. Solomon A. Berson, is not here to share this moment. As most of you know, he died in 1972, and that is the only reason he is not being awarded a Nobel Prize, but we all know that our discoveries could not have been made without him."

Had her work after Sol's death equaled their accomplishments together? Of course not. Their work with insulin, and their development of the radioimmunoassay method was the definitive discovery of both of their lives. But how many Nobel laureates have produced more than one body of work worthy of the prize? And now she had won, and it was richly deserved: a prize for the method and for the living person who had discovered it and done so much to develop its applications. A Nobel in medicine for a woman, only the second woman to win in medicine, and one of a handful to have won in science!

Calls, telegrams, letters of congratulations came pouring in, and she was deeply moved by the fact that so many were so very happy for her. "Radioimmunoassay deserved a prize," she would say. "You deserve the prize," would be a frequent rejoinder. She would smile, laugh, even giggle a bit. It was clear that a weight had been lifted. She had endured, and she had won it for herself, for RIA, and for Berson. Now all she needed was a dress.

You could see the joy and satisfaction in her eyes and smile, but she used few words to express her feelings. She still distrusted that. She has said that in her entire career, even at the times when she realized that an important discovery had been made, she never had a moment of wild excitement, never felt like shouting eureka. At those moments she would immediately begin to think of all the work that would have to be done to confirm and extend the discovery.

Rosalyn knew nothing about fancy dresses or ball gowns, but Sherman Lawrence always knows the right person. He had a client who was a big time dressmaker, and he took Rosalyn for her dress. The man made a beautiful dress, a fabulous dress, a dress in which Rosalyn Sussman Yalow, a "housewife from the Bronx," could dance with the King of Sweden. It was a long royal blue gown, with a vest of silver brocade, and she looked truly regal when she tried it on. It was the first and only piece of wearing apparel or adornment she had ever cared about, that is, until she received Rolf Luft's gift of the replica pendant. She was ready to go to Stockholm.

It was early December 1977, and snow was falling. The lights of old Stockholm twinkled as the new Laureates and their entourages checked into the Grand Hotel for Nobel week. It seemed unreal, a fairy tale setting for a rare experience. My plane was late, and when I entered the lobby of the hotel I saw Violet Mallory, Rosalyn's secretary and beloved den mother of the Berson Laboratory, negotiating with the concierge. She was her usual calm and collected self, as she reassured the concierge and helped him to retrieve her bags that had mistakenly been sent to Paris. They arrived safe and sound the next morning. Jesse Roth and his wife Susan had already arrived, so had Roger Unger, and the Yalow family. "Dr. Yalow is off being interviewed for European television. They were waiting for her when she arrived," Violet said, noticing that I was looking across the room. "I'm sorry Vi, but that's U. S. Von Euler!" I said. "He discovered substance P and prostaglandins!" Later in the week I was to sit next to him at a luncheon, and he would teach me about the development of the Swedish tradition of toasting, or skoling, including its sexual and social connotations wherein one man might skol another man's wife, but the other man might not have the stature to return the gesture. But now he was talking with Roger Guillemin of the Salk Institute in California, one of the other 1977 laureates. "Who are all those beautiful young women?"

I asked, referring to the five long-haired and elegant ladies who were flanking Guillemin. "They are Guillemin's daughters," said Violet. "Go over and say hello." Luckily, just at that moment Wiley Vale, Guillemin's brilliant and jocular associate, joined their group. I knew Wiley from the circuit of scientific meetings relating to brain peptides, and when he saw me he waved and flashed the great smile that even his magnificient mustache can't hide. Thus began the heady whirlwind of Nobel week.

There would be luncheons at the American ambassador's residence, lectures by the new laureates, tours of Professor Victor Mutt's laboratory at the Karolinska Institute in Stockholm where cholecystokinin, a gastrointestinal hormone with which we were working, was first purified and where many new and important regulatory peptides were discovered. There would be cocktail parties given by various scientific societies, and drives into the country in the limousines provided by the Nobel Committee, and, of course, the royal banquet, the royal ball, and the most important event, the awards ceremony.

Rosalyn was literally the belle of the ball. She was, of course, the only woman being honored, which quite naturally set her apart. Whenever the king appeared he would have Rosalyn on his arm. He escorted her in the procession to the royal banquet, while Aaron, beaming in his white tie and tails, escorted the queen. Rosalyn had been chosen to be the one to give the traditional address to the university students at the begining of the banquet.

One of the rituals of Nobel week is that a student walks through the hall to greet and escort the speaker to the podium. The young man had been given the seating arrangement and he strode down the banquet table in his crisp student's uniform and white hat to escort Dr. Yalow. But he came down the wrong side of the long table and stood behind Aaron. Having seen two Dr. Yalows on the seating plan he had assumed the laureate was the man. Rosalyn threw her head back and laughed, she said something to the king, winked at the queen, and then stood proudly in her beautiful gown. She marched off as the poor student, his honor squandered and face red as a ripe peach, absorbed the laughter of the assembled notables and walked along the opposite side of the table. At the end of the great table she stopped, and when the student caught up to her she took him by the hand, whispered something that restored his humor and pride. Then *she* escorted *him* to the podium. After she was introduced, she looked out at the audience, pausing for a moment and looking through the audience as if to indicate that she had heartfelt thoughts to share, and then she gave her speech:

Your Majesties, Your Royal Highnesses, Ladies, Gentlemen, and you, the Students, who are the carriers of our hopes for the survival of the world and our dreams for its future. Tradition has ordained that one of the laureates represent all of us in responding to your tribute. The choice of one among the several deemed truly and equally distinguished must indeed be difficult. Perhaps I have been selected for this privilege because there is certainly one way in which I am distinguishable from the others. This difference permits me to address myself first to a very special problem.

Among you students of Stockholm and among other students, at least in the Western world, women are represented in reasonable proportion to their numbers in the community; yet among the scientists, scholars, and leaders of our world they are not. No objective testing has revealed such substantial differences in talent as to account for this discrepancy. The failure of women to have reached positions of leadership has been due in large part to social and professional discrimination. In the past, few women have tried and even fewer have succeeded. We still live in a world in which a significant fraction of people, including women, believe that a woman belongs and wants to belong exclusively in the home, that a woman should not aspire to achieve more than her male counterparts and particularly not more than her husband. Even now women with exceptional qualities for leadership sense from their parents, teachers, and peers that they must be harder-working, accomplish more and yet are less likely to receive appropriate rewards than are men. These are real problems which may never disappear or, at best, will change very slowly.

We cannot expect in the immediate future that all women who seek it will achieve full equality of opportunity. But if women are to start moving toward that goal, we must believe in ourselves or no one else will believe in us. We must match our aspirations with the competence, courage, and determination to succeed, and we must feel a personal responsibility to ease the path for those who come afterwards. The world cannot afford the loss of the talents of half its people if we are to solve the many problems which beset us.

If we are to have faith that mankind will survive and thrive on the face of the earth, we must believe that each succeeding generation will be wiser than its progenitors. We transmit to you, the next generation, the total sum of our knowledge. Yours is the responsibility to use it, add to it, and transmit it to your children.

A decade ago during the period of worldwide student uprisings there was a deep concern that too many of our young people were so disillusioned as to feel that the world must be destroyed before it could be rebuilt. Even now, it is all too easy to be pessimistic if we consider our multiple problems: the possible depletion of resources faster than science can generate replacements or substitutes; hostilities between nations and between groups within nations which appear not to be resolvable; unemployment and vast inequalities among different races and different lands. Even as we envision and solve scientific problems—and put men on the moon—we appear ill-equipped to provide solutions for the social ills that beset us.

We bequeath to you, the next generation, our knowledge, but also our problems. While we still live, let us join hands, hearts, and minds to work together for their solution so that your world will be better than ours and the world of your children even better.

The speech was received with enthusiastic applause, and when she had finished she took her place next to the king (Fig. 26). He danced with her at the ball. But Rosalyn seemed more interested in the Queen, who was both very beautiful and unusually intelligent and well informed (Fig. 27). It was a pleasure to see Rosalyn enjoying her chats with the Queen of Sweden. They spoke about the role of women in Sweden and throughout the world, and there was no stiffness or formality. Rosalyn seemed more relaxed, more open, and more charming than I had ever seen her. That was the way she was for the entire week. At least two of the other laureates knew each other and didn't get along. But Rosalyn brought them together. "This is the time to enjoy," she said. They smiled and shook hands, perhaps for the first time

Figure 26. Rosalyn Yalow and the King of Sweden at the Nobel Banquet, 1977.

Figure 27. Rosalyn Yalow and the Queen of Sweden, 1977.

in many years. And it made Rosalyn happy to have done that. She had thrown away her shield, and she was bathing in the secret waters.

At the awards ceremony everyone, even the audience, which was filled with prior laureates, heads of state, European royalty, dignitaries of all sorts, were in white tie and tails and ball gowns. The stage was beautifully decorated with giant bouquets of large yellow flowers. There was triumphal music. The king and the royal family arrived. I got the feeling that during the fleeting moments of Nobel week, when the Swedish royals participate in the gala events, one may catch a glimpse of the role of royalty and the connection to a monarch that had once been such a moving force among the people of the world. Finally, those who were about to receive their prizes took their places on the stage looking serious, reflective, even a bit somber. But Rosalyn, the only woman among them, resplendent in her beautiful blue gown, a shock of color among the black and white of the men, was smiling, looking like her entire life had been prepared for that moment. She waved a big and unabashed wave to the center of the audience, to Aaron, who was in tears.

When she stepped forward her face radiated pure joy, and with a slight bow, received her prize from the King. After the ceremony was over, when we left the auditorium for the Royal Ball, I asked her how she felt. "It should happen to everyone," she said, and there were stars in her eyes, but no tears (Fig. 28).

The Nobel Prize changed Rosalyn Yalow by giving her a larger audience and license to speak on a wider range of issues. "Before the Nobel, nobody had heard of me," she says. "After I got the Nobel I was in the spotlight, people listened to what I had to say." She was awarded dozens of honorary degrees, and in 1988 she received the National Medal of Science, the nation's highest science award. She became even more controversial, speaking out against what she considered phobic attitudes regarding low level radioactivity, supporting nuclear power, and encouraging funding for medical research. She participated and took leadership positions among her colleagues in the National Academy of Sciences and in fora that are occasionally held for Nobel laureates (Fig. 29). On November 12, 1986, at a ceremony at

Figure 28. Rosalyn Yalow and the author at the Royal Ball, 1977.

Figure 29. Elie Wiesel, Shimon Peres, Isaac Bashevis Singer, Arthur Goldberg, and Rosalyn Yalow.

the New York Historical Society honoring 48 Jewish American Nobel laureates, Rosalyn was selected to speak on behalf of the assembled laureates, who included Julius Axelrod (medicine, 1970), Herbert Charles Brown (chemistry, 1979), Michael Stuart Brown (medicine, 1985), Joseph L. Goldstein (medicine, 1985), Herbert A. Hauptman (chemistry, 1985), Robert Hofstadter (physics, 1961), Isador Isaac Rabi (physics, 1944), and Eugene Paul Wigner (physics, 1963). In her speech she asked, "Why have our people enjoyed disproportionate representation among those deemed truly worthy of recognition for service to humanity?"

"Through the ages," she said, "we have taken pride in being known as the People of the Book. This phrase can be interpreted not only as our having carried the Book—our Bible and traditions—throughout history in spite of the Diaspora, persecution and the many travails inflicted by a hostile world, but also as a recognition of the fact that throughout those centuries of tribulations we have continued to honor wisdom and learning." She noted that before World War II quota systems "restricted free access of our talented to academia." Finally, she recognized the struggles of immigrants and children of immigrants to succeed through their dedication to learning, and that in that year the five top Westinghouse Science Talent Search scholarship awards went to children of Asian origin. "We are delighted that a new group of immigrants can aspire and succeed in the dream that America makes possible," she said.

But Rosalyn has not been universally admired, and that's an understatement. She has been called arrogant, belligerent, and worse. For someone like Yalow it goes with the territory. The Nobel Prize gives the recipient special status. To some extent it pushes the laureate out of her field because she is urged to speculate about a much broader range of issues, and her scientific data may be given a special status that is not helpful to the scientific process. There is also a tendency for her opinions to be elevated to the status of proven fact—in her own eyes if not in the eyes of others. In any case, it does not make the laureate immune to criticism. Some say that after the Nobel she became more scathing in her criticisms of other scientists, more personal in her attacks. One former colleague was quoted in a book as saying that, "She's become awesomely full of herself with a kind of a viciousness of style for dealing with people." Others have been quoted as saying that her reviews of journal articles and grant applications became "scathing" and "devastating." While it is certainly true that she is very opinionated and gives the impression that she believes she's always right, she rarely reviewed journal articles or grant applications, and such reviews are virtually always anonymous. Still, Rosalyn takes it like a woman; she will acknowledge the right to your opinion. And, as Ed Rall says, you'd better be prepared. But don't expect her to change her mind. She's still Rosalyn Yalow.

13

Recalled to Life

An old friend recently wrote me about his decision to withdraw from academic activities at the age of eighty-two. He writes: "I will vacate my office, distribute most of my books, and start contemplating my navel." By the age of seventy, or even ninety, my dear Ros will still not even know where that navel is.

ROLF LUFT, M.D.

I am going to stand up, I want to stand to talk to the girls . . . I want to tell you something of my history. There was a time when Jews and Blacks and women had a hard time getting jobs in physics and medicine . . . and you youngsters have to worry because there isn't as much money going into research as there was some years ago.

ROSALYN SUSSMAN YALOW
To the group of girls at the Hebrew Home for the Aged on "Take Your Daughter to Work Day," April 24, 1997

$\mathcal{R}$ain was falling. It was cold as the social worker pushed the wheelchair toward glass doors that looked out to the Hebrew Home's expansive lawn and across the Hudson River to the Palisades. Nearly sixty years earlier, Rosalyn Yalow and Sherman Lawrence had hiked along those cliffs. On this grey morning one could see that the land had changed less than the people who walked upon it.

"I should have brought your sweater or a jacket. We have to cross the courtyard to the other building, and you will be cold," said the social worker.

"That's OK. I don't mind the cold, but we're going to be late. It's a good thing I didn't try to walk such a long way," Rosalyn said. She had been at the Hebrew Home for two months now and she could walk 200 feet with her walker. She could transfer in and out of bed, and she could climb up and down six steps like the ones in front of the house on Tibbett Avenue. More than that, she began eating. She could think about the future, and she could smile. With the slow passing of the days, Rosalyn observed the struggles of the elderly infirmed as they worked to regain mobility and maintain social contact with those around them. She began to work and to defy the predictions that she would never make it out of the institution. It had been hard. She had to be coaxed through tiredness and pain, but she was proud of her accomplishments with her walker and in transferring from bed to chair and back.

Rosalyn Yalow was going home in a few days, but first they had asked her to speak before a group of young girls who were assembled at the Hebrew Home for "Take Your Daughter To Work Day." Ninety percent of the workers at the home are women. They are doctors, administrators, nurses, therapists,

251

cooks, cleaners, and teachers. They are black and white, Hispanic and Asian, and their daughters, sixty-five of them aged nine to fifteen years old, were gathered at a breakfast to hear some of the mothers talk about their work and to hear a distinguished woman who was a temporary resident.

Rosalyn arrived at the back of the auditorium. A female physician was finishing her talk. There was a small commotion as the press photographers and reporters who had been waiting for the famous scientist scurried to take Rosalyn's picture with the officials of the home. A yellow rose was pinned on her blouse. An administrator said, "Dr. Yalow we are very grateful, it is an honor for you to speak to the girls."

"Nonsense, I live here. Of course, I would want to speak," she said, but with a smile and a softness that were new. "I feel that it is now my duty to speak to young women, to encourage them to have careers, and particularly careers in science. I'm very happy to have the opportunity to speak to the girls (Fig. 30)."

She gave them a short history of her career, emphasizing the way in which her training in physics gave her a quantitative discipline that she brought to medical science. She told them something of the hardships she had faced: how they had told her to be a high school teacher; how she was told to learn stenography; how she was the only woman on the faculty in the graduate school; how they had fired pregnant women; how it had been hard for Jews and how it was hard for minorities. She explained how it would be hard for these young women, too, but that they should keep on working for their goals.

When she was finished and had sat down in her wheelchair, one girl asked if she had felt competitive with her husband. Another asked if she had felt torn between her career and her family. She was asked how her family had helped her to get through her schooling, and how she felt when she won the Nobel Prize.

Rosalyn told the girls that competition with a spouse could be a problem, although it wasn't one for her because Aaron had not gone into research. She admitted women could feel torn between career and family, but that if they wanted a career they could find ways of getting past these problems. She said that her parents had little formal education and were not wealthy, but

Figure 30. Rosalyn Yalow speaking to the young women at the Hebrew Home for the Aged, 1997.

they encouraged her, and good public education had been essential to her success.

She told them "it was a delight to win the Nobel Prize, but it gave me a responsibility to see that women become more interested in working in science and that they are able to work at a level that will allow them to achieve to their maximum potential." Twelve-year-old Stacey Jae Pouncy, daughter of nurse Monica McGibbon, walked to the front. Standing next to Rosalyn, she took the microphone and told the two hundred people, almost all women, how Dr. Yalow's talk had just inspired her to work to become a doctor (Fig. 31).

A few weeks later, on May 14, 1997, Rosalyn left the house on Tibbett Avenue for the first time in the weeks since she had returned. She was living there successfully, and this day she would take a two-hour drive to Monmouth University in Long Branch, New Jersey. She was going to receive her fifty-seventh honorary degree, the first since her health had begun to fail, and it seemed like a new beginning. On the way she got to know the driver, a jovial police officer who was an enthusiastic spokesman for the university and for its president, Rebecca Stafford.

When she arrived, President Stafford was gratified by Rosalyn's knowledge of her career, and grateful for her acknowledgment of the strides the institution had made under her direction. Stafford had transformed Monmouth from a college to a university. Yalow indicated that she knew this was a major accomplishment, and all the more remarkable for a woman who would have to organize and direct so many men. President Stafford just smiled and said, "I'm glad you understand."

It was the perfect day for an outdoor graduation, and Rosalyn climbed to her seat on the stage, looked out over the scene as the students marched in to the music of "Pomp and Circumstance." The parents and young family members were stretching and positioning to get a glimpse of their special graduate. Under a cloudless sky, buffeted by Atlantic winds, she winked a sly wink in my direction as if to say, "I'm back."

Dr. Robert Pinsky, a local man who went from a shaky student career to become Poet Laureate of the United States, gave an engaging commencement address with good humor and per-

Figure 31. Rosalyn Yalow answering questions at the Hebrew Home.

sonal revelation. When it was Rosalyn's turn to receive her degree, she encouraged the graduates to follow their dreams, and she brought the crowd to its feet by concluding with "I'd like to think that I serve as a symbol of the fact that women can make it in what was *once* a man's world."

Would that it were true. The pioneers must be followed by the building of a better road. More than two decades since Yalow's prize, and after the recognition of great scientists like Marie Curie, Irene Joliot-Curie, Lise Meitner, Emmy Noether, Gerty Radnitz Cori, Frieda Robscheit-Robbins, Rosalind Franklin, Maria Goeppert Mayer, Dorothy Crowfoot Hodgkin, Barbara McClintock, Rita Levi-Montalcini, Gertrude Elion, Chien-Shiung Wu, Mildred Spiewak Dresselhaus, and many others, it is clear countless women labor without the opportunity to build the careers that should be theirs, or are steered away from following their talents.

In May 1997, Drs. Christine Weneras and Agnes Wold published in the British journal *Nature* the first scientific study of sex discrimination in the awarding of a large number of research positions. They studied the awarding of postdoctoral fellowships by the Swedish Medical Research Council's peer review system. It should be noted that the United Nations has recently declared Sweden "the leading country in the world with respect to equal opportunities for men and women." Still, the researchers had to go to court to gain access to the confidential peer review scores, and they found that women had to publish much more often than men to compete successfully for scientific jobs. Women had to publish an average of three more papers in elite scientific journals such as *Nature* or twenty more papers in leading specialty journals to earn the same score as men from the peer review process.[1]

Rosalyn Yalow's legacy should be that future generations provide equal access to scientific careers for people of ability. She believes that a broad sample of society must be informed and participate in science. After all, we face issues regarding genetic engineering, the cloning of human beings, and the preservation of the earth's environment. We are at risk of having only a small elite with any involvement in changes that will be more dramatic and will come more quickly than anything that has happened in the past.

Rosalyn Yalow gave the world of science a good look at an alpha female, someone who could lead the pack. The world needed it, and she loved it. But there must be opportunity for the great diversity of female personalities, just as there is for males. Now science and other fields must be opened so that equal opportunity is for real. Men have to be brave and compete on an equal basis.

Yalow is satisfied with her life, but she feels the strain of unfinished business. She was a great scientist whose work and methods advanced medical science in the areas of diagnosis, treatment, and prevention of disease. This was done by providing breakthroughs in the understanding of diabetes, in the diagnosis and treatment of many glandular disorders such as dwarfism and cretinism, and through providing a method to save countless people from acquiring liver disease from blood transfusions. She fought for what she wanted and for her beliefs. And she did not shy away from adversity or controversy. She is a unique human being, with a singular position with respect to power structures and her approach to the issues that face women. A woman of great dignity and honesty, a complex individual who fits no preconceived pattern, her struggles and her triumphs should force us all to reconsider the current situation for women in science and society. Primarily, she is a person who was always more concerned with ideas, facts, analyses, than feelings or opinions. But she loved science and medicine for what it could bring to people's lives. She loved research and the process of discovery and its application in the relief of suffering. She sacrificed a great deal to be part of all that. Her life and her career should help us to understand how many talented girls and women are driven under. She wants the life of science and medicine to be available to all people who have the ability and the interest to participate. At this point she will be happy if her health allows her to attract people, especially girls and minorities, to love science and to make a place for themselves. It is her wish that her hard work and triumph will inspire others on this path to even greater discoveries.

On the morning of September 11, 1997, Rosalyn Yalow, with the help of her son, Benjamin, took a big step forward. On Tibbett Avenue the front door opened. Looking a bit frail and shaky,

Rosalyn was helped down the stairs and into the car that would take her over a highway and up the long steep hill to her desk at the Bronx V.A. It was 9:00 A.M., time for Benjamin to turn in after a night on-line fixing things for a fanish convention gone awry. But first he would accompany his mother to her office, just to be sure that her first day back would begin smoothly. By 9:30, he was back at home. He called me before catching his customary few hours of sleep.

"She's back at work," he said, heaving a great sigh of relief.

"They said it couldn't be done," I replied.

"Right," he snapped.

"It's a great accomplishment. Who knows how you both did it?"

"Right," his sharp retort.

"How are you?"

"Surviving," he said, his voice rising to the end of the word.

When I called the V.A., Rosalyn answered her phone. And when I asked how she was, her voice was full of wonder: "Great. I'm back!"

Appendix

CURRICULUM VITAE

Rosalyn S. Yalow, Ph.D.   Date of Birth: 7/19/21

Education

A.B.   Hunter College, New York, NY—Physics and Chemistry
    1941
M.S.   Univ. of Illinois, Urbana, IL—Physics   1942
Ph.D.   Univ. of Illinois, Urbana, IL—Physics   1945

Honorary Degrees (Partial List)

D. Sc. (Hon)   Univ. of Illinois, Chicago, IL   1974
D. Sc. (Hon)   Philadelphia College of Pharmacy & Science, PA
    1976
D. Sc. (Hon)   New York Medical College, NY   1976
D. Sc. (Hon)   The Medical College of Wisconsin, Milwaukee,
    WI   1977
D. Sc. (Hon)   Yeshiva University, New York, NY   1977
D. Hum. Lett. (Hon)   Hunter College, New York, NY   1978
D. Hum. Lett. (Hon)   Sacred Heart University, Bridgeport, CT
    1978
D. Sc. (Hon)   Southampton College, Southampton, NY   1978
D. Sc. (Hon)   Bucknell University, Lewisburg, PA   1978

D. Sc. (Hon)   Princeton University, Princeton, NJ   1978

D. Sc. (Hon)   Jersey City State College, Jersey City, NJ   1979

D. Sc. (Hon)   The Medical College of Pa., Philadelphia, PA   1979

D. Hum. Lett. (Hon)   St. Michael's College, Winooski Park, VT   1979

D. Honoris Causa   Universite Claude Bernard, Lyon, France   1979

D. Hum. Lett. (Hon)   The Johns Hopkins University, Baltimore, MD   1979

D. Sc. (Hon)   Manhattan College, New York, NY   1979

D. Honoris Causa   University of Rosario, Rosario, Argentina   1980

D. Sc. (Hon)   University of Vermont, Burlington, VT   1980

D. Sc. (Hon)   University of Hartford, West Hartford, CT   1980

D. Sc. (Hon)   Rutgers University, New Brunswick, NJ   1980

D. Sc. (Hon)   Rensselaer Polytechnic Institute, Troy, NY   1981

D. Med. Sc. (Hon)   Medical University of South Carolina, Charleston, SC   1981

D. Sc. (Hon)   St. Lawrence University, Canton, NY   1981

D. Sc. (Hon)   Colgate University, Hamilton, NY   1981

D. Sc. (Hon)   University of Southern California, Los Angeles, CA   1981

D. Sc. (Hon)   Clarkson College, Potsdam, NY   1982

D. Sc. (Hon)   University of Maryland Baltimore, Cantonsville, MD   1982

LLD (Hon)   Beaver College, Glenside, PA   1982

D. Sc. (Hon)   University of Miami, Coral Gables, FL   1983

D. Sc. (Hon)   St. Mary's College, Notre Dame, IN   1983

D. Sc. (Hon)   Washington University, St. Louis, MO   1983

D. Sc. (Hon)   Adelphi University, Garden City, NY   1983

D. Sc. (Hon)   The University of Alberta, Edmonton, Canada   1983

D. Honoris Causa   The University of Ghent, Belgium   1984

D. Hum. Lett. (Hon)   Columbia University, NY   1984

D. Sc. (Hon)   University of the State of NY   1984

D. Sc. (Hon)   Tel Aviv University, Israel   1985

D. Sc. (Hon)   Claremont University, Claremont, CA   1986

D. Sc. (Hon)   Mills College, Oakland, CA   1986

D. Phil. Honoris Causa   Bar-Ilan University, Israel   1987

D. Sc. (Hon)   Cedar Crest College, Allentown, PA   1988
D. Sc. (Hon)   Drew University, Madison, NJ   1988
D. Sc. (Hon)   Lehigh University, Bethlehem, PA   1988
D. Hum. Lett. (Hon)   College of St. Rose, Albany, NY   1988
D. Hum. Lett. (Hon)   Spertus College of Judaica, Chicago, IL
    1988
D. Sc. (Hon)   San Francisco State University, San Francisco,
    CA   1989
D. Sc. (Hon)   Technion-Israel Institute of Technology, Haifa
    1989
D. Sc. (Hon)   Medical College of Ohio at Toledo, OH   1991
D. Sc. (Hon)   Fairleigh Dickinson University, Teaneck, NJ   1992
D. Sc. (Hon)   Connecticut College, New London, CT   1992
D. Sc. (Hon)   Smith College, Northampton, MA   1994
D. Sc. (Hon)   Union College, Schenectady, NY   1994
D. Sc. (Hon)   Monmouth University, Long Branch, NJ   1997

Positions Held

Assistant in Physics, University of Illinois   1941–1943
Instructor, University of Illinois   1944–1945
Lecturer and Temporary Assistant Professor in Physics, Hunter
    College, NYC   1946–1950
Consultant, Radioisotope Unit, VAMC, Bronx, NY   1947–1950
Consultant, Lenox Hill Hospital, NYC   1952–1962
Physicist and Assistant Chief, Radioisotope Service, VAMC,
    Bronx, NY   1950–1970
Acting Chief, Radioisotope Service, VAMC, Bronx, NY   1968–
    1970
Research Service Professor, Mount Sinai School of Med., CUNY
    1968–1974
Chief, VAMC Radioimmunoassay Reference Laboratory   1969–
    1992
Chief, Nuclear Medicine Service, VAMC, Bronx, NY   1970–1980
Senior Medical Investigator, VAMC   1972–1992
Director, Solomon A. Berson Research Laboratory, VAMC, Bronx,
    NY   1973–1992

Distinguished Service Professor, Mount Sinai School of Med.,
    CUNY   1974–1979
Distinguished Professor-at-Large, Albert Einstein College of
    Medicine, Yeshiva University, NY   1979–1985
Chairman, Department of Clinical Sciences, Montefiore Medical
    Center, Bronx, NY   1980–1985
Professor Emeritus, Albert Einstein College of Medicine, Yeshiva
    University, NY   1985
Senior Medical Investigator Emeritus, VAMC   1992
Solomon A. Berson Distinguished Professor-at-Large, Mt. Sinai
    School of Medicine, CUNY   1986–present

Societies

Fellow, New York Academy of Science
Radiation Research Society
American Association of Physicists in Medicine
Association Fellow in Physics, American College of Radiology
Biophysical Society
American Diabetes Association
American Physiological Society
Endocrine Society
Society of Nuclear Medicine

Other Activities

National Committee on Radiation Protection Subcommittee 13
    1975
Secretary, U.S. National Committee on Medical Physics   1963–
    1967
Chairman, Biophysics Division, New York Academy of Sciences
    1964–1965
Editorial Board, *Endocrinology*   1967–1972
Medical Advisory Board, National Pituitary Agency   1968–1971
Endocrinology Study Section National Institutes of Health (NIH)
    1969–1972
IAEA Expert, Instituto Energia Atomica, Sao Paulo, Brazil   Dec.
    1970

Consultant, Subcommittee on Human Applications of Radioactive Materials, NYC Dept. of Health   1972–present
Board of Scientific Counselors, NIAMDD, NIH   1972–1975, 1978–1981
Task Force on Immunology and Disease, NIAID, NIH   1972–1973
Co-Editor, *Hormone and Metabolic Research*   1973–present
Member, Committee for Evaluation of the NPA, National Research Council   1973–1974
Endocrine Society: Council   1974–1980, President-elect   1977–1978, President   1978–1979
Member, Board of Directors, New York Diabetes Assoc.   1974
Member of the Editorial Advisory Council, *Acta Diabetologica Latina*   1975–1977
Editorial Board, *The Mount Sinai Journal of Medicine*   1976–1979
Editorial Board, *Diabetes*   1976–1979
WHO Consultant, Radiation Medicine Center, Bombay, India   Jan. 1978
Member, Editorial Advisory Board, *Encyclopaedia Universalis*   1978

Honors

Nobel Prize in physiology or medicine   1977
Member of the National Academy of Sciences   1975
Member of the American Academy of Arts and Sciences   1979
Foreign Associate of the French Academy of Medicine   1981
Designation of Berson Laboratory as American Nuclear Society Nuclear Historic Landmark   1986
National Medal of Science   1988

Honorary Memberships

Sigma Xi
Phi Beta Kappa
Sigma Pi Sigma
Pi Mu Epsilon

Sigma Delta Epsilon
Harvey Society (Honorary Member)
Clinical Society of the New York Diabetes Association (Honorary
    Fellow)
Medical Association of Argentina (Honorary Member)
Diabetes Society of Argentina (Honorary Member)
American College of Nuclear Physicians (Honorary Member)
The New York Academy of Medicine (Honorary Fellow)
The New York Academy of Sciences (Honorary Fellow)
American Gastroenterological Association (Honorary Member)
New York Roentgen Society (Honorary Member)
Society of Nuclear Medicine (Honorary Member)

Awards and Prizes

Annual President's Award, American College of Nuclear Physi-
    cians, Phoenix, AZ   1994
The Butler Award, Marymount School, NYC   1994
Gold Medal, American College of Radiology, New Orleans,
    LA   1993
Myrtle Wreath Award, Westchester Region of Hadassah, White
    Plains, NY   1992
Exceptional Service Award, Department of Veterans Affairs,
    New Orleans, LA   1992
Distinguished Scientist Award, The Kingsborough Community
    College Women's Center, CUNY, Brooklyn, NY   1992
Outstanding Women of Valor Award by Bronx Borough Presi-
    dent F. Ferrer, Bronx, NY   1990
Outstanding Contribution to Science Award by Bronx Borough
    President, Bronx, NY   1990
Abram L. Sachar Silver Medallion, Brandeis University, Wal-
    tham, MA   1989
Distinguished Scientist of the Year Award, ARCS, NYC   1989
Recipient of Golden Scroll Award, The Jewish Advocate, Boston,
    MA   1989
Special Award, Clinical Ligand Assay Society, Washington DC
    1988

Enshrinement by The Engineering and Science Hall of Fame, Dayton, OH   1987

Dorothy S. Levine Humanitarian Award, Bnai Zion   1987

Outstanding Mother Award, National Mother's Day Committee 1987

Sesquicentennial Commemorative Award, The National Library of Medicine   1986

Recipient of Bronze Medallion Award, AMIT   1986

Georg Charles de Hevesy Nuclear Medicine Pioneer Award 1986

Recipient of Milton Helpern Memorial Award   1983

Distinguished Research Award, Association for Retarded Citizens, Dallas, TX   1982

The President's Cabinet Award, University of Detroit, MI   1982

Theobald Smith Award   1982

Science Award, Big Brothers Inc.   1982

The Achievement Medal, Alpha Omega   1981

First Joseph Handleman Award, Jewish Academy Arts and Sciences   1981

Achievement in Life Award, Encyclopaedia Britannica   1980

Annual Gold Medal Award, Phi Lambda Kappa Medical Fraternity   1980

Sarasota Medical Award for Achievement and Excellence   1979

Citation of Esteem, St. John's University, New York, NY   1979

G. von Hevesy Medal   1978

Virchow Gold Medal, Virchow–Pirquet Medical Society   1978

Gratum Genus Humanum Gold Medal, World Federation of Nuclear Medicine and Biology   1978

Jubilee Medal, College of New Rochelle, NY   1978

Jacobi Medallion, Associated Alumni of the MSSM, NYC   1978

"Rosalyn S. Yalow, Research and Development Award" American Diabetes Association   1978

Banting Medal of the American Diabetes Association   1978

VA Exceptional Service Award   1978

Torch of Learning Award, American Friends of the Hebrew University, NY   1978

American Academy of Achievement Golden Plate Award for Salute to Excellence   1977

"La Madonnina" International Prize of Milan   1977

The President's Award for Distinguished Federal Civilian Service   1977

Albert Lasker Basic Medical Research Award   1976

Sustaining Membership Award of the Association of Military Surgeons   1975

The A. Cressy Morrison Award in Natural Sciences of the New York Academy of Sciences   1975

VA Exceptional Service Award   1975

Scientific Achievement Award of the American Medical Association   1975

American Association of Clinical Chemists Boehringer–Mannheim Award   1975

Medical Society of the State of New York Albion O. Bernstein, M.D. Award   1974

Detroit Association of Analytical Chemists Anachem Award   1973

Recipient of Commemorative Medallion, American Diabetes Association   1972

The Koch Award of the Endocrine Society   1971

The Gairdner Foundation International Award   1971

University of Pittsburgh, Dickson Prize   1971

University of Chicago, Howard Taylor Ricketts Memorial Award   1971

American College of Physicians Award   1971

Van Slyke Award and Medal, American Association of Clinical Chemistry   1968

Lilly Award of the American Diabetes Association   1961

First Veterans Administration William S. Middleton Award for Medical Research   1960

Endnotes

PREFACE

1. Eve Curie, *Madame Curie* (New York: Doubleday, 1937)
2. Ruth Lewin Sime, *Lise Meitner, A Life in Physics* (University of California Press, 1996)
3. Anne Sayre, *Rosalind Franklin and DNA* (New York: W. W. Norton, 1975)
4. Margaret W. Rossiter, *Women Scientists in America, Struggles and Strategies to 1940* (Baltimore: Johns Hopkins University Press, 1982)

1. THE WITNESS

1. Rolf Luft, Festschrift for Rosalyn S. Yalow: hormones, metabolism, and society. *Mount Sinai Journal of Medicine* 59:1992
2. Erica Jong, Hillary's husband re-elected! *The Nation*, November 25, 1996
3. From a list of scientists who visited and took courses in RIA given by Berson and Yalow at the Nuclear Medicine Service of the Bronx Veterans Administration Hospital from the mid-1950s through the early 1960s.
4. Solomon Berson advised the author, among others, to be extremely cautious about collaborating with other scientists because one could never be sure how work was being conducted in someone else's laboratory.

5. Kurt Eichenwald, Push for royalties threatens use of Down syndrome test. *New York Times*, 1997

2. DUMPED

1. Rosalyn S. Yalow, Unwarranted fear about the effects of radiation leads to bad science policy. *The Scientist* 2:1988
2. Report by the Director of Military Application, Summary of Relationships between the A.E.C. (Atomic Energy Commission) and the Photographic Industry Regarding Radioactive Contamination from Atomic Weapons Tests, from January through December 1951
3. Joseph N. Mangano, Why was government silent on bomb tests? *New York Times*, July 31, 1997; see also Matthew L. Walk, U.S. alerted photo film makers, not public, about bomb fallout. *New York Times*, September 30, 1997

3. WOMAN IN THE DUNES

1. J. Edward Rall, Festschrift for Rosalyn S. Yalow: hormones, metabolism, and society. *Mount Sinai Journal of Medicine* 59:1992
2. Conversation with Maurice Goldhaber, June 28, 1996
3. Maurice Goldhaber, Reminiscences from the Cavendish laboratory in the 1930s. *Annual Review of Nuclear Particle Science* 43:1993
4. James Chadwick and Maurice Goldhaber, *Nature* 134:237, 1934

4. PAPER, TWINE, AND COLLARS

1. Conversation with Sherman Lawrence, March 11, 1996
2. Information regarding the Zipper family obtained from Rosalyn Yalow's cousin Ruth Wollman.

5. MAKING A WAY AND A PLACE

1. Conversation with Mildred S. Dresselhaus, Ph.D., April 8, 1996
2. Conversation with Estelle Sussman, April 16, 1996
3. Robert Kanigel, Sussman's his name: jobs are his game. *New York Daily News*, October 24, 1975

6. THE SHIELD AROUND THE MAIDEN

1. Jordan J. Cohen, M.D., Medical schools challenged to improve record on women leaders. *Academic Physician and Scientist*, June/July, 1996.
2. The quotes from Zacharias and his claim that Heisenberg had buffaloed the dean at Columbia to hire Rabi are taken from *Rabi Scientist and Citizen*, by John S. Rigden (New York: Basic Books, 1987), and verified by Dr. Rabi in conversations with the author in 1989.
3. Statistics from the Association of American Medical Colleges, Washington, D.C.
4. Reprinted with the permission of the author.
5. Random Samples (Constance Holden, ed.) *Observations From Project Access, Science*, 127:1996 page 295

7. A GOOD DEAL AND TRUE

1. Conversation with Johanna Pallotta, M.D., April 19, 1996
2. Elizabeth Stone, A Mme. Curie from the Bronx. *New York Times Magazine*, April 9, 1978; this and other newspaper stories have compared Yalow to Curie, while others have emphasized her involvement with "womanly" duties with headlines like, "She Cooks, She Cleans, She Wins The Nobel Prize"
3. Rosalyn Yalow's ideas and opinions are well known to me through countless conversations during the many years that we worked together and through our close association since

that time. Nonetheless, these ideas and opinions, and the passages that are direct quotations, are included in the many hours of conversations that I tape recorded 1994–1997.
4. Brenda Wineapple, Ph.D., Gertrude Stein reads JAMA. *Journal of the American Medical Association*: 276:1132, 1996. Gertrude Stein's essay, Degeneration in American Women, can be found in B. Wineapple, *Sister Brother Gertrude Stein and Leo Stein* (New York: GP Putnams, 1996:411–414).

8.   LAB RATS TANGO IN THE BRONX

1. Gabriel Rosselin, M.D., Festschrift for Rosalyn S. Yalow: hormones, metabolism, and society. *Mount Sinai Journal of Medicine* 59:1992
2. Paul B. Magnuson, M.D., *Ring The Night Bell* (Birmingham: University of Alabama, 1960)
3. S.A. Berson and R.A. Yalow, The use of K^{42} or P^{32} labeled erythrocytes and I^{131} tagged human serum albumin in simultaneous blood volume determinations. *Journal of Clinical Investigation* 31:572–580, 1952
4. Copies of Advisory Committee on Human Radiation Experiments: Final Report (stock no. 061-000-00-848-9) and copies of its three supplemental volumes can be obtained from the Superintendent of Documents, U.S. Government Printing Office, 202-512-1800. This report is also available from Oxford University Press under the title *The Human Radiation Experiments*, 1996.
5. J.A. Barondess, Medicine against society: Lessons from the Third Reich. *Journal of the American Medical Association* 276: 1657, 1996
6. J.M. Harkness, Nuremberg and the issue of wartime experiments on US prisoners: The Green Committee. *Journal of the American Medical Association* 276:1672, 1996; see also J. Katz, The Nuremberg Code and the Nuremberg trial: a reappraisal. *Journal of the American Medical Association* 276:1662, 1996; and V.W. Sidel, The social responsibilities of health professionals:

lessons from their role in Nazi Germany. *Journal of the American Medical Association* 276:1679, 1996

7. S.A. Berson, R.S. Yalow, J. Sorrentino, and B. Roswit, The determination of thyroidal and renal I[131] clearance rates as a routine diagnostic test of thyroid dysfunction. *Journal of Clinical Investigation* 31:141, 1952

8. I.A. Mirsky, The etiology of diabetes millitus in man. *Recent Progress in Hormone Research* 7:437, 1952

9. Lawrence K. Altman, Drug firm, relenting, allows unflattering study to appear. *New York Times*, April 16, 1997; see also *JAMA*, April 16, 1997

10. Reproduced in R.S. Yalow, Radioimmunoassay: A probe for fine structure of biologic systems. *Les Prix Nobel En 1977*, p. 245, The Nobel Foundation

11. S.A. Berson, R.S. Yalow, A. Bauman, M.A. Rothschild, and K. Newerly, Insulin-I[131] metabolism in human subjects: demonstration of insulin binding globulin in the circulation of insulin-treated subjects. *Journal of Clinical Investigation* 35:170, 1956

12. R.S. Yalow and S.A. Berson, Assay of plasma insulin in human subjects by immunological methods. *Nature* 184:1648, 1959

13. R.A. Yalow, S.A. Berson, Immunoassay of endogenous plasma insulin in man. *Journal of Clinical Investigation* 39:1157, 1960

14. V. Herbert, Studies on the role of intrinsic factor in vitamin B_{12} absorption, transport, and storage. *American Journal of Clinincal Nutrition* 7:433, 1959

15. S.P. Rothenberg, Assay of serum vitamin B_{12} concentration using Co^{57}-B_{12} and intrinsic factor. *Proceedings of the Society for Experimental Biology and Medicine* 108:45, 1961

9. MOTHER

1. From, *Random Samples, Constance Holden*, ed. *Science* 271:295, 1996

2. Conversation with Mildred S. Dresselhaus, Ph.D., April 8, 1996

3. Conversation with Elanna Yalow, Ph.D., February 12, 1996
4. Conversation with Benjamin Yalow, July 18, 1995

10. PROFESSIONAL MOTHER

1. Enoch Gordis, M.D., Festschrift for Rosalyn S. Yalow: hormones, metabolism, and society. *Mount Sinai Journal of Medicine* 59:1992
2. Conversation with Jesse Roth, M.D.
3. Conversation with Sheldon Rothenberg, M.D., September 15, 1996
4. Conversation with Seymour Glick, M.D., April 19, 1996

11. DEATH

1. Letters and memoranda of Solomon A. Berson are from the archives of the Solomon A. Berson Laboratory

12. TRANSFIGURATION

1. Rolf Luft, M.D., Festschrift for Rosalyn S. Yalow: hormones, metabolism, and society. *Mount Sinai Journal of Medicine* 59:1992
2. Frieda Robscheit-Robbins, Ph.D., worked with George Hoyt Whipple, M.D., from 1917 until her retirement from the University of Rochester Medical School in 1955. They wrote many scientific papers together, and she was the senior author on some of the most important of these. Nonetheless, she never rose above the rank of an associate in pathology, while Whipple won a Nobel Prize in 1934 for their work in developing a cure for pernicious anemia.

13. RECALLED TO LIFE

1. Lawrence K. Altman, Swedish study finds sex bias in getting science jobs. *New York Times*, May 22, 1997

Index